Internal Quality Auditing

Meeting the Challenge
of ISO 9000:2000

Internal Quality Auditing

Meeting the Challenge
of ISO 9000:2000

William A. Stimson, Ph.D.

Paton
Press

Chico, California

Most Paton Press books are available at quantity discounts when purchased in bulk. For more information, contact:

Paton Press
P.O. Box 44
Chico, CA 95927-0044
Telephone: (530) 342-5480
Fax: (530) 342-5471
E-mail: *books@patonpress.com*
Web: *www.patonpress.com*

ISBN 0-9713231-0-0

Staff

Publisher .... Scott M. Paton
Senior Editor .... Taran March
Assistant Editor .... Heidi M. Paton
Book Cover Design .... Thomas G. Vallance, Jr.
Graphic Designer .... Caylen Balmain

Dedication

To Wilhelmina Metzger—mother of 18, pianist, font of love and joy, inspiration for courage and love of God. Here it is, Grandma, a little late, perhaps:
"Hooray for Minnie!"

Contents

Introduction

Something new has appeared in the world of quality—a complete shift in the focus of quality initiatives from *compliance* to *performance*, from doing things right to doing the right things. This new direction will have a profound effect upon the purpose of quality audits and upon the skills and techniques needed by quality auditors.

This book addresses the changes in quality standards and discusses the broader view that quality auditors must have to remain effective in a performance-oriented environment. In the past, quality auditors were concerned with the details of document control. In the future, these details will be much less important—perhaps even irrelevant. The focus will be on the bottom-line measures of effectiveness that executive management have long been concerned about.

Traditionally, the purpose of any audit was to compare an existing system with a standard one to verify system conformity relative to the standard. The kind of system this book is concerned with is a *quality management system*, literally a system established within an organization to manage the quality of what it does—its performance, products, and services. There are many standards of good business practices that can be used as a basis for comparison, but the most universally accepted standard for quality management systems, and the one referred to throughout this book, is the ISO 9000 series.

In keeping with the traditional view, until recently the ISO 9000 series of standards focused on the compliance of a quality management system to its requirements. But in the year of 2000, in response to demands from customers and in competition with quality programs such as the Malcolm Baldrige National Quality Award, ISO 9000 was changed significantly in both form and substance. Fundamentally, it has shifted away from being a compliance standard to one of performance. The new focus is on customer satisfaction and continual process improvement, and the new measures of performance are effectiveness and efficiency. Effectiveness is not measured by whether a document is signed off properly. It is measured by such things as inventory turnover and setup times. Efficiency is measured by cost reductions coherent to quality retention. Many of these new measures will be unfamiliar to quality auditors.

Auditors are going to have to learn this new system. ISO 9000:2000 retains the requirement that an ISO 9000-certified company must have an internal quality audit system, in keeping with the philosophy that a company's most effective auditor is the company itself. Internal auditors can become the eyes and ears of executive management, but only if both parties look at and listen to the same things.

But quality auditors must also be the customer's eyes and ears because too many managers don't concern themselves with quality. Consider, for example, the parameter of efficiency. One way to reduce cost is to use cheaper materials in the product; this has become so common that it's scarcely necessary to provide examples. The coffeemaker that I have is an identical model to the one my sister owns, but hers is 10 years older. The quality of the materials used in hers is patently superior to mine. This is why I qualify the measure of efficiency, to emphasize that it is measured by cost reductions *coherent to quality*. The quality auditor must look at cost reduction as a measure of quality in order to provide service to the company. But management, too, must broaden its traditional views on performance to include achieving and maintaining quality products and services. The new terminology here is "value," the strong correlation between price and quality that is made known to the customer.

Auditing is a professional endeavor with its own philosophy, methods, and code of conduct. Because fundamentally it compares a system to some reference or standard, auditing is easier to understand when studied in that context. Therefore, in discussing the planning and conduct of quality audits, it's also useful to refer to some standard. This book's strategy is to combine the two tasks—learning how to conduct internal quality audits and understanding the latest revision of ISO 9001.

This book is addressed to quality auditors or those who would be quality auditors. It will be useful to speak in terms of a hypothetical company in some context of ISO 9001. Our hypothetical company is not necessarily considering ISO 9001-registration but does want a comprehensive and effective quality management system built around an ISO 9000 structure. In other words, the company wants to be ISO 9000-compliant.

PURPOSES OF THE BOOK

Auditing is an art that requires knowledge of the system to be audited, the standard that serves as the audit's basis, and auditing techniques. An auditor must be skilled in administrative, technical, and human relationships. All of these aspects of auditing and auditors are important and are discussed extensively in the following chapters. However, to be effective as a learning tool, this book is written with certain objectives in mind.

Objectives

The first objective is to teach concepts, not bean-counting. For this reason, we stress big-picture notions—principles, policies, and objectives rather than paragraph numbers or a list of requirements. An auditor should ask, "What is the company quality policy and how is it implemented?" rather than being concerned with checking off paragraph 4.1 or 5.3 from the standard. We tend to check off numbers more or less mindlessly, yet the importance of a process such as contract review is whether a company has a system for it, and if so, how it is structured. This book focuses attention on concepts and structures.

The book's second objective is to review the major requirements of ISO 9001 in light of customer requirements and continuous improvement because these are the new features of ISO 9001:2000. The third objective is to show how to compare an existing quality management system to the standard. The former is a real-time, operating system, installed and working. The standard is a document, not unlike the U.S. Constitution, which is a standard of governance. For example, how do you establish that the city of Peoria, Illinois, is working according to the Constitution? Comparing a company's quality system to the standard poses a similar challenge.

An existing quality management system is by definition implemented in some way. The auditor should prepare for every audit with this big picture in mind: "What does this system do? How well does it do it? Can it be improved?" Otherwise, the auditor will lose sight of the audit's true purpose and most likely end up with a nitpicking list of nonconformities with no findings and little or no indication of how to improve the system.

Therefore, a fourth objective of the book is to encourage a big-picture view of a quality management system by providing images of process structures that achieve stability, capability, and improvability, and by suggesting metrics that are appropriate to the larger view, a necessary perspective to encourage opportunities for improvement.

An auditor must be skilled in human relationships because by its very nature, an audit can be perceived as an inspection. However, quality audits are not meant to be inspections. True, they compare what is to what should be, but the objective is not to find errors or defects but bring about an improvement in the quality system. This is achieved through a cooperative effort between auditor and auditee to establish whether the audited process is working as well as it should, and whether improvements can be made. Raphael Fiorentino and Michel Perigord define this type of audit as *formative*.[1] A formative action is one that contributes to form. In a formative audit, the auditor and auditee work together to "reform" or improve the system. Learning how to conduct formative audits is the book's fifth objective.

A final objective follows from the others. By learning how a standard such as ISO 9001 interacts with your job, you can better integrate job and standard, not just as an auditor but also in your daily work. Thus, the audit experience will benefit you as an employee as well as an auditor.

For Want of a Nail

Not too many years ago, every American school kid had to learn Benjamin Franklin's words, in *Poor Richard's Almanack*, (1758), about how a little neglect can breed mischief:

> *For want of a nail, the shoe was lost;*
> *For want of a shoe, the horse was lost;*
> *For want of a horse, the rider was lost;*
> *Being overtaken and slain by the enemy,...*

Franklin's words could easily be extended: "For want of a rider the battle was lost; for want of the battle the war was lost." The idea here is germane to auditors: A loose nail is a nonconformity; a lost war is a finding. Auditors spend their lives looking for loose nails because they can lose wars. You cannot predict the harm that a loose nail can cause; having lost the war, you cannot always find the root cause. Auditors go back and forth in their work, using inductive reasoning at one time, then deductive reasoning at another.

The point here is that although auditors should take a big-picture approach to auditing, they cannot totally abandon the details of a quality system; it's in the details that things begin to break down. The idea behind an audit devoted to customer satisfaction and continual improvement is to avoid nitpicking. Things must be kept in balance. Auditors will still be responsible for knowing the detailed requirements of ISO 9001—and you can't know too much—but many books have been written about them. This book is about auditing. The use of a standard as an audit-teaching device is necessary, but the standard itself is not this book's objective. Therefore, we offer the top-down view, focusing on the larger aspects of this latest version of ISO 9000. You won't find the minutiae here.

BOOK OUTLINE

The material in this book covers all aspects of an internal quality audit (IQA). The first seven chapters discuss the processes of internal quality auditing: introduction to auditing, pre-audit activity, opening meetings, auditing techniques, closing activities, and post-audit activity. The pre-audit activity includes planning and preparing for an audit. The chapter on auditing techniques includes tactical approaches to audits, creating and using checklists examining documentation, interviewing personnel, and assigning and reporting nonconformities constructively. This book also discusses organizing and conducting opening and closing meetings, establishing findings, writing a final report, and closing out an audit.

Audits are literally a sequence of observations compared to some standard. There is necessarily a question of compliance in every audit. Chapter 5, covering assessment, is where the role of the auditor diverges from compliance to performance. The evaluation of observations in light of effectiveness and efficiency is the heart of the formative audit.

Chapter 8 provides a background on quality management standards in general and includes an overview of ISO 9001, which will be our reference standard. Obviously, if you are going to audit a quality system, you need to be familiar with what you are going to compare it to.

Chapter 9 is devoted to the notion of continual improvement, what it is and how you measure it. The term is found frequently in corporate quality policies, and it has a nice ring to it. However, auditors must go beyond subjective opinion to that which is measurable and auditable.

Chapters 10 through 14 provide an analysis of the ISO 9001 quality management system. Chapter 10 concerns the quality system itself, while chapters 11 through 14 discuss its four core responsibilities—management responsibility; resource management; product realization; and measurement, analysis, and improvement. Each of these areas contains many requirements, many of which are carried over from earlier versions of ISO 9000. They reflect good business practices but have been written about extensively elsewhere. In this book, we focus on auditing the new requirements in terms of the customer and continual improvement.

Chapter 15 summarizes the book's concepts, but rather than reviewing previous chapters, the reader is asked to step back and look at the audit process from the top down—the big-picture view.

Although the book can be perceived in two parts, audit and standard, it's constructed to combine the two. The chapters on auditing make frequent reference to ISO 9001. Conversely, the chapters on ISO 9001 focus on those things that are auditable and make frequent reference to auditing techniques. In this way, as the reader gets into these techniques, the objectives and procedures make sense because they are referenced to good business practices. The standard makes sense because it is analyzed through measurable things. Abstractions and lists of rules and regulations are avoided.

Every quality audit uses some form of sampling, explicitly or implicitly. In recognition of this, it's best to consider a formal sampling approach so that valid conclusions can be drawn from the audit findings. Although nonstatistical sampling is more appropriate to internal audits, many terms used in it come from statistical sampling. Therefore, certain terms used in statistical sampling and nonstatistical sampling plans are described in the four appendices.

CONVENTIONS

While working for IBM in the mid-1960s, I attended a meeting of IBM management and a director of the National Aeronautics and Space Administration at the Marshall Space Flight Center. As a junior engineer invited there simply to observe, I listened as one of the IBM managers used the term "controllability" in its everyday sense. Of course, we were all control systems engineers, as was the director, and he was incensed. "Controllability" has a precise definition in systems theory, and we had been guilty of lazy English and probably lazy thinking, too. Things went downhill from there; the meeting was aborted and we all returned to IBM well chastised.

The lesson I learned that day is to forever define words I intend to use if I believe there is no general agreement to their meaning, or if I use them in a sense contrary to general agreement. Therefore, the reader is entitled to be told of the conventions used in this book.

Terminology

Many readers will be familiar with the ISO 9000 series of standards and know that there were three of them dealing with requirements: ISO 9001, ISO 9002, and ISO 9003. However, the 2000 revision contains only one: ISO 9001: Quality management systems requirements. It is the reference for this book and will be referred to either as ISO 9001 or simply the standard.

The International Organization for Standardization is an awful term from an English-language point of view, and although the International Standards Organization is much more pleasant to the ear, we cannot change what has been done. Throughout this book, ISO refers to the International Organization for Standardization.

The terms "supplier," "organization," "subcontractor," and "company" have no standard meaning in business and industry; they mean different things to different people. Even ISO 9001 has changed its meaning of these terms at various times. In this book, "organization" refers to the company, institution, or agency that the auditor works for. We use the word "company" interchangeably with "organization" because it is shorter. Brevity has its charm. We also use the term "quality system" interchangeably with "quality management system," which is abbreviated as "QMS."

In the past, the labor hierarchy in organizations was defined as manager, supervisor, and worker. Recent trends in social psychology have been toward a more democratic terminology. In some companies, managers are called "facilitators," supervisors are called "coordinators," and workers are called "associates" or "operators." In this book, we retain the term "manager" because of its close association to management responsibility, a key area of ISO 9000. However, in recognition of its 19th-century caste, we avoid using "worker," preferring the term "operator," which seems to be more accurate in the modern workplace.

Systems and Processes

The terms "system" and "process" have no standard meaning in business and industry. Historically, they have carried different meanings. Indeed, ISO 9001:2000 defines them differently. However, in modern systems thinking they are regarded as the same thing, and will be treated so in this book. The rationale follows.

For many years, a system was defined as a collection of elements so interconnected as to contribute to a defined goal. We referred to audio systems and video systems, even when their power was off. In other words, "system" came to represent a set of elements, whether or not they were doing anything. A "process," on the other hand, suggested activity; something was being done. These notions changed during the 1960s when Rudolph E. Kalman, one of the founders of modern systems theory, defined a system as a mathematical concept with inputs, outputs, a set of states, and a state transition function.[2] Thus, a dynamical property was assigned to the notion of a system. Because this coincides closely with how we think of a process, it no longer makes sense to distinguish between system and process. It might be argued that a system is a mathematical concept, whereas a process is real. Yet, engineers design things from mathematical models. If it is a system when it is designed, then it is a system when it is built.

Whether an entity is a system, a subsystem, or an element of a system is all a matter of perspective. For example, the solar system is a subsystem of the universe and an element in the cosmos. The heart is a subsystem of the cardiovascular system and an element in the biological system. A national banking system consists of subsystems of local banks, each having operations systems, filing systems, and so on. In all of these cases, the word "process" could have been used instead of system.

Control

Much of the literature on audit techniques comes from the financial world and certified public accountants (CPAs). Basically, a CPA reviews the books of an audited company, looking for not only fiscal balance, but for controls in place and working. Indeed, the evaluation of a financial audit is often in terms of "high risk" and "low risk" on the effectiveness of a control. So, too, in quality audits we find that ISO 9001 seeks assurance that "processes are under control."

In recent years, the term "control" has taken on a pejorative flavor. For example, we hear of "control freaks," and the idea that a human-machine system is under control offends us. Thomas Pyzdek tells us that control has been the dominant theme of the 20th century but it has its limits.[3] During the 21st century, he contends, quality will move away from control toward greater freedom. While I usually agree with Pyzdek, in this case I believe it is more accurate to say that we will move away from controlling those functions that are best left free. The human race is nothing if not pedantic and systematic; certainly control has been overdone. Controls that are placed on activities that require creativity, for example, may well be counterproductive.

To mix a few metaphors, in our haste to throw off our clothes and be free, let's not throw the baby out with the bathwater. There are circumstances that must remain under control—dispensing drugs, licensing physicians, distributing nuclear devices. And there are processes that are best left under control—documentation changes, inventories, deliveries, spending company money—all those activities that when left to lackadaisical management, or no management at all, could result in poor performance or even chaos. In the aggregate, these processes constitute what is known as a quality system, which is "managed," if you will, by a quality management system. It is this system that will remain the auditor's domain.

Section Numbering

The ISO 9000:2000 standards consist of three parts: definitions, requirements, and guidelines. ISO 9001 is the requirements standard and therefore the focus of auditors. As we have stated, it is the reference standard for this book. However, the requirements are greatly expanded upon in the guidelines, ISO 9004, which is more descriptive yet more concise than ISO 9001. The power of ISO 9000:2000 as a performance standard lies in integrating the guidelines and requirements.

Standards and codes having to do with quality, law, medical, or fiscal protocols often number their paragraphs for ease of reference, a facility important to auditors. ISO 9001 also numbers its requirements by the section and subsection in which they appear in the document. However, numbering has two drawbacks. The first is that a section numbering system tends to identify a requirement with a number rather than with a meaning, opening the door to bean-counting. We want to avoid that approach to auditing. Second, if the structure of a code or standard is changed significantly, then a completely new numbering system is necessary, which is exactly what has happened between the 1994 and 2000 versions of the standard. This has introduced confusion and added work.

Nevertheless, the deed is done, the requirements appear in sections, subsections and even sub-subsections. Therefore, to aid the reader in research, the requirements in this book, too, are numbered according to the section in ISO 9004:2000 in which they appear.

Why use the numbering system of ISO 9004, the guidelines, rather than that of ISO 9001, the requirements? In my view, while ISO 9004 remains concise, its expanded description of the requirements is necessary to an auditor's full understanding of them. For example, although ISO 9001 describes resource management in four sub-requirements, ISO 9004 uses eight.

Major requirements are numbered in sections as follows: 4.0 Quality management system; 5.0 Management responsibility; 6.0 Resource management; 7.0 Product realization; and 8.0 Measurement, analysis, and improvement. The subsections are numbered accordingly, for example: 7.4 Purchasing. We do not number sub-subsections in the book because doing so would encourage bean-counting and because once in the appropriate subsection, the auditor should be able to find his or her way around.

Even without numbered sub-subsections, it will become apparent to the reader that not all of them are discussed. The purpose of this book is to offer a top-down view, concentrating on the new requirements of ISO 9001:2000 and *what they mean*, in particular, in terms of customer focus and continuous improvement. We recognize that auditors tend to have a library of several books on the standard and on auditing, so it would be redundant to discuss all the standard's elements and minutiae. As a result, the new requirements introduced by the 2000 standard are discussed, but some of the detailed requirements carried over from the 1994 standard are not if there is no new interpretation of them.

REFERENCES

1. Fiorentino, Raphael, and Michel Perigord. "Going from an Investigative to a Formative Auditor." *Quality Progress*, Oct. 1994, pp. 61–65.
2. Kalman, Rudolph E.; Peter L. Falb; and Michael A. Arbib. *Topics in Mathematical System Theory*. New York: McGraw-Hill, 1969.
3. Pyzdek, Thomas. "Quality Profession Must Learn to Heed Its Own Advice." *Quality Progress*, June 1999, pp. 60–64.

CHAPTER

1

Auditing

And how his audit stands who knows save heaven?
—William Shakespeare, *Hamlet* (3.3.82)

Audits, as Shakespeare's words imply, have been around for a long time. Indeed, they have become a routine part of many institutions' operations. During the course of a year, companies complete numerous audits of one kind or another—for example, financial and inventory. Companies using toxic chemicals must undergo periodic audits to ensure safe handling, usage, and distribution of their products. Banks and other financial institutions participate in financial audits to meet legal requirements. If a company operates under a quality system, then it undergoes a performance audit from time to time, and if the system is ISO 9001-certified, then periodic audits by the company's registrar are mandated.

The word "audit" derives from the Latin *audire*—to hear. Dennis R. Arter tells us the word originally was used to describe the process when a ship's captain declared aloud his cargo, item by item, so that an auditor, representing the king, could record the inventory for tax purposes.[1] As this anecdote suggests, through the centuries an audit became associated with a listing of some sort that required verification. Effectively, an audit represented a kind of inspection.

Today, particularly in the quality world, we have moved away from the notion of an audit as essentially an inspection, considering it instead a method of enhancing the continual improvement of whatever is being audited. This idea represents a profound change in quality philosophy and is the nucleus of this book.

The internal quality audit (IQA) is particularly effective in improving a quality system. Larry Tate, vice president of quality at Comdial Corp. of Charlottesville, Virginia, maintains that the power of the internal quality audit offers the very best way for a company to sustain and improve its quality system. This view is widely held by quality experts. Rafik H. Bishara and Michael L. Wyrick claim the internal quality audit at Eli Lilly improves quality, enhances the fitness of the product, and avoids delays in launching new products.[2] Raphael Fiorentino and Michel Perigord write that the impact of an internal quality audit reaches beyond evaluation, promoting motivation, cohesiveness, and continuous learning.[3]

In the course of this book we will discuss the mission and implementation of internal quality audits as a tool for improving quality management systems. Beginning with a few definitions and characteristics of auditing in general, we'll then describe a comprehensive and effective audit program. You will learn how to organize and conduct the pre-audit phase: planning and scheduling, and assembling an audit team. You will learn the techniques necessary to conduct an effective audit, including critically reviewing documents and effectively interviewing personnel. You also will learn the post-audit process, which includes the all-important follow-up activities. When you finish this book, you will be an able participant in an effective IQA program as a member of an IQA team.

Because auditing is fundamentally a comparison of a system to some standard, it's easier to understand when studied in that context. The most widely accepted standard for quality systems is the ISO 9000:2000 series. In this book, we integrate the discussion of auditing with ISO 9001:2000 requirements as a means of clarifying the techniques and objectives of internal quality auditing.

INTRODUCTION TO AUDITING

There are two basic kinds of audits. The first is a *compliance audit*, during which the performer must *comply* with a set of rules. Examples of well-known compliance audits include tax audits, financial audits, and regulatory audits. The government usually conducts regulatory audits—a city health official may visit a local restaurant, for example. We read about financial audits in the daily newspapers and are aware of the important role that certified public accountants play in the business world. And because we are all subject to tax audits, we have a first-hand understanding of compliance audit requirements—you better be in compliance, or else. Unfortunately, the punitive notion of audits as something to be feared has given auditing a bad name.

The second type of audit requires conformance to a standard, but also evaluates how effective that conformance is in achieving intended goals. A *management audit* falls in this category. Whereas a compliance audit is a form of go/no-go evaluation, the management audit looks at things from the standpoint of improvement. It's constructive. Quality, environmental, and safety audits are management audits.

However, the true purpose of any audit is to examine, adjust, and verify a process in some sense. Notice the train of thought here—we examine the process with the *objective* of making necessary adjustments to bring the process to a performance level that can reach intended goals. Both auditor and auditee benefit from an audit of this kind.

Audits are conducted in several ways and can be categorized by how they are conducted: internally, externally, and extrinsically. Internal audits, which we are studying in this book, are first-party audits that an organization conducts of its own processes. A company may conduct second-party audits of its suppliers or agents— auditing a supplier's quality system, for example, rather than conducting a receipt inspection of products purchased from the suppliers. Third-party audits of a company's processes are conducted by an outside agency, often a regulating body. An audit of Food Lion Corp. by PriceWaterhouseCoopers is a third-party financial audit; an audit of Motorola Corp. by the British Standards Institution is a third-party quality audit.

Quality Audits

There are many different names for audits, some of them indicating a genre, some a scope, some a purpose. We are primarily interested in quality audits, and a definition may clarify things for us. ISO 10011:1994 defines a quality audit as:

> *A systematic and independent examination to determine whether quality activities and related results comply with planned arrangements and whether these arrangements are implemented effectively and are suitable to achieve objectives.*

This definition indicates that a quality audit is also a management audit. It requires compliance to "planned arrangements" and also verifies effectiveness. Improvement of the audited function is implied. The planned arrangements usually represent some sort of standard. By its very nature, an audit must be conducted according to a standard. If financial auditors had different standards—say Deloitte & Touche used one standard and PriceWaterhouseCoopers another—then financial markets would be plunged into chaos because company ratings could not be compared. In the global marketplace, quality is no less important. Every product has both price and quality levels attached to it, and the two together establish its value.

To ensure that quality can be sustained in a dynamic environment, a company must maintain an IQA program. The program monitors the dynamic quality system in real time, with the IQA team functioning as the eyes of management. This combination contributes to improvement because systematic problems can be identified through feedback and eliminated by management decision in a bootstrap cycle: self-evaluation fosters self-improvement.

Quality audit elements include training, planning, and scheduling; a checklist; the audit itself; analyzing the audit's results, reports, and records; and follow-up activities. Clearly, there is much more to a quality audit than just conducting it. Let's examine each of these elements, some of which apply directly, some indirectly, to the quality audit.

Types of Quality Audits

It's useful to classify quality audits according to their objective. Every auditee's first question is, "Why am I doing this?" The objective answers that question and gives direction to the enterprise. Given the nature of any business organization, an audit can focus on the product or service, a basic process used to accomplish the product or service, or the overall system in support of this activity. In simple terms, the *type* of audit implies its objective. Figure 1.1 outlines types of audits and gives a brief description of each.

A product (or service) quality audit examines specified quality characteristics of a product or service to verify that they meet specifications. A product quality audit is, in this sense, much like an inspection, but the purpose is quite different. The product is examined *after* final inspection, and the audit's purpose is to verify whether any findings are common or special, and whether improvement is possible. The examination may be an inspection or a full operational test and measures whether the system can correctly accept or reject product.

A process quality audit verifies that an activity or operation used in generating a product or service is stable and capable of producing output that meets specifications. Software, hardware, and personnel employed in the activity are considered a functional part of it. Simply speaking, a process audit has the breadth of a system audit, but it focuses on a single activity—for example, a stamping machine, a paint operation, or a financial department. All controls are examined for effectiveness.

Figure 1.1 Types of quality audits
Product
Examines a product or service for conformance to specifications and standards
Process
Examines an activity to verify that inputs, actions, and outputs conform to requirements
System
Examines the entire quality system for conformance and effectiveness

A system audit, as its name suggests, examines the entire quality system to verify its conformance to company policies, procedures, and controls. It looks at products, processes and services, management responsibilities, and the effectiveness of all activities in ensuring a stable, capable, and improvable system.

Purpose of Quality Audits

Every measurement comes down to a comparison. An audit, too, is a measurement "to determine whether quality activities and related results comply with planned arrangements." In fact, different comparisons can be made, and the nature of the comparison defines the audit's purpose. Figure 1.2 provides concise meanings for the three purposes of an audit.

A *suitability audit* is an in-depth comparison of the quality system documentation to a reference standard. Comparing, for example, a company's quality manual in its entirety to ISO 9001:2000 requirements is a suitability audit. This is often called a desk audit because much of it can be accomplished at the auditor's desk or in the auditee's office. The latter case would occur when it's necessary to go into work areas to verify work instructions, for example.

A *conformity audit* is an in-depth comparison of a quality system's activities to the system documentation. It verifies and validates implementation of the quality manual. It is not unusual to conduct both kinds of audits if that is the objective, first doing the desk audit, and then doing on-site verification.

Suitability and conformity audits also can be conducted at the product, process, or system level.

You can compare a document to a standard, or an activity to its controlling document, either to verify that it is adequate in some minimal sense, or to verify

Figure 1.2 Reasons for quality audits

Suitability
An audit to compare the quality documentation against a reference standard

Conformity
An audit to compare quality activities against quality policies and procedures

Effectiveness
An evaluation of a quality activity relative to the achievement of quality objectives

that it is effective in achieving quality goals. It's a question of degree. Effectiveness is best determined by measuring capability, but capability is rather rigorously defined and measured. The auditor must examine the objective of a control, then attempt to determine the extent to which it is effective. Simply noting that a control is "in place" is a weak criterion of quality.

THE IQA PROGRAM

We began this chapter by saying that internal quality auditing can be an effective instrument for quality improvement, but this effectiveness comes neither free nor easily. An IQA program must be implemented properly, within a structure shown in Figure 1.3. Readers with a background in control systems will recognize this structure as a closed-loop control system. This is not mere coincidence: The stability, capability, and improvability of a system depend upon feedback, and much more will be said about these system characteristics in later chapters. For now, we want only to stress two issues with regard to Figure 1.3. First, this is a very general flow chart; the closed-loop process is capable of delivering either a product or a service. Second, the IQA program overlays this operating system, which should operate normally during an audit. An old axiom states the act of measuring should never affect the measurement itself or the dynamics of the thing measured. This ideal is not easily obtained; statisticians recognize that some of the noise measured in a process may well be caused by the measurement itself, and they include the probability of this occurrence in their experimental design.

It should be noticed, too, that an IQA team fits within the structure as the customer requirements do. As Fiorentino and Perigord put it, the IQA teams are the eyes and ears of the customer.[4]

Management

The management representative responsible for the quality management system should serve as the IQA program manager—the person responsible for defining IQA policies, procedures, plans, and program execution. For small companies, IQA management may be a corollary duty of one of the company managers. If so, this should be specified in the quality manual. Although the management representative is the IQA program manager, he or she might not be the IQA team leader or take part in the auditing. That depends on the team's competence and size, and the team leader's own availability.

The IQA program plays two very important roles. First, it is the driving force that achieves and maintains a dynamic quality system. It continually monitors the quality system for compliance to the standard. Second, an IQA program provides the vehicle for analysis and review of operations from the viewpoint of quality, enabling the potential for improvement. Though continual improvement works well as a theory, an empowered and properly implemented IQA program, in which executive management uses the IQA function as its eyes and ears, can make it a reality.

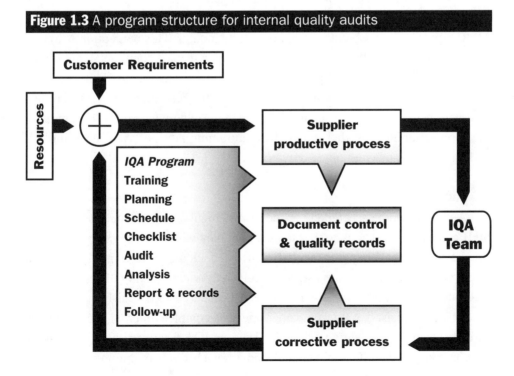

Figure 1.3 A program structure for internal quality audits

Training

Besides their personal skills, internal quality auditors need to know the standards and auditing techniques. Specifically, the auditor should be trained in setting up a schedule, developing and using a checklist, effectively and efficiently conducting an audit, reporting on nonconformities, writing a report, and verifying follow-up activities.

Internal auditing must be both efficient and effective. Efficient auditing involves sampling, because not every item of a quality system can be observed due to time constraints. The audit plan should accommodate this reality. Effective auditing requires acceptable techniques for examining, questioning, and evaluating. Therefore, auditor training includes exercises in comparing a quality system to a standard, defining an audit's scope, conducting meetings, performing the audit itself, describing nonconformities, determining findings, and writing reports.

Formal training provides the means for gaining auditing expertise, but mastery comes with on-the-job training. Both the auditors and the auditee learn to see the operations of the company with a customer's perspective. Auditors achieve this perspective by acting in a customer's role. The auditees, most of whom will never see an external customer if they work in a manufacturing plant, get the customer's perspective through the auditor-as-customer-agent.

Through the auditing experience, the auditor also learns the process is, as Craig M. Rice puts it, for problem solving, not fault-finding.[5] This perception is important to improvement. If the auditor is seen as an inspector, then the audited functions may well try to hide symptoms, thus obscuring systematic problems. Auditees may even deny the auditor's observations, with the resulting blame, denial, and obstruction escalating up the chain of command. Audit team leaders must monitor the cooperation level of their audits from a training point of view, ensuring that auditors develop tact and objectivity.

Schedule

Audits should be scheduled repeatedly and regularly. Companies seeking ISO 9001 conformity may look to the standard, but they will not get much guidance on frequency. ISO 9001 requires regularly scheduled audits, but does not specify how often. For companies that are ISO 9001-certified, or that intend to become so, the frequency of internal audits is more or less dictated by their registrars. They will almost always insist that the company achieves a complete internal audit cycle before they come in for their annual audit. Thus, an IQA frequency of at least once a year has become the ISO 9000 standard and is not a bad rule of thumb for everyone.

Annual quality audits can be accomplished in several ways. One method is to do it the hard way, i.e., once per year auditing everything. An alternative is to divide the company operations to be audited into groups of two, four, or 12, for example, and then perform partial quality system audits monthly, quarterly, or semi-annually. At the end of one year, the entire quality system will have been audited at least once, thus meeting the requirement.

Scope and Basis

The scope of an audit depends both on the activities to be audited and the reason for the audit. In the first case, only certain departments might be audited because of an annual cycling system. Beyond that, an audit might specify sampling rate or purview—only so many procedures, instructions, and interviews, for example.

The reason for an audit is called its *basis*. We have discussed scheduled audits, but there may be some other rationale: customer complaints, results of statistical analyses, or an increase in nonconformities in a given area. These kinds of problems amount to system-level special causes and may require an audit effort to track them down.

Checklist

An auditing checklist is composed of several columns. The first might be a specific requirement of the standard. The second might be a space for a simple yes or no, relative to compliance. The third column might be used for auditor comments. The checklist is made up in accordance with the scope and basis of the audit, but understanding the top-down structure of a process helps in generating a checklist.

Planning

The management representative is responsible for an audit plan, which covers schedule, scope, basis, and checklists. The audit plan also includes strategy: which departments will be examined, and where and why. Previous audit results, special cause reports, and auditor training are factors in deciding how to execute an audit. The planning phase allows the management representative to select and meet with the audit team to discuss objectives; do some brainstorming; and define, develop, and finalize the plan.

Report

The audit report may be written by the audit team leader, but it is the management representative's responsibility. A copy of the report becomes a quality record, but a copy should also be provided to the managers responsible for the audited activities. The report should be dated and include the names of those who conducted the audit.

The IQA team's report is much different than that of an external audit team. A fundamental purpose of any report is to discuss nonconformities, so it should identify items to be taken for corrective action and suggest a schedule for doing so. The report should be in a standard form, especially that part devoted to reporting nonconformities. One possible format might include the audit number, responsible department, responsible auditor, nonconformity, issue date, and response due date. However, the internal audit has a second purpose: to improve the system. In an audit conducted formatively, ideas for improvement will have been discussed at various workstations and offices, in closing meetings, and elsewhere. Agreement and conclusions about these ideas are extremely important and should also be enclosed in the report. Doing so raises them to a formal level and enhances the probability that positive steps will be taken.

Follow-up

The minimum goal of an internal quality audit is to verify conformance of a quality system to its standard. In the event of a nonconformity, corrective action is required and must be verified. Corrective action is always in addition to the planned and scheduled regular activities of the productive unit found in nonconformance, so the responsible manager may take his or her time responding. One way of encouraging compliance to the audit report is to make things clear about the matter in a policy recorded in the quality manual. For example, in its section on internal audits, the quality manual might say: "It will be the company policy that corrective action items will be assigned a response date by which time the identified problems must be resolved. Problems remaining uncorrected beyond this date will be brought to the attention of executive management for resolution."

Continual improvement ideas, too, extend through the follow-up period and should be formalized. J.P. Russell and Terry Regal identify the "audit function improvement process."[6] This is a formal mechanism by which those who conduct an audit are brought into the follow-up process. The auditors, the audited, and other stakeholders work together in teams to ensure a constructive resolution to systematic problems identified in the audit. S. Sakofsky and David Vitale express it this way: The purpose of an internal quality audit is to improve the value of the audited activity.[7]

SUMMARY

A quality audit is defined as a systematic and independent examination to determine whether quality activities and related results comply with planned arrangements, and whether these arrangements are implemented effectively and are suitable to achieve objectives. Beyond this, an IQA can be a process for continual improvement within a company because of the congruity of objectives shared by the auditors and the auditees.

Above all, auditing requires a belief that the IQA, representing the customer, is the company's trump card in self-evaluation and improvement. This notion encourages executive management's investment in the IQA in terms of personnel training and program influence. Auditors will be trained in auditing techniques and in understanding the requirements of a quality management standard, in addition to their expertise and skills in their regular responsibilities. The management representative will provide scope and direction to the IQA.

We have examined the definition of a quality audit, discussed some of the characteristics and variety of audits, and have considered the utility of the internal quality audit as a tool for continual improvement of the quality management system. It was also established that an auditor compares the audited entity to some standard, and so must understand quality standards. In the next chapter, we will look at the very important initial phase of an internal quality audit.

REFERENCES

1. Arter, Dennis R. *Quality Audits for Improved Performance*. Milwaukee: ASQ Quality Press, 1994.
2. Bishara, Rafik H., and Michael L. Wyrick. "A Systematic Approach to Quality Assurance Auditing." *Quality Progress*, Dec. 1994, pp. 67–70.
3. Fiorentino, Raphael, and Michel Perigord. "Going from an Investigative to a Formative Auditor." *Quality Progress*, Oct. 1994, pp. 61–65.
4. Ibid.
5. Rice, Craig M. "How to Conduct an Internal Quality Audit and Still Have Friends." *Quality Progress*, June 1994, pp. 39–41.
6. Russell, J. P., and Terry Regel. "After the Quality Audit: Closing the Loop on the Audit Process." *Quality Progress*, June 1996, pp. 65–67.
7. Sakofsky, S. and David Vitale. "Value-Added Audit Training." *Quality Progress*, May 1994, pp. 45–47.

The Pre-Audit Phase

John Gibson, of the University of Virginia's School of Engineering, used to say that when confronted with a challenge people often have an overwhelming tendency to just jump in and do something. He would give the example of software programmers who, when given a new project, would want to "throw together a few lines of code, just to get started."[1] This notion is almost always a bad idea, and never more so than when conducting an audit.

Before you can begin a quality system audit, there are many things that must be done first. Doing them constitutes the preliminary or pre-audit phase of activity. You must decide the "who, what, where, when, and how" of the audit; in other words, you need a plan. To begin with, the system, process, product, or service to be audited must be operating—there is no point in auditing a quiescent process. Therefore, people need to be working and the company making money. The audit must be planned so that it can be effective and yet not affect the audited system.

Another aspect of the plan is the audit team itself. Collectively, it encompasses a wide spectrum of skills, yet individual auditors may well audit processes with which they have little or no experience. We will show that this is entirely feasible and professional, and even though the team might not be experts in the areas they audit, they can maintain credibility if they conduct a well-organized and well-planned audit.

A plan answers the question of what to do and includes a schedule for when to do it. You need to put together an audit team, and then decide whom you are going to audit. You need a checklist of events and requirements that will define the audit's basis and scope. Of course, the plan also will explain why a given action is taken, which is the most important factor of all. Sometimes an event is repeated for years, long after its utility is expired, simply because people have stopped asking why it is being done. There must be a purpose to an audit, and if the purpose changes or expires, the audit must be planned anew.

Because there are many different kinds of audits, there are also a wide variety of reasons for conducting them and an equally varied list of skills required for them. Most of the overall planning will be done by the management representative, although the internal quality audit (IQA) team leader will be responsible for helping to plan a particular audit. Because each IQA team member is a potential team leader, it behooves all members to learn how to plan and prepare for conducting an audit.

In this chapter we'll learn how to generate an audit plan and schedule, examining all the factors to be considered in scheduling. We'll consider auditors and teams, and learn how to assemble an effective one. We'll discuss the basis and scope of an audit, because it is in keeping with the top-down approach to auditing. Because the audit is implemented by a checklist, we'll also learn how to create a checklist from a given scope and basis. Thus, we have two reasons for understanding how scope and basis are considered.

PLANNING

A plan is a set of ideas that define an action to be taken. In simple terms, a plan explains the why, who, what, when, where, and how of the action. *Why* are we doing this audit? Why refers to the audit's objectives. These are expressed in its basis and scope. The basis is the reason for the audit. It may be a regularly scheduled audit with the objective of verifying conformance to the standard, or it may be a special audit for some other rationale—customer complaints, results of statistical analyses, or increase in nonconformity in a given area.

Who refers to the scope of the audit—the functions or processes to be audited. The strategy of the plan is the key to who gets audited. For example, if a company does only one audit per year, then everybody is audited. If it does quarterly audits, then roughly one-fourth of the processes are audited, and so on. If the audit is special, then the objective implies its scope.

Figure 2.1 The elements of the audit plan
Why   Objectives
Who   Functions to be audited
What   Applicable requirements
When   Schedule, frequency
Where Functional itinerary
How   Procedures, observations/roles, responsibilities, IQA team

What refers to the basis of the audit—the applicable requirements of the standard. The scope has a major impact on which requirements are active because the standard's requirements are mapped into a company's functions in a logical way. Clearly, if you are going to audit the purchasing function of the company, then requirements applicable to the purchasing function are appropriate, and the requirements applicable to, say, design reviews are not.

When is determined by the schedule and the frequency of the company's audit strategy. The frequency should be as evenly spaced throughout the year, as operations will allow, to verify the consistency of the quality system.

Where refers to the location of the functions to be audited. Often they are not in the same building, and may not even be in the same town. For example, VSE Corp. maintains an IQA team at its headquarters in northern Virginia, which conducts audits of branch offices throughout the state. So an audit plan should designate the location(s) of the audit. At the very least, each auditor should know where to go and when to be there.

How is defined by the procedures that are applicable to the audit. There may be some ambiguity here. Audits can include the audit of procedures, when the auditor reviews them to see how things are done. But the auditor also conducts the audit according to procedures. How the auditor conducts the audit is guided by the controlling policies and procedures of the standard related to internal auditing. Thus, you follow procedures when auditing procedures; how another person does his or her job is no more important than how you do yours.

The ISO 9000:2000 auditor guidelines, Q10011-1, 2, and 3 (1994), require that an audit plan include:

- Scope and basis of the audit
- Identification of all individuals with direct responsibilities in the audit
- Identification of reference documents, such as the standard, the quality manual, and applicable procedures and work instructions
- Identification of the audit team members
- Language of the audit
- Date and place of the audit
- Identification of the functions to be audited
- Expected time and duration of each audit activity
- Schedule of pre- and post-audit meetings to be held with audit management
- Confidentiality requirements
- Audit report distribution and expected date of issue

Some of these items are obvious, but others may require an explanation. "Language of the audit" does not refer to the language spoken within the company but to any specific or technical terms that have meaning to quality experts. For example, if the audit plan discusses a *unit under test* or a *measuring device*, these terms should be defined. If evidence of process *stability* or *capability* is required, these terms also should be defined. "Expected time and duration" is a more detailed requirement than simply designating the time needed for the overall audit. Each audited unit has a right to know the impact of audit time on its operations.

The distribution of the audit plan is as important as the plan itself. Usually, the management representative will make this determination, but every auditor should understand that personnel who are responsible for the scheduling and production of audited processes must see the audit plan, if for no other reason than it will affect their operations. Also, the plan should be distributed to them sufficiently in advance of the audit for their review, in order to permit objections to any of the provisions. In this way, a revised plan can be proposed, with the required audit continuing on or near schedule.

It cannot be stressed too strongly that confidentiality must be a personal principle for auditors. Companies often classify information as proprietary or confidential, if knowledge of it by a competitor would have adverse consequences. Data that reflect operations, particularly capability, are often confidential, yet this is precisely what an auditor will examine. Auditors must honor confidentiality, both in speech and writing. There is an old Army maxim: "What you see here, stays here," which is a good auditing strategy. Auditors should not discuss confidential information; indeed, it is a good idea to not talk about audit observations to anyone who does not need to know. Discretion is an excellent virtue for auditors. This reticence applies to writing, too, in private notes and in audit plans and reports. If a document contains confidential information, its distribution must be limited to those authorized to see it.

SCHEDULING

ISO 9001-certified companies are usually required by their registrars to accomplish a complete internal audit cycle prior to undergoing their annual third-party audit. As we have assumed the readers are interested in an ISO 9000-conformable quality management system, we shall also assume an annual audit schedule. The company will establish a policy on the audit frequency—declared in its quality manual—that is amenable to its business operations. The IQA is responsible for verifying that such a policy exists in the quality manual, and that it is implemented in procedures.

Internal audits must be scheduled around operational and maintenance requirements. The IQA program is a tool to improve quality throughout the company and not an interference with daily operations. Work-around is easy to do for planned operations and maintenance, but unforeseen events such as work backlog or equipment failure will affect the schedule also. One of the advantages of a formative audit is that it adds value to company operations. Once this level of confidence is established, internal audits become identified as an operational asset, and scheduling or adjusting schedules will be a cooperative effort. In addition, the audit should accommodate the various work shifts because all shifts operate under the same quality system. Few auditors are happy about night-shift work, but if quality is going on there, it could use improvement, too.

DIMENSIONS OF AN AUDIT

Many auditors-in-training, when asked to map standard requirements into an organization to be audited, assign all the requirements. Such an audit would get completely out of hand because time constraints are applied to any audit, and first-party audits often have rather severe time limits. After all, if the business of the audited organization is delayed or adversely affected, the audit becomes a hindrance rather than a beneficial evolution. Therefore, purpose, scope, and basis have been developed to work together to keep the audit manageable and effective.

The *purpose* is the reason for the audit, and provides the first parameter. The *scope* is the items, groups, and activities to be audited, and provides the second parameter. The *basis* constitutes the applicable requirements of the standard and provides the third parameter. You must carefully consider the minimum set of requirements that will verify the quality of the processes of the audited function.

Hence, an audit is a bounded activity—you don't go in with carte blanche and look at anything you please. Moreover, not only must you limit the audit, but you must also sample the things that you are authorized to audit. Audits are sampling activities. For example, if you want to verify a training process by examining training records of a company with 500 employees, you examine only a handful of records, not all 500. Sampling activities require great thought in their preparation in order to maintain statistical integrity. The purpose, scope, and basis of an audit help us to maintain the integrity of the audit, as well as its effectiveness.

Figure 2.2 The dimensions of an audit: purpose, scope, and basis

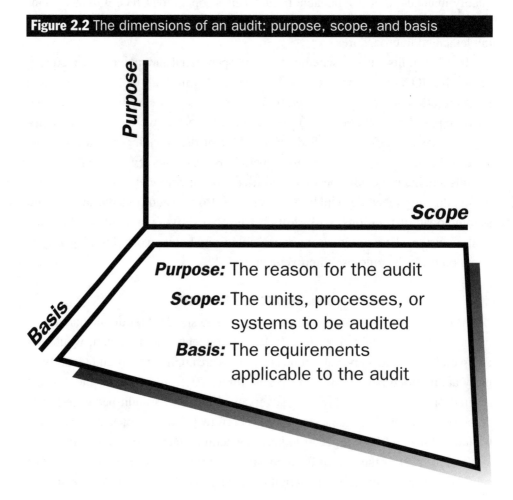

Purpose: The reason for the audit

Scope: The units, processes, or systems to be audited

Basis: The requirements applicable to the audit

The Audit Purpose

There are many well-known techniques used in root-cause analysis: Pareto diagrams, affinity diagrams, and cause-and-effect (fishbone) diagrams, to name three. An internal quality audit, too, is a useful method. It can detect and identify problems, measure effectiveness, and lead to solutions and process improvement. With this in mind, we can identify three reasons for conducting a quality audit.

■ *Regularly scheduled audits.* Walter Shewhart said that product is always subject to a certain amount of variation as a result of chance.[2] It's reasonable to assume that this notion applies to service also. Indeed, by definition every dynamic system sustains change, random or not. In the words of G. K. Chesterton:

> *All conservatism is based upon the idea that when you leave things alone, you leave them as they are. But you do not. If you leave a thing alone, you leave it to a torrent of change.*[3]

Therefore, a quality system should be monitored and its performance evaluated from time to time, because it, too, is a dynamic process. Not long ago, a friend told me that his company had moved beyond control charting to design of experiments (DOE). I hope he did not mean that DOE was replacing control charts in his shop, because the two have different objectives. DOE is used to design or develop a system for optimality in some sense, or to improve capability. Control charts are used to indicate stability because nothing ever stays optimal. That is why ISO 9001 requires regular measurement of process effectiveness and calls for audits of the quality system as part of that measurement. A regularly scheduled audit of the quality system, in whole or in part, offers a major contribution to the measurement of system effectiveness.

■ *Exploratory audits.* Most quality systems include various methods of self-assessment, such as run charts, control charts, acceptance testing, or supplier evaluation. From time to time, one of these early warning systems may discover the presence of a special cause without identifying what it is. Internal audits are an important addition to the strategies for root-cause analysis, along with other techniques such as brainstorming and cause-and-effect diagrams. Conducting an exploratory audit of the process that is out of compliance is one of the feasible tools for locating and identifying the cause.

■ *Assessment audits.* A company may be contemplating a change in one of its processes and want to establish a baseline evaluation of the existing process as a basis for comparison. Or perhaps the company may have already installed an improved technique in one of its functional organizations or processes and want to determine its effectiveness. An assessment audit is one of the ways in which a baseline level or an improvement can be determined.

For example, the purchasing department of a manufacturing plant may initiate direct, computerized access from the factory floor to generate a purchase order and want to evaluate the new process for its effect on lead time and impact on correlated parameters such as overall cost. Or the operations department of a financial service may initiate an electronic payments process in its billing procedures and want to evaluate the impact on cycle time.

The Scope of an Audit

The scope of the audit refers to the functions or processes to be audited. In the case of assessment and exploratory audits, or for any special audit, the audit's objectives tend to define the scope. In the case of regularly scheduled audits, the scope of each audit depends on the audit strategy. There are several effective strategies for auditing all functions and processes at least once each year. Some compa-

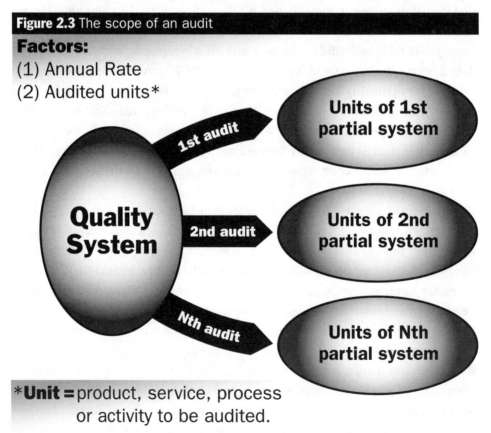

Figure 2.3 The scope of an audit

Factors:
(1) Annual Rate
(2) Audited units*

Quality System

1st audit → Units of 1st partial system

2nd audit → Units of 2nd partial system

Nth audit → Units of Nth partial system

*Unit = product, service, process or activity to be audited.

nies do this by dividing the quality system into parts, as shown in Figure 2.3, and then conducting a periodic audit on each part.

The scope of an audit will influence the audit basis because the standard is mapped into the functions of a company in a logical way. Once the audit purpose and scope are determined, then the applicable requirements of the standard are easily inferred and the audit basis is implied.

But there is a certain ambiguity here that must be clarified. We have shown how the audit of a quality system can be partitioned into groups of processes or activities, as indicated in Figure 2.3, to facilitate the audit task. It's also possible to partition the audit by the applicable requirements of the standard; indeed, many companies do this. Strictly speaking, then, the audit is partitioned by basis and not by scope. There is nothing wrong with this approach. On the one hand, you partition the audit task by activity, and then map the applicable requirements into each activity. This is called conducting a vertical audit. On the other hand, you partition the audit task by requirement, and then map the appropriate activities into them. This is called horizontal auditing. Comdial Corp. of Charlottesville, Virginia, conducts audits that are a mix of the two approaches: several functions audited for several requirements. We shall revisit this issue again in chapter 4, covering audit techniques, to ensure that it is clear.

The Basis of an Audit

Some quality authorities define the basis of an audit as the reason for one. Most, however, define the basis as we choose to do in this book—it is the set of applicable requirements relative to its scope. Purpose, scope, and basis are all interrelated and provide boundaries for the enterprise. To appreciate this interaction, consider that a company might need a regularly scheduled audit with the objective of verifying conformance to the standard, or it may need a special audit for some other rationale—customer complaints have risen, results of statistical analyses indicate an unstable process, or perhaps the number of nonconformities in a certain process has increased inexplicably.

If, for example, a series of customer complaints implies the need for an audit, then the company may require a special audit in addition to regularly scheduled audits. A special audit does not replace a regularly scheduled audit because the two have different objectives. In every case, however, there is a specific set of processes, groups, or activities to be audited, and therefore a specific set of applicable requirements.

This is an important point because it is not intuitive. Most students of auditing, when asked as an exercise to assign standard requirements to the processes or functions in their company, will assign them all to each activity. It takes experience, a good understanding of the purposes of each requirement, and an appreciation of the limits of time to correctly determine a basis for an audit. There is a good rule of thumb to help determine which requirements are to be selected for a given audit: *Select only those requirement(s) that are applicable to the audited unit's role in the quality system, as defined in the quality manual.*

For example, consider the partial audit of a purchasing department. Obviously, the standard requirements concerning purchasing are applicable. But so also are the requirements on document and data control. The purchasing department uses documentation related to quality—parts descriptions, for example, and so must have control of its documents and data. Some of the documents, such as supplier's evaluations, will fall under the requirement for quality records. And its personnel must be able to do their jobs; hence training requirements are also applicable.

The relation between scope and basis should be established early in the planning of a regular audit program, when the partitioning of the audit program is decided. This relationship will not change unless the quality system changes, so you don't have to decide what a regular audit's basis might be every time.

We have discussed the basis of an audit, given its scope. Starting with a set of functions or processes to be audited, we ask, "What should be the basis of the audit?" It's equally reasonable to start with a *basis*—a set of standard requirements whose implementation is to be verified, then ask, "What should be the *scope* of the audit?" The purpose, scope, and basis of an audit are interrelated, but you start with the purpose as the independent factor. Given the purpose and the scope, the basis can be inferred, and given the purpose and the basis, the scope can be inferred.

THE IQA TEAM

Team Selection

Several factors must be considered when selecting members for an IQA team. The first is the company's population from which team members will be drawn. An IQA team is usually drawn from a pool of employees representing all the company's activities because a mixed composition enhances independence and provides fresh, objective views of procedures and work instructions. Auditors with different backgrounds will observe the same activity from different perspectives, even when subject to the same rules of evidence. This breadth of view enhances the possibility of process improvement that derives from unbiased observation.

IQA team members usually work at their normal jobs—the ones they were hired for. Serving as an auditor is a part-time and corollary duty. When an internal audit is called for, the audit team is formed by drawing members from functions within the company that are *not* being audited. No person may serve on an audit team for an audit of his or her own function.

Audit team members, of course, have the technical skills they use to perform their everyday jobs. As a general rule they will not use those technical skills in an audit because they will not be auditing their own functions. But most jobs contain some common characteristics, such as following standard operating procedures and work instructions, and examining one's own work to determine if it meets quality criteria. In addition, auditors are trained to understand the requirements of the standard, a necessary skill to verify compliance. Finally, auditors are trained in audit skills because auditing is a profession in its own right, with its own rules, techniques, and code of conduct.

Each team has a designated team leader who is trained as a lead auditor. The team leader reports to the company's management representative, or to the quality assurance manager if the company uses some other quality management system standard.

Auditors

Auditors must be independent. This means they must be objective in their evaluations and judgments of the processes they are auditing. Independence is not arrived at by self-declaration or by promises, but by creating policies that encourage this virtue. For example, independence is enhanced by selecting team members from departments other than those scheduled for the present audit. An auditor observing an unfamiliar sequence of events may lack depth of understanding, but because the auditor probably will have no preconceived notions, he or she will be able to see what is *really* happening rather than what *should* be happening.

Auditors must demonstrate a capacity for good judgment and the ability to arrive at a decision about what they see relative to the standard. Moreover, they must be able to maintain that decision in the face of pressure from a tight schedule or from other operators or managers. Independence helps here because as the auditors come from another department, they don't rely on the audited personnel for companionship or the audited supervisor for performance evaluation.

Auditors must have tact. This is so important that lack of tact is sufficient basis to exclude a person from the auditor pool. Audits are absolutely not inspections and must not be perceived as such by those being audited. Otherwise, the audited persons will become defensive and hide evidence that could be helpful for process improvement.

Independence contributes to tact. Most of us tend to be tactful when observing a process in which we are not experts. We aren't anxious to make fools of ourselves. So when we see something that appears contrary to a standard, we prefer to bring it up as a point of clarification, improving the chance of constructive agreement about an observation with the audited person.

The old saying, "The devil is in the details" is never truer than during an audit, so an auditor must demonstrate a capacity for great attention to detail. Lacking expertise in the audited process, auditors will tend to see what is there rather than what should be there, if they see it at all. Auditors are not subject to production schedules or job routine. They are not making anything. They are simply comparing a performance to a procedure, and a procedure to a standard.

Documentation is particularly detailed—some documents are as difficult to read as a contract. Yet, documentation review is an important part of the auditor's job and requires careful examination. Auditors are not looking for technical correctness; they usually are not competent in the process being audited. They are looking for consistency between performance, documentation, and standard, and this consistency, or its lack, is often found in the details.

CHECKLIST

A checklist is a list of events or conditions that the auditor looks for in comparing the implemented and documented quality systems to the standard. The comparison of the documented system to the standard is called a *suitability audit*. The comparison of the implemented system to the documented system is called a *conformity audit*. Some IQA managers retain complete checklists for each major requirement of the standard. If so, and if a partial audit is scheduled, then only the part of the checklist is used that corresponds to the scope and basis of that particular audit.

In the introduction, we stated that one of this book's objectives is to teach concepts, not bean-counting. We want to focus on the big picture, on concepts and structures, rather than on the paragraph numbers of a list of requirements. Therefore, a word of warning is appropriate at this point: checklists tend to do just the opposite. They tend to encourage the auditor to check off, item by item, a lengthy list of bean-counting criteria. This unhappy circumstance is not so much the fault of the checklist per se, but lies in the way humans tend to do things. For example, you, the auditor, tell yourself that, in examining the purchasing department, you want to keep your eye on the big picture. Is the right material arriving when it is needed? But at the same time, you don't want to overlook anything. So you go to the various sections of the standard and find, under Planning, Resource management, and Product realization, a number of requirements, criteria, and suggestions on the purchasing function. You write them all down in bullet form and put them in your checklist. You now have a list of beans that must be counted!

In fact, however, whether you treat this list of criteria as so many beans to count, so many hoops to jump through, or as a list of reminders to help guide you to a big-picture inference is up to you. I once had an excellent man on one of my audit teams, who could not get over the tendency to nitpick. He had a checklist of about 45 questions, and he would ask every one of them of a person being audited. It was impossible for this team member to come to a conclusion until he had finished the list. Induction was beyond him.

In ensuing paragraphs, we are going to discuss how a checklist is generated. How you *use* your checklist is up to you, but the best auditors have good powers of induction, so you should strive to develop that ability.

The standard contains four areas of responsibility, with a total of about 25 major requirements. However, each major requirement contains more detailed ones. Indeed, there are more than 200 of them if you count all the nested requirements, which some auditors may well be tempted to do when making up their checklists. As an example of nested requirements, consider the area of responsibility titled Measurement, analysis, and improvement. One of its major requirements concerns improvement, and a sub-requirement concerns corrective action, which contains a half dozen sub-sub-requirements.

A checklist should include these detailed requirements as reminders of the dimension of the audited operations, but by judicious sampling from the detailed list and by making use of inferences, the auditor can provide a formative audit, looking for areas for improvement rather than getting bogged down in a microview of operations.

Requirements are checked off by the auditor making observations of processes and procedures, and by asking questions. General Electric Capital Services recommends asking open questions, those that require a narrative response rather than a simple yes or no.[4] As another example, Robert W. Brown compares a traditional question ("Are records maintained for qualified processes, equipment, and personnel?") to a preferred narrative style ("What is the evidence that records for qualified processes, equipment, and personnel are on file?").[5] A partial checklist adapted from Brown appears in Figure 2.4, and serves as an example for creating a checklist.

In some companies, checklists are provided to auditors; in others, auditors make up their own, in which case each auditor will choose a favorite approach. Writing down open questions on a checklist is convenient because you can pose questions directly from your list. However, this might tend to discourage a big-picture view. In the checklist of Figure 2.4, an auditor is reminded to verify certain conditions, and then must think, on the spot, of appropriate open questions to do so.

Figure 2.4 A one-page sample audit checklist

Major unit audited:_____   Auditor_____

Sub unit audited: _____   Date_____

Key: Yes = satisfactory; No = deficient; NA = not applicable; NC# = nonconformity number

Q9001	Requirement Title	Yes	No	Comments
7.3	**Design and/or development**			
7.3.1	*Planning.* Verify that design stages are planned			
	Verify review, verification, and validation procedures are appropriate to each design stage			
	Verify that responsibilities are defined and authorities assigned for design activities			
	Verify interfaces between groups at each design stage are effective in communication and clarity of responsibilities			
7.3.2	Verify that the inputs needed to meet product requirements are defined and documented			
	Verify that all inputs are reviewed for adequacy, completeness, and clarity			
7.3.3	Establish that design outputs are documented such that they may be verified against design inputs			
	Verify that the design outputs meet design objectives and constraints			

SUMMARY

There is much preliminary work to be done prior to conducting an internal audit. The pre-audit phase includes planning the audit, scheduling, putting together an effective audit team, and generating an appropriate checklist. The planning phase includes defining the scope and basis of the audit, identifying participants, and announcing the schedule, duration, and place of the audit, as well as identifying necessary documentation required for the audit and reports following after.

REFERENCES

1. Gibson, John E. *How To Do Systems Analysis*. Workbook. Charlottesville: University of Virginia School of Engineering, 1990.
2. Shewhart, Walter A. *Economic Control of Quality of Manufactured Product*. Princeton, N.J.: Van Nostrand, 1931.
3. Chesterton, G. K. Orthodoxy. New York: Lane Publishing Co., 1908.
4. *Training the Trainer*, symposium at General Electric Capital Services, Stamford, CT, Jan. 7–9, 1998.
5. Brown, Robert W. "How to Develop a More Effective Checklist." *Quality Progress*, Feb. 1997, p. 144.

Opening Meeting

Most of the form, substance, and customs of an audit derive from third-party audits, which are the most common kind and necessarily the most formal because the major players represent different organizations. One of the customs of this formality is the opening meeting. A moment's reflection will show why opening meetings are important.

An audit of any kind almost always involves many people. A quality audit is usually conducted by a team of several persons, sometimes as few as two, sometimes as many as five or more, depending on the audit's type and scope. Among the group of those audited will be managers, supervisors or facilitators, and operators or associates. The size of the audited group may involve dozens of people.

The audit has been planned, of course, and the audit plan distributed to the internal quality audit (IQA) team and to the function or department to be audited. However, two factors can contribute to misunderstanding. The first involves expectations. Both auditor and auditee expect support from each other, and expectations can best be expressed through direct communication. The second factor is the sheer complexity of auditing a dynamic system. Close coordination is needed, and this, too, can best be achieved through direct communication. For this reason, tradition and common sense call for an opening meeting to precede most audits, with both auditors and the auditees attending.

Over time, the opening meeting has become well-defined and formalized, although there are some who neglect the latter. When it comes to internal audits, some persons advocate informality in open meetings and in general, as a means of building amiability between the auditors and those audited. "After all," they argue, "we all work for the same company." Others say that informality can breed familiarity, carelessness, omission, and neglect. Comdial Corp. of Charlottesville, Virginia, maintains a formal audit process in its internal audit program as a means of maintaining consistency, comprehensiveness, and respect for the quality system. Klöckner Pentaplast of America, of Gordonsville, Virginia, utilizes a formal audit process in recognition of the importance of the quality system itself.

Thus, it is important to define what we mean by "formality" with regard to internal audits. In this book, formality does not refer to social formality, but to adherence to *form*. It means that the steps of a formal audit are maintained: pre-audit phase; opening meeting; audit phase; closing meeting; post-audit phase; close-out. Moreover, all the components of these steps are maintained. For example, the components of an open meeting, irrespective of internal or external audit, are:

- Purpose
- Scheduling
- Structure
- Attendance
- Action items

However, the activity of an internal audit differs from that of an external audit in two ways: Most critically because the objective of an internal audit is improvement, and the accent is on cooperation and constructive critique. Also, because the activity of internal audits may call for smaller groups, communications are adapted for effectiveness. For example, in a meeting of a group of 25 persons, it's often necessary to use visual aids. On the other hand, when the group is small, say six people, as may be the case in the opening meeting of an internal audit, it is usually more effective to converse around a table. Also, with everyone working in the same organization, there is more intimacy and less reason for reserve. But with large meetings or small, the courtesies of rules of order should be maintained. An IQA is a professional activity.

As a part of this professionalism, an IQA requires an opening meeting just as a third-party audit does. Your co-workers are your internal customers and deserve the same courtesy as they would be shown by an external agency because internal audits will impact their operations, too.

In this chapter we shall discuss the components of an opening meeting—purpose, schedule, and structure. We will discuss the attendance required of an effective meeting and the action items that must be accomplished by the attendees. Where the format of an IQA differs from that of an external audit, we will examine the differences because an IQA team member will sooner or later witness both and should understand why they exist.

THE PURPOSES OF AN OPENING MEETING

The first purpose of an opening meeting is to review the basis and scope of the impending audit. Whether the basis is a regularly scheduled audit or one called to verify correction of a nonconformity from a previous audit, the auditors and auditees should know its purpose so they can understand what is expected of them. It's worth repeating that an agreement of expectations is fundamental to a successful audit, as is agreement on the necessary coordination to achieve the audit's objectives. This includes major objectives, such as the audit basis, and minor objectives, such as identifying who goes where, who does what, and which documents, data, and personnel must be made available for the audit.

Each IQA team member will have a responsibility—processes to observe, documents and data to verify, and personnel to interview. These tasks require a liaison between the team member and the audited personnel, and may even require an escort. The opening meeting provides the opportunity for the IQA team and the audited supervisors to identify the necessary liaison of personnel.

The outcome of an internal quality audit is a quality record under the terms of the standard. Therefore, there must be one or more formal reports. Nonconformance reports and follow-up reports are required to identify problems and verify

Figure 3.1 The purposes of an opening meeting

- Review audit purpose and scope

- Define tour and interview schedule

- Agree on objectives

- Understand responsibilities

- Identify interviewees, documents, and processes to be audited corrections. Therefore, another purpose of the opening meeting is to identify the recipients of these reports. For example, the manager of a deficient process must know what to correct. An executive steering committee must obtain a copy of the report, in compliance with the standard requirements on management review.

The opening meeting might be viewed as an occasion for social chat or exposition of company affairs. After all, everyone knows everyone, and there may be a temptation to visit. However, visiting is definitely *not* the purpose of the meeting. An opening meeting should stay focused, with a duration of no more than one hour because it necessarily subtracts from the time available to conduct the audit itself. One hour should be enough time to achieve meeting objectives.

SCHEDULING THE OPENING MEETING

The opening meeting of a third-party audit is usually a major, formal affair. The company has been preparing for the audit for some time, implementing and grooming the necessary processes, policies, and procedures. If the purpose of the impending audit is for certification, the lead auditor from the registrar may have made several pre-audit visits to the company for pre-assessment purposes. In any case, a letter from the registrar goes out about 30 days prior to the audit, announcing the audit plan. The opening meeting takes place as the kickoff event on the first day of the audit. Company leaders will attend the meeting, including the chief executive officer or general manager, functional managers representing activities that directly affect quality of product or service, and many of the supervisors and key personnel from operations.

In contrast, the opening meeting of an IQA isn't like this at all. The company has not been preparing for the audit. Instead, it's been pursuing its daily business with status quo operations. Presumably, the everyday operations conform to the standard, but in any case, the period prior to an internal audit is routine. The impending internal audit is a quality activity, used as a supplement to operations. The audit team is composed of employees and the audit should be seen as an adjunct to routine operations. Therefore, people are concerned with their routine duties and aren't thinking much about outsiders coming in to review events.

The opening meeting of an internal audit is usually an informal affair, attended by the supervisors, key personnel, and the highest-level management that are concerned with its scope. Just as with third-party audits, IQA procedures also require sending out the audit plan about 30 days prior to the audit, but the scheduling of the opening meeting itself varies from company to company. Nevertheless, there is a common framework within which most companies will arrange the opening meeting of an internal audit. Generally, the scheduling follows the rule-of-thumb outlined below:

Event	Days to Audit
Announcement notice to the auditee	~30
Opening meeting	0 to 7
Audit	0

Some companies prefer that the opening meeting take place prior to the day of the audit, anywhere from the day before to one week ahead. The reason for an advance meeting is precisely because the company has not been preparing for the audit and now must consider how best to integrate it with the pace and direction of daily work activity. The advantage to an early opening meeting is that auditors and auditees can iron out any misunderstandings or misgivings about the audit plan before the day of the audit. For example, the audit schedule may coincide with a late-date delivery of a major product. Because such deliveries may well be a part of operations, they aren't necessarily a good reason to postpone the audit; nevertheless, the coordination challenge is increased.

Other organizations prefer to hold the opening meeting on the first morning of the audit, just as a third-party audit does. As a kickoff event, the opening meeting serves as a motivation for quality awareness. It's an opportunity for the team to present itself as part of an improvement effort rather than a band of outsiders arriving for inspection. The underlying assumption in this approach is that the audit plan, previously distributed, contained enough detail so that any potential conflicts to the company operations can be resolved in a kickoff-day opening meeting.

STRUCTURE OF THE OPENING MEETING

Every meeting must have a chairperson who provides direction and pace. The team leader, responsible for accomplishing the audit's objectives, will chair the opening meeting of an IQA. This meeting provides two benefits. First, it permits the team leader to declare and seek agreement on the agenda. Second, the meeting provides the visibility and status the leader will need in order to accomplish the task.

Probably fewer than 12 persons will attend this meeting, which suggests that an informal approach is the most effective. This means that the attendees sit around a table. Discussion is conversational. But the team leader should not be lulled into thinking that informal means haphazard. Conversation should be loud enough that everyone can hear, people take turns speaking, and, above all, there must be an agenda.

Figure 3.2 Structure of the opening meeting

Chair	IQA team leader
Agenda	Audit purpose, action items, assignments
Informal	Around table
Presentation	Handouts, Vu-graphs, discussion

The agenda consists of reviewing the purpose and objectives of the audit, stating the action items that must be accomplished in the audit, and appropriately assigning personnel. This includes identifying participants on both the audit team and among those to be audited. Essentially, the audit plan is presented for all to review, understand, and agree on.

The team leader will use whatever visual and narrative aids are most effective. Ordinary discussion will be the most important medium of communication, but this may be supplemented with visual aids and handouts if they help to clarify complex ideas. Quality documentation may be used, too, to explain the conduct of the audit, but care must be taken here. In some cases, auditors may not have completed their desk audit and may have asked that certain documents be brought to the meeting for later audit review. The review of this documentation shouldn't be confused with the opening meeting itself, which should close before the work of the audit begins.

ATTENDEES

The attendance at an opening meeting of an IQA is usually smaller than that of a third-party quality audit; nevertheless, the same categories of personnel are represented: management, auditors, and auditees. Generally, the attendance consists of the following:

- IQA team
- Highest-level audited manager
- Audited supervision
- Audited key personnel
- Owners, stakeholders of the audited processes

This can be a large group if the audit is an annual one of the entire quality system, but in general that isn't the case. Usually the internal audit will be a partial one of the quality system and only 10–15 people will be involved. Nevertheless, it's important that everyone engaged recognize each other. Some audited processes are in secure areas where unauthorized or unrecognized personnel are not permitted to wander around. The areas may have classified or proprietary information, or they may be clean rooms. Auditees must be able to recognize IQA team members so that they can be accorded the freedom of movement their task requires.

Therefore, all of the IQA team should attend the opening meeting, and the team leader should introduce each member. The highest-level manager of the audited process or activity should attend as well because he or she is the accountable person. Key personnel are rather difficult to define, but we know them when we see them. They are the high-level performers so skilled at getting a process to hum along that they are often in charge, effectively if not nominally.

The owners and stakeholders of a process are usually, but not necessarily, the accountable managers. A company may organize around process centers, business units, or profit centers. Then, in order to ensure horizontal integration of operations, an owner may be assigned to a specific job order. The Naval Surface Warfare Center at Dam Neck, Virginia, has assigned persons as *standard owners*, responsible for the implementation of requirements related to their processes.

Thus, at the opening meeting, the auditees identify the IQA team and the IQA team, too, meets the persons whom they will be auditing. Everyone can put each other into context. Society is organized around these little subtleties, and businesses are no exception. The opening meeting provides the occasion for all players to discuss their expectations and audit responsibilities on a one-to-one basis with each other.

ACTION ITEMS

Action items are the tasks and events that enable the audit, and they must be defined and assigned during the opening meeting. Very simply, they are the actions that will achieve the audit's purposes. Usually, there are more action items than purposes because actions are achieved at a lower level of aggregation than purposes.

The first action item is to identify the person-to-person liaison that will be required to achieve the audit. Attach names here—the auditors will be working with individuals, not titles. One week before the audit, the team should be able to identify the persons involved in the audit. Of course, the auditor must know the title of the liaison person, too, so that he or she will have some idea of that person's

Figure 3.3 Action items of the opening meeting

■ Identify person-to-person liaison

■ Identify interviewees

■ Identify documents and processes

■ Identify report recipients

■ Clarify responsibilities

■ Define the process itinerary

responsibility and authority. Thus, if the auditor is to audit the purchasing function, the auditor will be introduced at the meeting to Robert Roe, purchasing officer. In his turn, Robert Roe will know that on that date, at an agreed upon time and place, he will meet with the auditor, Joanne Doe.

An auditor usually conducts interviews with managerial and supervisory personnel, as well as with operators on the line or in the office. That there will be interviews of management and supervision is usually understood because the auditor will need to supplement observation and reading with first-hand description. However, it's a good idea to clarify this point with them at the opening meeting. At the same time, it's appropriate to inform management that there may be interviews of opportunity with the operators.

The audit will include a review of documents and data relevant to the audited operations. There are two schools of thought here. One is to keep intentions secret, then "surprise" the audited personnel on the day of the audit by asking for a document that should be there. This tactic is not formative and will result in a we-vs.-they attitude about all audits. A better idea is to build cooperation between auditors and audited personnel to lay the groundwork for improvement. At the opening meeting, give the persons to be audited a good idea of what to expect, including what documents and data will be required.

A quality system includes not only policies, procedures, and plans, but also the set of responsibilities, authorities, and accountabilities that make them all work. Auditors must know the distribution of these controls in order to pursue the thread of quality operations. The opening meeting, with all the key players attending, is an ideal place and time to settle these issues.

We have already discussed the need to identify the reports that may result from an audit, who will receive them, and when. Later in this book we'll discuss how a report is written and who writes it; an effective report has several contributors.

Finally, it's a good idea for the IQA team to familiarize themselves with the physical layout of the processes to be audited so that they can conduct the audit with a minimum amount of wasted time. Because many work areas may have safety zones, noisy machines, or clean rooms, the auditors can pursue the audit more effectively if they are familiar with any constraints on movement.

SUMMARY

An opening meeting should precede an IQA. Usually, the meeting serves as an audit's initial event, but it may be effective to conduct the meeting a day or so in advance, particularly if some of the audit activities might adversely impact the audited operations. The meeting is chaired by the IQA team leader and attended by the IQA team as well as managers and key personnel of the processes to be audited. The opening meeting is the time to introduce the players, review the audit's scope, and clarify the details of the impending audit.

Audit Techniques

How an audit is conducted makes all the difference in whether it is effective and formative. An *effective* audit achieves objectives. A *formative* audit leads to improvement. Both conditions are dependent upon the auditor's skill and technique. From our own personal experience, we know that the way questions are answered depends on how they are asked. The time needed to find certain information in a library depends on the technique we use to seek it out. And so it is with audits. The information you, the auditor, obtain depends on how you go about getting it.

The audit will achieve its objectives through comprehensiveness and consistency. A good checklist helps the auditor attain these properties. The checklist lays out the audit's dimensions and serves as a memory-jogger. By using a checklist, you are reminded to investigate the entire system defined by it, and if you and other auditors use the same checklist for audits of the same purpose, scope, and basis, then consistency is maintained as well.

In the introduction, we introduced the notion from Raphael Fiorentino and Michel Perigord that when auditors contribute to the improvement of a process, they have accomplished a formative audit.[1] If they are able to solicit the support of the persons audited, then improvement is possible because cooperation opens the door to constructive observations. This means that auditors and auditees work together, even though, as a general rule, they do not know each other. How do you get cooperation between strangers? First, both auditor and auditee must understand that the audit's objective is improving the process, not inspecting and condemning it. A good audit technique can improve this understanding while a bad one can ruin it. Second, communication between auditor and auditee should be relaxed and directed toward clarification and solutions. Communication depends entirely upon technique.

Constructive observation is enhanced by using proper interviewing techniques. The auditor solicits critical information by posing carefully worded questions that lead to a spirit of cooperation. In this way, the auditor comes across not as an inspector but as someone genuinely interested in the process, appreciative of the interviewed person's skill, and anxious to hear suggestions on how things can be made better.

Of course, the implemented quality system is only one-half of the job; the documented system must be examined, too. In all of this, the auditor will find that people play games. Things are not always what they appear, and answers are not always straightforward. The auditor must get through this façade to the real quality system. In this chapter, we will examine proper auditing techniques: formulating checklists, conducting the review of documents, posing questions, and dealing with games.

THE CHECK-OFF PROCESS

A checklist helps the auditor achieve a comprehensive and consistent audit. A comprehensive checklist includes all the factors necessary to evaluate the audited processes. It is consistent when it is used over and over again for the same kind of audit; a similar checklist is used for other kinds of audits. Auditors often compose their own checklists, but in some companies the quality assurance department provides them. Using the list, the auditor literally checks off the requirements as they are verified.

The auditor uses the standard as the basis of comparison. The standard's requirements are listed on the checklist as open questions. In some cases, the questions serve as memory-joggers for the auditor, questions to ask when searching documents or examining procedures and processes. As a requirement is met by the quality system, the auditor checks it off. The same question is posed for the documented system.

Thus, the audit is accomplished by a requirement-to-requirement check off, comparing the documented system to the standard, then comparing the implemented system to the documented system. As Figure 4.1 shows, the third comparison of the triad, i.e., the implemented system to the standard, is inferred by the principle of transitivity. Some auditors prefer to verify the two systems simultaneously while others choose to verify them one at a time, turning to the implemented requirement first. If the requirement is not being implemented, there is little point in looking to see what the written system has to say. Generally, though, in a suitability audit, it is more efficient to verify the documented system first because much of this comparison can be done during a desk audit prior to the physical audit.

In either case, the old maxim applies. The audited process must "say what you do; do what you say; prove it." Once a company's documented system is validated against the standard, a suitability audit is no longer needed unless the quality manual is changed. For this reason, internal audits are usually conformity audits.

Figure 4.1 The check-off process

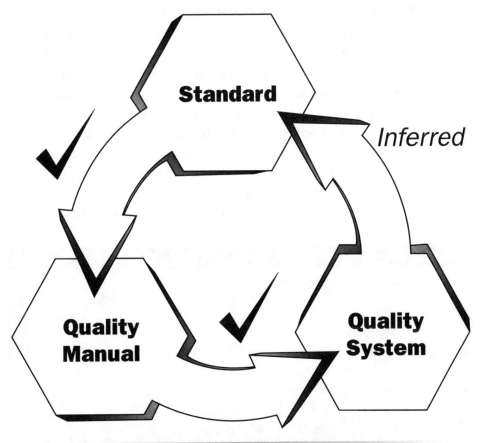

We noted earlier that the quality assurance office might provide the checklist for an internal audit, rather than require individual auditors to compose their own. Uniformity, consistency, and comprehensiveness are the advantages gained with this method. Individual auditors may be very competent at generating their own checklists, but this method increases the possibility of variation from audit to audit, and increases the risk of not covering the entire quality system.

USING CHECKLISTS

The checklist is composed of the standard requirements formed as open questions. For example, purchasing requirements include the company evaluating and selecting suppliers on the basis of their ability to meet contractual requirements. The checklist may state: "7.4 Purchasing. Describe the process you use to evaluate and select suppliers." The checklist helps you gather the necessary evidence to verify that the quality system is in compliance. A completed nonconformance form, for example, is evidence of nonconformity control as well as corrective and preventive actions. You may want to see a calibration log in support of calibration requirements, or examine a training record when verifying training requirements.

The checklist does not iterate requirements. If you, the auditor, want to know exactly what the requirement says, carry a copy of the standard with you. In fact, it is a good idea to carry this document with you as a resource and because an auditee might ask for clarification from it. Rather than quote the standard, the checklist should use language that helps to pose open questions. For example, Robert W. Brown uses questions about the quality system such as, "Verify that a quality manual exists and record the title, document number, and issue date," and, "How does the

---

Figure 4.2 Using the checklist

- Review intent of the standard

- Collect evidence

- Verify implemented system

- Verify documented system

- Make notes of observations

- Record nonconformances

organization determine that the quality system and procedures are effectively implemented?"[2] Checklist entries written in this format will generate the important details that the auditor requires for verification.

Your checklist doesn't mean much to the auditees and shouldn't be shown to
them because you will be making candid and private comments on it. Be liberal in
taking notes and listing evidence. An audit can overwhelm the memory, and notes
help to recall what you saw. However, don't take notes during observation; you
might miss something. Complete the observation, then, before going on to the next
subject, record your thoughts.

CONDUCTING THE AUDIT

Words such as "behavior," "deportment," and "conduct" have taken on a nuance of infantilism in the modern language, and some people might be slighted to
have these properties associated with them. Let's settle on "demeanor" as the manner in which an auditor carries himself in exercising the dynamics of the audit.
This demeanor is expressed by the auditor's communication, professionalism, interviewing style, and judgment.

Communication

I used to believe the burden of communication was on the transmitter but have
since changed my mind. Communication is the process of transmitting *and* receiving messages. You, as the speaker, have the obligation to express your thoughts so
that your listeners can understand them. You risk being misunderstood if your words
are too complicated or your expressions too vague. The listener, too, owes the
speaker his or her attention and willingness to try to understand. How many times
have you gotten the impression, when speaking, that your listener wasn't really
listening? The kind of messages that we are primarily interested in are data and
information. You are communicating when you express your thoughts so that your
audience understands what you say and what you mean. You are communicating
when you understand what it is that others mean, which may not be at all what they
are saying.

In the movie *Cool Hand Luke*, there was a great line used by Martin Strothers,
a fine actor who played the part of a prison superintendent who loved to punish
recalcitrant prisoners: "What we have here is a failure to communicate." Failure to
communicate happens all the time, especially within institutions. For example,
generals and admirals often are not told the truth by their subordinates but are told
what the subordinates think their superiors want to hear. In business, lack of com-

munication between management and labor is well identified as a major impediment to success. Good decisions can't be made on the basis of bad information, so many businesses go to great lengths to improve communication, including abandoning formality. When I worked at IBM, everyone from the CEO down to the lowliest employee was on a first-name basis. This wasn't done because IBM was an egalitarian institution (it wasn't). The chain of command was well understood. It was done because we tend to tell our superiors what is really happening when we address them by their first names. When we address them by their title, we tend to tell them what they want to hear.

People will tell you the truth in an audit if they believe that (1) you care, (2) you are wise enough to understand, and (3) you will respect confidentiality. The burden is on the auditor to appear self-confident, respectful of the auditee, and objective in judgment. All this can be communicated to your listeners by how you talk to them. Don't talk down, don't pose as an expert in a process unless you really are, and then do so as a peer and use everyday language. Pose your questions directly to the person you are talking to, and if the person is a subordinate, try to communicate apart from supervision. You want to hear what he or she has to say to you, not what he or she wants the boss to hear.

As a novice auditor, I once conducted an audit at a large shipyard. I interviewed a test engineer who had returned from sea trials during which not all the required tests had been run. The purpose of the interview was to determine if he had the authority to conduct the entire test package. His boss was present at the interview. Indirect questioning failed to get anything deductive, so I asked him point blank: "Did you have the authority necessary to run the all the tests?" He looked at his boss, he looked at me, then blurted out: "In this state, you either work for this shipyard or you don't have a job."

I had made several errors during this interview. The first was in failing to grasp the significance of the order of priorities inherent in the shipyard organizational structure. Although this interviewed person was the chief test engineer, his boss was head of production. Manufacturers usually separate production from acceptance testing, but many shipyards do not. Test programs must compete within the production schedule, and if testing affects that schedule, it is aborted. The second error followed from the first, in that I supposed the test engineer to be taciturn, when in fact his reticence was due to fear of his supervisor.

There are two lessons in this story. The first is that the auditor is well advised to examine the company's organization chart and then try to determine how authority is distributed within that organization. Why is this important? Because decisions are made on the basis of authority, and almost all modern systems are decision systems. In many companies, authority is not distributed in a logical way, i.e., equal authority among peers. Sometimes it follows the money. If production is where money is made, then the production boss will have most of the authority. Sometimes authority is distributed in proportion to the force of personality, the most forceful person assuming the lion's share. The auditor must understand the distribution of authority in the organization because authority is a system control.

The second lesson in this story is that it's best to interview people alone. It's asking too much of human nature to expect objective answers from a person being interviewed in front of the boss. The opportunity for self-promotion or the fear of offending the hand that feeds is just too great.

Modern quality systems include humans in the loop, and this person's role is at least as critical as any machine or documentation. Human performance must be understood, too, and the auditor's task is to find some tactful way to evaluate this performance. In some cases, as in the shipyard example, it may be best to discuss operations with the operator, away from supervision. This isn't always easy to do, either because the supervisor won't permit it or because an auditor may be in mid-interview before it becomes apparent that the questions are creating apprehension. The ability to think on your feet is an important asset to an auditor. It comes with experience, but if you find yourself at an impasse, it will be necessary to look for alternate evidence.

You improve communication by thinking carefully what it is you want to know, and how best to frame the question so that it's easily understood and unambiguous. Above all, do not send mixed signals. A frown can be interpreted to mean that you expect or want a negative answer. Try to match the objectivity of the question with objectivity of expression. When you hear the answer, think about it. If it isn't a satisfactory answer, either the respondent didn't understand the question or the answer is deliberately oblique and you must try to figure out why.

Suppose, for example, a company uses control charting on a certain machine and has documented the policy that if six events in a row occur on the same side of average, then the supervisor must be called for possible machine shutdown. You ask a machine operator what the triggers are to stop production. The operator answers, "I don't know." Either the operator hasn't been trained—a nonconformity under standard training requirements—the operator thinks the supervisor should answer the question, or the operator doesn't understand the word "trigger."

Of course, communication isn't always spoken. Letters, reports, facsimiles, and e-mail are also included. Good communication requires that you know your audience, keep the message as simple as possible, match the communication to the objective, and choose the appropriate time, place, and medium.

Professionalism

During the late 1960s and early 1970s, engineers in California's Silicon Valley suffered massive layoffs. There were 3,500 unemployed aerospace engineers in Santa Clara County in 1970. The situation became so serious and so prolonged that the Institute of Electrical and Electronic Engineers (IEEE) stepped in to set up a means for re-employment. Among other steps, IEEE tried to define what a professional is. In retrospect, it appears that it was unsuccessful in finding a generally acceptable definition.

I believe that many people, Americans particularly, are reluctant to define professionalism because of a fundamental revulsion to caste or class. We simply refuse to accept a definition that categorizes people. But I also believe that we know it when we see it, so without bothering to define the notion, we shall discuss some points of demeanor that are worth an auditor's attention.

The burden of establishing who you are as the auditor is on you. In general, the person with whom you are talking is an expert in the process and you are not. The auditee knows that. The auditee suspects that you are not a friend, and fears there may be a negative result to your visit. In addition, the auditee fears that a nonconformity at his or her workstation will reflect badly on him or her. At the very least, you are interfering with the auditee's routine. None of this is necessarily true—much, in fact, is totally untrue. But that is the environment you are walking into. Now you begin to see why demeanor is important.

Therefore, wear clothing that is acceptable within the company and appropriate to the audit site. For example, wear dungarees if you normally wear them and if you are auditing sites in which they are the norm, but don't wear them to impress the auditees. Never try to pass for someone you are not. On the other hand, don't wear a suit to an auto repair shop. And in any clothing, be clean and well-groomed.

Be friendly and courteous. Project a positive, uncritical interest in the audited process. John T. Burr stresses the importance of body language.[3] You aren't there to judge anyone. The auditee may appear indifferent, but that isn't a nonconformity. If the person seems frightened, lighten up. If the person seems hostile, explain what you are doing there, that your purpose is to work together with him or her. In my experience, people on the line are not often well-versed in what the audit is all about. Some of them associate quality with job loss. Do not suppose that the company has prepared operators properly for your visit; be prepared to do it yourself.

However, friendliness does not mean that you have to become friends with the person you are auditing. Consider that the auditee is worthy of respect and so are you. Let that be the basis of your communication. It is not a good idea to take notes in front of the auditee, who may assume that you are citing him or her in a report. Also, you may fail to observe some event or hear some evidence while you are writing. If possible, wait until the observations at that workstation are complete, then go to some neutral corner to record your observations. If your notes at a particular workstation are so extensive that you can't remember everything, then of course you will have to take notes onsite, but try to reassure the auditee of the objectivity and neutrality of your notes, that they are not critical of him or her. Above all, never swear, criticize, or be sarcastic. Never compare the auditee to others or make personal comments about the company.

Interviews

Everything discussed previously about communication and professionalism applies to the interview process. An interview is a conversation with an auditee, who may be a manager, supervisor, or operator. Interviews supplement the gathering of information through observation, measurement, and documentation. The idea is to assemble evidence that the quality system either conforms to the standard or does not. If not, what are the nonconformities? The right approach will encourage cooperation, but the auditee may not know what it is that you want to know.

Ask your questions systematically. You can start with the process input and work to the output, or do it conversely. Each approach has its own merit, and the one you select should conform to the way you think. I like to start at the beginning and work to the end. Others prefer to start at the output because they are bottom-liners, and the output is the bottom line. However, if you jump around, you risk confusing yourself and the auditee about what it is you are seeking.

Use prompts in your questioning style. "What if this happened?" or, "I'm sorry, I did not understand that." These statements elicit further comment from the auditee. Sometimes silence is a good tactic. The auditee answers a question that you may consider incomplete. Say nothing, but smile expectantly as though waiting for more information.

Sooner or later failure occurs. The auditor must look into correction processes but must do so without creating apprehension or appearing as an inspector. So ask hypothetical questions when you are looking for a downside event. For example, you might put a question this way, "*If* a nonconforming unit were produced, what would you do with it?" In this way you can verify the implemented system subject to nonconformity requirements without implying that the operator ever produces defects.

Look the auditee in the eye when talking to him or her when he or she is talking. Looking around indicates either that you aren't listening or that you're inspecting. When you have completed the interview, write down the person's name, along with the time and where the interview took place, i.e., the department and workstation.

Judgment

Few things are black and white. Some nonconformities are obvious, but others are not. For example, a company has an apparently high rate of bad product but does not measure the capability of the process. ISO 9000's data analysis requirements are ambiguous about measuring capability. Is it a nonconformity? It may be, if not under data analysis, then perhaps under management responsibility, quality system requirements, or requirements for continual improvement. Many times an auditor must use plain old-fashioned judgment. In the past, some companies could be cavalier about their capability or about consumer risk, but ISO 9001:2000 now includes requirements on measuring customer satisfaction. This increases the variety of evidence available to auditors in forming judgments.

Sometimes the difference between a major and minor nonconformity is subtle. When a quality policy or procedure is totally missing, the difference is clear, but when a procedure exists but is not followed the day of the audit, how do you establish that the failure to act is one-time or systematic? The issue becomes one of either common or special-cause failure, and few discernment issues are more important to the auditor. Generally, you look for corroborating evidence of a similar type, either in this audit or a previous one.

Keep in mind auditors must use judgment without being judgmental. This can be done by painstaking attention to detail and collection of evidence. After you hear testimony and reach a conclusion, verify it. Remember that there is no record of conversation. Verbal testimony can lead you in the right directions, but there should be corroborative documentation. Documented evidence provides the objectivity that is the basis of sound judgment. At the closing meeting, some of your conclusions that are based on conversation will be challenged. You can't count on auditees repeating their testimony at the closing meeting, even if they are present. You need documented evidence to support the testimony.

For example, you conduct an interview of a customer service representative who describes the routine used to respond to calls from customers. Because of the nature of the job, every call is a potential sale or potential complaint, so that most of what the customer service representative does should have a form associated with it. Ask to see those forms—chits, order blanks, technical service requests, complaint forms—all the paperwork involved with direct customer communication.

There must be procedures describing the use of the forms and policies for conditional responses. Everything ties together, and you must determine how well this integration is achieved. You are ready for the closing meeting when you have assessed this integration.

Direction

As the auditor, it's your nickel. You are responsible for the direction of your part of the audit and for the interviews you conduct. The objective is improvement, so how do you get there? On a few occasions, ways of improvement may be clear to you, but in general that will not be the case. You are not the expert—the operators are. So ask them. Many operators have good notions of how to improve their process but are either reticent about approaching their superiors with their ideas, or they have already done so in the past and were ignored for one reason or another.

If you can create a confidential atmosphere, the operator might well be willing to discuss his or her ideas with you. In fact, it's not uncommon for an operator, or even a supervisor or manager, to use an audit's power for his or her own agenda. The operator knows that the audit reviews and reports will get high-level visibility, possibly offering an end-run around some lower-level obstruction.

DOCUMENTATION REVIEW

The implemented quality system is described by a documented quality system, which provides its form. You can think of the implemented system as the substance and the documented system as the form of the total quality system. The first gets things done; the second ensures consistency. Both systems must be verified. Some auditors prefer to do this simultaneously. They compare an implemented process to the standard, then see if it is supported by documentation. Others prefer to start with the documented system because they can get started on it as a desk audit well before the scheduled audit begins.

If that's the case, you start with the quality manual, which provides the policies and lists the procedures that correspond to each of the standard's requirements. The quality manual may be subdivided by a standard requirement, such as 5.0 Management responsibility, with each division listing responsible positions, affected departments, and associated policies. An alternative, used less frequently, is to subdivide the quality manual by department, with each division listing the applicable requirements and associated policies. In a partial audit you will be auditing some of the company's quality operations, though not all. By starting with the quality manual, you will know what policies to expect, you identify the owners of the various standard requirements, and you learn what documents to look for when you arrive at the department or function to be audited.

Quality manuals are controlled, which means that there shouldn't be an excessive number lying around. Each department head will have a copy and will also have the departmental procedures that describe what his or her department does. You must scan through these procedures, bearing in mind that you don't have time to read them in detail. Auditing requires gathering evidence through sampling documentation and operations to verify the existence and effectiveness of controls. We will discuss sampling in the appendix, but for now you should be aware that your initial review of departmental procedures is done critically but rapidly. You know in advance the kinds of controls you are looking for, and you scan through the documentation looking for them. You learn what the responsibilities of the department are, you identify its processes, and you verify the list of work instructions applicable to the processes.

Sooner rather than later you will arrive where the rubber meets the road—at the workstation where production or service is actually being done. There will be a

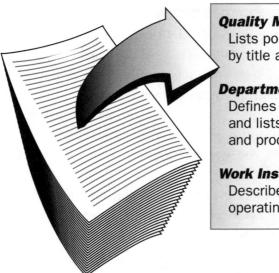

Figure 4.3 Review documentation

Quality Manual
Lists policies and responsibilities by title and department

Department Procedures
Defines department procedures and lists work instructions by title and process

Work Instructions
Describes set-ups, safety, standard operating procedures

performer or operator, and there should be a work instruction. The instruction may be in a computer, but in every case it must be current and applicable to what the workstation does. An interview with the operator establishes whether the operator is trained in the process and familiar with the work instruction. Familiarity implies, but does not prove, that the operator performs in accordance with the instruction. As familiarity with a task reaches a maximum, it is human nature to take shortcuts. Sooner or later shortcuts depart from the work instruction, and it's not unusual for even good performers to stray from the book. Nevertheless, unless the auditor observes a clear violation of safety, procedure, or work instruction, the assumption must be that the operator is performing correctly.

Let's take an example of document review. The scope of the audit can be defined in terms of a department or in terms of a standard requirement. We'll take the second case—the basis of the audit is Section 8 Measurement, analysis, and improvement. As an IQA team member, you are assigned to audit Section 8.3 Control of nonconforming product, which has several parts, or sub-clauses. Presumably, these parts are all on your checklist, and you begin with one of them, perhaps the part concerning the process for handling nonconforming units. This handling is done in two steps: correction and re-verification. Correction means the nonconforming unit will be pulled off the production line for repair. Afterward it must be re-verified.

You start with the quality manual to understand company policy concerning the first step and find there is a policy of isolating nonconforming units from the production line to prevent their inadvertent reinsertion into production. The policy says that such units will be physically isolated until some convenient time when they can be transferred to the repair bench. While still in this section of the manual, you also look up the policy on the re-verification of nonconforming units. The policy may say that after a unit is repaired, it is tested at the repair station and then it is reinserted into the production line at the workstation following the one where the nonconformity was discovered—we'll call that one Test Station B.

Or perhaps the repair station has no test capability, so that the policy may require the unit to be returned to the production line at Test Station B for re-testing. As an auditor, you have no authority to invalidate the policies—that is a management decision. However, you *do* have the authority to verify that a policy exists and appears to be comprehensive and complete. You also verify that the policies are supported by procedures appropriately located, for instance, in the production department office.

Verifying a policy involves obtaining the procedure and determining how the policies of correction and re-verification are implemented. You verify that the procedure seems adequate to the task. You then note from the procedure that the task of isolation is described in a work instruction located in the desk at Test Station B, and the tasks of re-verification options are located in a desk at the repair station. You go to Test Station B and interview the test person, asking how the operator ensures the removal and isolation of a nonconforming part from the production line, how and when it is taken to the repair station, and whether the operator has a work instruction for this process. You subsequently verify that the work instruction is in agreement with procedures.

You then go to the repair station and interview that person, in order to verify the policies and procedures of re-insertion of the unit back into production. You verify that he or she understands the policies and how they are implemented, and that this action is in agreement with the work instruction.

In this way you have verified all the documentation concerning the correction and re-verification of nonconforming units while at the same time verifying the implemented system. You have gone to the workstations and have interviewed the people responsible for the procedure. Work instructions support procedures and operators' testimonies agree with the work instructions. The correction and re-verification processes are operational and routine. This part of the quality system is alive and well.

However, remember the big picture. Test integrity requires that a repaired unit be retested according to specifications. If you find either the policies, procedures, or their implementation do not ensure this, then you have found an opportunity to improve the system.

TACTICAL APPROACHES

Tactics is the art of maneuvering or managing an action to achieve an objective. Auditors often ask how best to do the audit. There are several tactical approaches that are used so often that we have traditional names for them: *horizontal* and *vertical* audits.

In the case of a horizontal audit, imagine a matrix in which the rows represent the standard's many requirements, and the column represents the company's many departments. It is already decided that the audit will be a partial one of the total quality system. The audit team selects one or a few requirements, and then audits all the departments to which they are applicable. Suppose, for example, the audit's basis consists of requirements applicable to design and development. Depending then on how the company is structured, marketing, purchasing, product engineering, or manufacturing engineering or operations may be audited.

The vertical audit represents an alternative approach. Again, you need to refer to the matrix to understand the term. The audit team will select one or a few departments, depending upon how partial audits are distributed during the year, then choose the appropriate requirements as the audit's basis. In Figure 4.4, there are M departments and N requirements. At some point in the IQA program, these requirements and activities were mapped one into the other, so that once the departments are selected for a vertical audit, the requirements follow. Of course, the same is true for the horizontal audit. The choice of a horizontal or vertical approach is one of convenience. The matrix concept is particularly useful in companies where internal audits are conducted year-round in a series of partial audits. The matrix helps to map requirements against functions so that no part of the quality system is inadvertently omitted. As we noted earlier, some companies, such as Comdial Corp., use both vertical and horizontal assignments simultaneously. As a general rule, a mix of the two approaches is very efficient.

Figure 4.4 Tactical approaches to conducting a quality audit

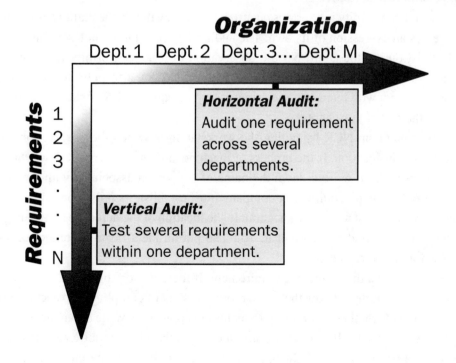

REPORTING NONCONFORMITIES

A nonconformance, or *nonconformity*, is an event in the quality system that is not in compliance to the standard. For practical reasons, some companies distinguish between major and minor nonconformities. A major nonconformity is the total absence of a required procedure or a total breakdown of a procedure. A minor nonconformity is a single observed lapse of a procedure, which in the estimation of the auditor is not a systematic malfunction. If the auditor estimates that the single observed failure is systematic (i.e., the cause is persistent), then the nonconformity is classified as major. Some companies refer to a major nonconformity as a finding, and a minor one as an observation. Still others use "observation" when describing a potential nonconformity.

Fortunately, these local usages are disappearing as the quality profession moves to a universal vocabulary. Q10011:1994 defines an observation as a statement of fact made during an audit and supported by objective evidence. Thus, the observation made by an auditor is much more than a passing glance. "Objective evidence" is qualitative or quantitative information, or records, pertaining to product quality or service that can be verified by observation, measurement, or testing.

Nonconformance Report

A nonconformity is a serious occurrence when evaluating a quality system and deserves an expression of its own. The auditor has been taking notes on his or her checklist during the audit, but the observation of a nonconformity must be formally documented on a *nonconformance report* (NCR), a form or document that auditors carry with them and use as necessary. A sample NCR is shown in Figure 4.5 at the end of this chapter.

You begin an NCR by noting the workstation at which the observation was made, and its location. If the process or machine has a name, write it down. Some registrars prohibit writing down the name of the person associated with the nonconformity; others require it. A company must establish its policy on this matter. It's very important to describe accurately the location of the defect so that management can later find and correct it. You also put an identification number on the NCR for easy reference.

Write down the applicable requirement. If there is more than one, write them all down, pointing out how the nonconformity is out of compliance to each. If you are unsure of whether several requirements are applicable, write down the one that you are sure about. If you are unsure about exactly which requirement is applicable, be prepared for a fight because the NCR will surely be challenged. The rationale for listing several requirements, if they are all applicable, is to make as broad an impact as possible on management to encourage a systematic approach to a solution.

An example of applicability to multiple requirements would be a workstation whose procedures fail to inform the operator what to do with nonconforming product. If the operator observes that the product is nonconforming, he or she reworks it or scraps it on his or her own initiative. Possible applicable requirements include 7.5 Production and service provision, 8.2 Measurement and monitoring, and 8.3 Control of nonconforming product. The only way to be sure about all of these is to track down the evidence. You must consider the applicable requirements. If you find evidence with respect to only one of the requirements, then write it down as the applicable one. However, when the NCR is finally resolved, you may want to verify that the corrective action has eliminated the nonconformity with respect to other requirements.

Describe the nonconformity as accurately as possible. If there are several ways to describe it, use words that describe the most serious condition. For example, if a pool of oil lies on the ground in an area where operators are carrying material, don't just say that you observed a pool of oil; include the safety risks in the description. Burr gives another example: If a document revision is out of date, a properly worded report will force management to resolve the problem completely.[4] The easy fix is to issue a current revision, but a better solution would be to determine what flaw in the quality system allowed a document to become outdated without automatically issuing a current one. Note that the NCR includes an entry for corrective action. The quality of this action often depends upon how well the nonconformity was described.

Disputes

An NCR is based upon an auditor's observation, someone outside the process being audited. It sometimes happens that the NCR is challenged and the nonconformity disputed. If the defect is major, there may be a great deal at stake. Therefore, the auditor must take care to use correct wording in the NCR. Despite the strong evidential nature of an NCR, a badly worded one can spell disaster. For example, you notice that a nonconforming unit has been held at its in-process workstation overnight, and you ascribe the observation as out of compliance to the requirement on 8.2 Measurement and monitoring. You should have ascribed it to 8.3 Control of nonconforming product. The person who failed to haul it away isn't going to come forward and say, "I'm sorry." The person on the production line is going to say, "Hey, I did what I was supposed to do; I put it over there for pick-up." The department manager will defend the employee vigorously by challenging your competence to do your job. After much haranguing and swearing, the NCR will be torn up, you will have lost face, and there is a good chance that the defective system will not be corrected.

In 1996, a ValuJet aircraft crashed in the Florida Everglades, killing 105 passengers and five crewmembers. Investigators found that the crash was caused by full oxygen generators that had been loaded aboard without their safety caps. Without the caps, the generators activated, producing intense heat that subsequently ignited the aircraft. Mechanics working for an airline maintenance company were supposed to follow their policy and procedures for transport of oxygen generators. The policy required that the generators have safety caps if they were not empty. The procedure called for labeling empty generators. During a long period while criminal charges were pending, no one would admit to anything, but even in circumstances much less serious than this, auditors will run into stonewalling from time to time. The best approach to take is to gather credible evidence and to be correct and specific when writing the NCR

Distribution

The NCR is signed on the spot by auditor and auditee, and the latter signature is important. If the auditee refuses to sign it, then you must call his or her superior because you need a witness to the NCR. If no one will sign it, then this event must be noted on the NCR. Following this, copies of the NCR are distributed according to company policies and procedures. Typically, the process supervisor, the department head, and the quality assurance manager receive copies.

GAMES PEOPLE PLAY

During my days at IBM, the company had a course called "Management by Role-Playing." It tacitly recognized that image is important in leadership, and that a certain amount of acting is involved. For that matter, a certain amount of acting is involved in life. The current notion that "It's OK to cry" doesn't go over very well in business, and a stiff upper lip in a calamitous environment may well be the role to adopt.

There is much ego at stake during an audit, and perhaps money, too. Therefore, you are going to see a certain amount of acting with hidden objectives; you are going to see games being played. If you recognize them, then you can respond professionally, even in an apparently heated environment. Things are often not what they seem.

■ *Anger.* A genuine emotion, anger sometimes develops naturally from the frustrations of an audit going badly. No one wants to lose his or her job or wind up in court; in any case, most managers are capable of holding true anger in check. However, some will use feigned or checked anger as a weapon of intimidation. The display is meant to make the auditor back down from an adverse decision. The angry actor is not trying to generate fear in the auditor—that would be counterproductive and possibly result in the manager losing his or her job. Rather, the objective is to make the auditor reflect on any doubts, and make him or her unsure whether the decision is worth the apparent conflict.

An angry atmosphere can become quite hostile and personal. I've had managers curse my decisions and my competence in a stream of four-letter words. The invective barely missed insulting me personally. That is when I became aware that the assault was acting, and that I need have no fear of physical attack. A person who is angry with you curses you, not your decisions. We see this strategy played out regularly on the ball field, even in Major League sports. Handle it the way the umpires do: Stand your ground and refuse to get involved in the argument. Do not reiterate or plead. Do not back down. You have presented the evidence and made your case.

■ *Flattery.* A form of bribery, flattery is a favorite weapon of management for two reasons. First, unlike bribery, it doesn't cost anything. Second, most people are susceptible to a certain amount of flattery. In proper dosages, it is highly effective. The purpose of flattering an auditor, of course, is to make him or her congenial to the audited manager's objectives. Moreover, flattery comes in simple or subtle forms. For example, most people want recognition, particularly from others higher on the totem pole. When an executive-level officer of your company throws an arm around your shoulder and calls you by your first name, it's hard to believe that it's just acting. You want to believe that you're being treated as a peer.

The way to deal with flattery is to maintain an amiable but professional demeanor and stay totally focused on the audit's objectives. Do not believe nor disbelieve the audited manager's offers of camaraderie. The manager is neither your friend nor your enemy. Instead, treat the manager as a fellow professional, and the only worthwhile objective is arriving at an improved quality system. You should both share this objective; it's the only necessary and sufficient condition of your relationship.

■ *Pity.* The opposite tactic of anger, with pity the audited manager retreats, with the objective of making you ashamed of yourself or unsure of your decision's fairness. Most of us want to be fair, and pity challenges that ideal. The manager might say, "Don't you realize that with your decision I will have to lay off 20 people? People who have bills to pay and kids to feed?"

Pity is hard to overcome. No one wants to be responsible for laying off dozens of people. You can meet this challenge by recognizing that, as the auditor, you are *helping* the audited process in its self-evaluation. You cannot be sure whether, in the short term, layoffs or adverse consequences will occur for some people. You *can* be sure that in the long term, everyone will benefit from improved operations.

■ *Bribery*. Although widespread in some cultures, out-and-out bribery is seldom used in the United States. It's not part of the American culture and in any case it's against the law. It's not likely that anyone will attempt to slip a few bills into your pocket or offer you seats on the 50-yard line of a big game. There are, however, milder and subtler bribes that you, as an auditor, might be offered. One is the free lunch, often sumptuous and expensive. The objective is to put you under obligation.

Whether you can accept free lunches or gifts of any type depends upon your employer's policies. This is a particularly subtle issue within the context of an internal audit because it's not unusual for managers and operators to go to lunch together, even when they are from different departments. And, of course, most employers will allow a working lunch because it is efficient, even though it may be the audited department that pays. The subtlety, and the departure from appropriate behavior, occurs when the audited manager invites you to lunch *because* you are the auditor. You have no way of knowing this—the manager's not going to tell you. It's all supposed to appear perfectly normal; we all work for the same company. The problem is, when lunch is over, if the manager has paid, then you are in his or her debt.

Your response to gratuities is to refuse them unless the refusal is awkward and stupid. A manager who offers you a ham sandwich and Coke during a working lunch is probably trying to be gracious and at the same time keep the audit going. It's not likely that the manager is thinking of buying your conclusions. The proper thing to do is to accept the sandwich in the spirit in which it apparently is offered, keep working, and, of course, recognize that you remain under the single obligation to do your job according to your conscience.

■ *The cook's tour*. An audit is a sampling evolution with a severe time constraint. Auditees know that, too, and they understand the implicit realities: Unless you find a major nonconformity, you will declare for quality system approval. Some auditees will be tempted to take up as much of your time as possible in noncritical activities. One of them is the "cook's tour" of a facility or process, which is designed not to reveal how well the system works, but to use up time.

You can identify a cook's tour by its irrelevance to the audit's objectives. A tour of the company's souvenir archives is a cook's tour. A tour of an operating process that is not on the audit schedule, or a high-speed tour, too fast to make valid observations, of a process that *is* on the schedule—these are cook's tours. You avoid them by politely and firmly sticking to the audit schedule and itinerary.

■ *The long lunch.* The long lunch is another tactic designed to use up the time available for you to conduct your observations. Again, you avoid the long lunch by politely and firmly sticking to the audit schedule and itinerary. In initially making up this schedule, a good strategy is to make every lunch a working one, with a fixed and explicit duration.

■ *The absentee.* An audited manager may know in advance that he or she has a process out of compliance with the standard. The manager is working to resolve the problem, but for the time being it is there, and it must not be audited. The manager is working under a policy of management by objectives and cannot afford any hits on his or her fitness report. So the manager tells you that this particular process is not a problem, never has been, but the supervisor is on leave or in the hospital, and there are no knowledgeable persons on hand who can discuss it with you. However, that person should return in a few days, so let's put the process on the next audit, please.

You get around this ploy as you do the others—stick to your schedule and your itinerary. Presumably, executive management and the participants approved the audit plan well in advance. Getting advanced approval from all parties is one of the reasons why scheduling the opening meeting a week in advance is a good idea. Let's abandon political correctness a moment. Many processes *are* individual-dependent. Certainly many historical events went one way because of certain persons and would probably have gone another way had other persons been there. It's the same with business processes. Some people are more effective than others. But products and services supposedly consistent in quality cannot be individual-dependent. If they are, then the quality system is not stable, and its capability cannot be defined. If the process is on your audit schedule, then do the audit and reject the notion of the indispensable absentee.

Some of the games we have discussed may seem improbable to an IQA auditor. It's not likely an internal auditor will be approached and cultivated by a high-level executive, if only because much less is at stake than with a third-party certification audit, for example. Moreover, that same executive, as a member of the management review committee, will have a major influence on how an internal audit's findings are perceived. Nevertheless, people work hard and have a strong personal investment in the processes within their purview. They also may have their professional reputation at risk if a nonconformance report finds its way into their personal performance evaluation. Egos, beliefs, and understandings all get challenged, even during an internal audit.

Let the games begin!

Figure 4.5 Sample nonconformance report form

| **Company Name** |
| **Nonconformance Report (NCR)** |

| Customer | Job Order Number | Job Order Owner |
| NCR Number | Date of NCR | Issuer of NCR |

Description of Nonconformity

Signature of NCR Issuer
Signature of Owner

Part A: Fault Analysis

Signature/Date

Part B: Corrective Action

Signature/Date

Part C: Preventive Action

Signature/Date

Quality Assurance Department Evaluation

Signature/Date

Company Form NCR03, Rev. 5, 16 October, 2001

SUMMARY

A properly conducted audit achieves objectives and can lead to improvement. Some of the factors that go into conducting an audit are (1) use of a checklist to compare the implemented and documented quality systems to the standard; (2) a professional demeanor, using well-recognized communication and interview techniques; (3) working together with the auditee to build a cooperative association, with the objective of improvement; (4) systematically reviewing documents; (5) understanding the strengths and weaknesses of nonrandom sampling; (6) writing carefully considered and accurate descriptions of nonconformities; and (7) properly dealing with any games and gambits that may be introduced by auditees. The best policy in the presence of such games is to maintain a professional demeanor and stick to the audit.

REFERENCES

1. Fiorentino, Raphael, and Michel Perigord. "Going from an Investigative to a Formative Auditor." *Quality Progress*, Oct. 1994, pp. 61–65.
2. Brown, Robert W. "How to Develop a More Effective Checklist." *Quality Progress*, Feb. 1997, p. 144.
3. Burr, John T. "Keys to a Successful Internal Audit." *Quality Progress*, April 1997, pp. 75–77.
4. Ibid.

Assessment

A formative audit requires the internal quality audit (IQA) team to assess carefully the observations of the audit and, working in cooperation with the auditees, the process experts, analyze the findings for ways to improve the system. The ISO 9001:2000 standard places internal audits in the category of measurement, analysis, and improvement, which reinforces what we've said all along: An internal audit is a measuring activity. Comparing what we've done so far, planning and conducting the audit represent the measuring part; data analysis is the assessment; and improvement is achieved by the follow-up activities resulting from the analysis and mutual considerations with the auditees. In this chapter, we shall focus on the assessment of a quality management system.

IQA TEAM PREPARATION DEBRIEFING

When the physical audit is complete, the IQA team leader meets privately with the team and conducts a cursory review of the audit results. Based on this quick look, the team leader estimates how much time will be necessary to prepare for the closing meeting. Then the team leader meets with the lead manager of the audited processes, and they schedule the closing meeting.

Then the IQA team meets in earnest, again privately. They begin with the evaluation's compliance phase, reviewing the discrepancies and determining whether each is major or minor. The team leader is responsible for looking for symptoms of trends or systematic problems, and establishing findings. The symptoms of problems are their gravity and their patterns, either within a single department or process, or across departments or processes. The wise team leader will rarely overrule team members because if they get the impression that their efforts are taken lightly, they will not come back. Being an IQA team member is, after all, a corollary duty to their regular company responsibilities.

Nevertheless, the team leader is responsible for the big picture—for the direction in which the post-audit action will go. The team report must be cohesive and defensible relative to the evidence. If there is dissension among the IQA team, the audited group will sense it, and the closing meeting will go badly. An IQA team that loses credibility will suffer for it not only in the present audit but also in the future because once lost, credibility is difficult to reestablish. All IQA team members must work together to ensure the audit results are constructive, supported by the evidence, and lead to improvement.

After completing the compliance phase of the evaluation, the IQA team begins its assessment of system performance, including suggesting possible corrective actions and identifying areas for improvement. The basis for this discussion will be described in the next sections.

Following the team assessment, the team leader then drafts the final report. The draft is informal in the sense that it is written on the spot, probably in longhand or on a laptop computer. There is no review by quality assurance because there is no time. Nevertheless, the draft is a crossing of the Rubicon. The final report may be prettier, but its conclusions essentially will be the same. The quality of the draft's content and analysis must be of a high order.

Figure 5.1 IQA team preparation debrief for the closing meeting

IQA Team Only

■ Review discrepancies

■ Categorize major/minor

■ Formulate findings

■ Identify areas of improvement

■ Draft final report

ASSESSMENT COMPONENTS

At one time, the purpose of a quality audit was to verify the compliance of a system to the requirements of a standard. Auditors examined the objective evidence and assessed the effectiveness of the controls. In a poorly conducted audit, the auditee might receive a laundry list of defects. In a professionally conducted audit, the auditee would receive an assessment of compliance in terms of findings—a systematic view, if you will, of the nonconformities. This approach is still used today in many kinds of audits and is even used in formative audits.

Measures of Performance

However, a top-down assessment of the quality system's *compliance* is a necessary, but insufficient, component of a formative audit. The other necessary component is an assessment of system's *effectiveness* and *efficiency*. Effectiveness measures the extent to which planned activities are realized and planned results achieved. Efficiency measures the relation between results achieved and resources used. The degree to which planned activities, results, and resources used all meet or exceed customer expectations indicates how well the quality system is performing. Therefore, effectiveness and efficiency are necessary and sufficient measures of quality system improvement.

Auditor Considerations

Although the auditor begins a formal assessment during the IQA meeting, the auditor has, in fact, been forming a rough assessment throughout the audit itself, framing observations within the context of four questions:
- How does this process work?
- Is the process performance acceptable?
- What are the key measures of how well it works?
- Can the process be improved?

The system's compliance to requirements is the lowest level of interest and requires the least auditing skill. This evaluation is straightforward, being a relatively simple process of verification and validation of system *form* against the requirements of the standard. Performance assessment is a higher level of interest and uses greater skill because it requires evaluating system *substance*, determining appropriate metrics, making measurements, and analyzing results. System improvement is the highest-level interest and calls for the greatest skill because it requires inductive and deductive reasoning in forming findings for improvement.

You begin your assessment when you have finished the onsite measuring. You seek some quiet place and reflect on what you saw and what it means. If there were nonconformities, you roughed out an NCR and obtained the auditee's signature, but now you must complete the NCR and prepare for a closing meeting. You meet privately with other members of the IQA team to discuss your observations and to identify trends, systematic problems, measures of performance, and areas of improvement. The team works together to arrive at a top-down audit report, which will be presented verbally during the closing meeting, and then presented formally in a written report. You must use effective wording during the closing meeting, especially with regard to nonconformities. If there is going to be a dispute over a nonconformity, it's more likely to occur at the closing meeting than onsite. The reason is that the operator or person at the workstation that is out of compliance may not feel equipped to argue with you, but his or her superiors will have no such reservation.

The whole purpose of the audit was system improvement, so closing the audit includes follow-up activities to ensure that improvements are implemented. In the closing meeting and during the follow-up period, it will be necessary to identify three levels of improvement. Corrective action is at the first level. Fixing something that is wrong is obviously an improvement.

Preventive action is at the next level. At the time of this writing, there is considerable debate about whether an action is preventive or corrective, particularly with respect to eliminating root causes. This argument is not germane here, but we have agreed to adopt ISO 9001:2000 as our standard and so will also adopt its definition of preventive action: *An action taken to eliminate the cause of a potential nonconformity or other potentially undesirable situation.* Generally, preventive actions require expertise in a given process sufficient to anticipate potential problems. Usually, auditors won't have that level of technical expertise in the systems they are auditing. Yet, valid preventive actions do improve a system, and the IQA team should consider those that arise, either through an auditor's insight or an auditee's suggestion.

The third level of improvement is, for want of a better term, reengineering—doing things in a better way. The first two levels of improvement are "involuntary" in that they are required in order to be ISO 9001-compliant. Doing things in a better way is "voluntary"; there may be no enforcement. Yet, if the better way is arrived at by metrics that are appealing to the executive management, then they are likely to be approved.

Figure 5.2 Analyzing observations to form decisions

Objective Evidence
Data supporting the existence or truth of something
Examples: measurements, records, testimony

Observation
A statement of fact based upon objective evidence
Example: auditors' notations derived from evidence

Findings
Results of assessment of audit evidence
Example: document control system not effective

FORMING DECISIONS

Auditing is a decision-making process. The auditor reads documents and observes activities solely in order to conclude whether the quality system's controls are effective. It is a heavy responsibility, but it helps if you understand the traditional language that is used to describe what you see. There are three terms that are extremely important for auditors to understand. The integrity and utility of the audit depends upon them.

Objective evidence is the data and information that the auditor gathers during the audit. The data must be verifiable. Statements can be considered as objective evidence, but only if they are verifiable. Hence, rumor and hearsay are excluded. You can use word of mouth as a basis to hunt down verifiable information, but you often cannot trust the statements themselves. Employees may boast of their performance to promote their own positions, or conversely, they may bad-mouth their employer for some real or imagined transgression that has nothing to do with the audit. Examples of objective evidence include measurements, records, and testimony, *if* the latter is verifiable.

An *observation* is sometimes defined as the objective evidence of a nonconformity. In other words, an observation is a deficiency. In my view, this isn't a good definition because it leaves undefined the evidence that *verifies* the controlled activity. A better definition is given by the American Society for Quality: "An observation is an item of objective evidence found during an audit." On the other hand, a *finding* is the auditor's conclusion about a control and is usually taken to mean a statement of a major nonconformity, supported by observations. It's the logical and concise formulation of all observations summarized to a probable cause. As an example, grease on the floor is not a finding; unsafe working conditions is. Similarly, an out-of-date document at a workstation and an unsigned job order are observations leading to a possible finding of "document control system not effective."

Figure 5.3 provides additional clarification of the differences between an observation and a finding. Notice in the figure that the absence of sign-off activity was endemic—found in three different departments. Each is an observation, perhaps made by different auditors. Yet, there is only one finding. Findings are the very important summary conclusions that go at the beginning of a formal audit report. Executive management focuses on them. Usually, there won't be too many findings even if there are many observations. Indeed, it's a good idea for the lead auditor to restrict the audit report to no more than six of the most critical findings, determined by a Pareto analysis. Too many findings overwhelm the audited activities and may result in an ineffective correction program.

This doesn't mean that the auditors should ignore findings, but only so much can be achieved as a result of a given audit. It may be wise, in the presence of wide-scale failure, for the audit team to take a long-term approach to correction. This strategy means that you get some findings corrected with the first audit, and other findings corrected with a second audit, and so on. The other extreme classifies

---

Figure 5.3 The nature of a finding

Finding

Document control procedures are inadequate. Specifically, the document authorization procedures do not support corporate policy.

Observation 1

Design change *Eng 06*: Engineering Change Order #1522, dated 18 October, did not have an authorizing signature on the signature sign-off plate.

Observation 2

Job order #2618, dated 30 November, located at the shipping dock, was not signed off by the production manager per procedure *Prod 222*.

Observation 3

Purchase Order #095, issued to vender Bravo on 27 October, did not have an authorizing signature on the signature sign-off plate per procedure *Pur 15*.

Figure 5.4 The elements of nonconformance description

What	Nature of the NC
Where	Process nonconforming
How	Manifestation of the NC
When	Date and time of the NC
Who	Operator or performer
Why	Apparent cause of the NC

each observation as a finding, which is technically wrong, or presents a massive number of findings, if such were the case.

The problems with presenting a large number of findings at once are both economic and psychological. Companies work on a budget, and only so much money will be allocated to resolve findings during any given quarter. In addition, there will be negative reactions. Some people will be overwhelmed with the unanticipated disappointment and give up on the quality program. Others will say, "Hey, we've been making money. These guys [the auditors] don't know what they're talking about!" Such reactions work against improvement and can kill the quality initiative.

Finally, Figure 5.3 indicates one of the benefits of conducting a private meeting of auditors prior to the closing meeting. They can compare notes and discover systematic problems.

DESCRIBING NONCONFORMITIES

We learned earlier that a plan answered six questions: what, why, who, when, where, and how. A report answers the same six questions. You describe nonconformities on an NCR, and the description is critical to resolving the problem. The best way to describe a nonconformity is systematically, which is why the six-question approach is effective. When you have answered the six questions, you have described the nonconformity so that it can be correctly identified, found, and corrected, with an enhanced opportunity for process improvement.

■ *What* refers to the nature of the nonconformity (NC). This description goes beyond whether it is major or minor. Examples include no documented procedures for a process, no follow-up action on NCs, no calibration program, no approval process for changes in drawings or specifications, or no master list of departmental procedures. A policy exists concerning subcontractor evaluation, but there is no procedure. Both policy and procedures exist for subcontractor evaluation, but there are no records.

■ *Where* refers to the specific workstation, machine, or process where the NC was found. It's important to get this right because it indicates the owner of the problem and because it helps the auditees to locate it at a later time. Carelessness can lead to a dispute. For example, a department may have three identical stamping machines. You audited only one of them, and at that machine you found an out-of-date work instruction. Inadvertently, you record the wrong machine number. Later, the supervisor goes to the machine you recorded and finds a current work instruction there. Hence, the true NC may go uncorrected.

■ *How* covers the NC's physical appearance—how it is manifested. Often this is the same answer as "what," but not always. For example, suppose you find that a forklift operator has laid several large sheets of steel on a small box. The sheets, intended as siding for a steel cabinet, have become bent and are useless for their purpose. No one wants a cabinet with creases on the side. Therefore, the "what" here is a nonconformity to the handling requirements of Section 7.5.5. But the "how" is the defective placing of the sheet steel so that it became permanently bent. The act described by "how" not only helps to locate the NC, it also indicates an appropriate solution.

■ *When* is the date and time of the observation. This may not be the same date and time of the nonconformity; if not, both entries are required. For example, on May 15, 2000, at 0930, you review a standard operating procedure (SOP) dated June 1996, but you observed earlier that the departmental procedure listed this SOP as having been revised in June 1998. Put all of these dates in the description.

Or perhaps on May 15, 2000, at 0430, you observed a worker reaching *through* a strapping machine to secure the box about to be strapped. The dynamics of the operation have convinced you that this is a safety violation. The work instruction specifically describes the correct manner for securing a box, thereby prohibiting the action of this operator. Yet, it is a single incident. You record this NC by date and time so that management can identify the work shift during which it occurred because some additional training may be in order.

■ *Who* refers to the person associated somehow with the NC. It also refers to you—you must sign your own NCR. The "who" may not be the co-signer of the NCR, who may have refused to sign it. Therefore, if you name a person, his or her role in the nonconformity should be identified. This is not done to attach blame but to exactly identify the scenario. For example, if an assembler is drilling holes in sheet metal, which isn't the assembler's job, in order to insert bolts in the correct locations, which is, the assembler should be identified. Yet, the assembler can scarcely be blamed for what is apparently a systematic problem.

Some quality managers are opposed to entering worker identities into an audit report, but without this information subsequent solution of the problem may be impossible. In the assembler scenario, suppose you had simply written "I saw an assembler drilling holes, which is not part of an assembler's job." If there are 125 workers on the plant floor, how do you proceed on the follow-up? In a similar scenario, at a recent quality congress, a compact disc was to have been delivered by FedEx to my hotel. It arrived on time, but the hotel clerk misinformed me about it. I never discovered the clerk's name, but when I described to the hotel management the details of what appeared to be a procedural problem of logging incoming packages into a computer, they insisted on knowing the day and time of the incident so that they could track down the culpable clerk. A policy that pretends to avoid identifying people, but requires identifying data, is disingenuous to say the least.

■ *Why* refers to the apparent cause of the nonconformity. This information, too, will help to identify and locate the NC, although you may be wrong on the why. For example, you audit a billing office and notice that billings are consistently late. This is a systematic problem. Policies are defined and procedures established. Clearly, something is wrong with the implementation. You interview several of the billing persons and find a significant variation in their responses. You examine training records and find the same variation in training. It's tempting to ascribe lack of training to the nonconformity, but subsequent corrective procedures carried out by the audited department may address some other root cause. It may be necessary to work together with them to find a root cause that you can both agree on.

MEASUREMENT AND ANALYSIS

The audit team completes its quality system compliance evaluation, which is the lowest level of concern, then moves on to measures of performance. The system's working, but how good is it? Traditional quality measures have concerned system dynamics—stability and capability. This should not change. Stability and capability are the core measures of a system; without them, performance has no meaning. In fact, capability *is* a measure of system performance, perhaps better than most, although executive management may be unfamiliar with it.

Capability is the ratio of acceptable deviation to process deviation, expressed in common units. From an engineering viewpoint it's a beautiful measure of performance because once you know capability, you can identify improvement. However, it has several shortcomings as a management indicator. The first is that until the system is stable, its capability has no meaning. So you must explain to management what stability means, and, even worse, how you measure it, because it's not free. Second, although capability can be linked directly to cost of quality—Genichi Taguchi does it all the time—the measurement is not as widely taught in business schools as are indicators such as return on investment, inventory turnover, or productivity measures.[1]

So quality auditors must learn to integrate new measures of performance into their quality considerations. Some of them are intuitively appealing, such as inventory turnover rate and production line setup times. Basically, these metrics imply a sense of just-in-time production, a notion most quality people appreciate. Other measures, such as market share and contacts-to-bookings ratio, may be less familiar and their connection to quality not readily apparent.

Quality auditors should bear in mind that every function in the company contributes to quality in the sense that quality is how well they do what they do. Even if they have no direct connection to the external customer, they do deal directly with internal customers. For example, a quality auditor may not be interested in the accounts receivable in the accounting department, but this metric relates to customers, suppliers, and company personnel.

Look at it this way: Capability is a parameter of quality. The capability of the accounting department will be measured in terms of account balances. The capability of the sales group might be measured in terms of quotes-to-bookings. The executive management of the company will have each function define its own appropriate metrics. Measurements will be made and statistics of performance determined. All this is auditable by quality auditors.

Auditors are not responsible for defining the performance metrics any more than they are responsible for defining production and service processes. Executive management is responsible for this part of the quality system, and the resulting measured data are provided to the auditors. The task of the auditor is to understand them. This book is designed to assist the auditor or auditor-trainee by introducing ideas at the appropriate time. Later chapters discuss in significant detail the requirements of ISO 9001:2000 from an auditing viewpoint. In particular, chapter 14 is concerned with measuring, analysis, and improvement, and discusses metrics for measuring the capability of various functions found in most companies.

IDENTIFYING AREAS FOR IMPROVEMENT

Part of the task of identifying areas for improvement is achieved when the IQA team has assessed the conformances and established its findings. Corrective action is the first level of improvement. The IQA team alone cannot identify the other levels. Preventive action will require a familiarity with the process that exceeds that of the audit team, so improvement derived from this strategy will follow largely from the expertise of the auditees.

The internal audit team should not underestimate its role as a catalyst in the third level of improvement—making things better. Depending upon the auditors' rapport with the auditees, some ideas have been forthcoming, and because the audit team members are fellow employees, an internal audit is an appropriate forum for their discussion. It ought to be possible to discuss freely the ideas that have arisen, from auditor or auditee, during the course of the audit.

This isn't always the case, however. Sometimes a person suggests an idea to a superior and is overruled. To bring up the subject again can cause a very strong reaction. I remember once supporting a technician who had an idea to improve a transmitter's power. As an auditor, I was innocent of the past history of this notion and was completely unprepared for the vehement rejection, by the technician's supervisor, of reconsidering it. But if you don't try, you can't win.

In some cases, an audit team member may make a direct contribution. It's true that, by rule, auditors cannot audit their own processes but must serve as auditors elsewhere. Yet, the functions of accounting, publications, and computer programming all use a metric of defect density, so if an auditor is familiar with processes that suffer this defect, then steps for improvement in one process might well work in another. Similarly, change orders are a part of engineering processes, contracts, and publications. Again, improvements in one process might work in another.

Sometimes an idea that improves a process might also improve another of a totally different kind. A particularly exotic example is that of phase plane analysis, which comes from physics and has to do with analyzing the kinetic theory of gases. It has been applied with great success in engineering, in analyzing state space, and is now being adapted to medical analyses, in assessing heart damage. Usually, the more novel the idea, the more necessary a brainstorming session becomes. If, while auditing a process, an idea for a better way to do things comes to you, first discuss it with the person closest to the problem. Begin to build up some support for the idea. If you get this first level of support, discuss it with the IQA team and with the operator's superior. Go into the closing meeting with some backing. Do not propose an idea "off the wall." In general, auditors aren't considered experts in the processes they are auditing, and given the environment of a closing meeting, which is often accompanied by some apprehension, a novel idea from you, unsolicited and unsupported by the locals, may strike the auditees as arrogance on your part.

When the system compliance and performance considerations are completed, findings and recommendations are determined, and the rough draft is presentable, the IQA team is ready for the closing meeting. This can be an excursion into harm's way, or it can be a very constructive event in the evolution of the quality system. It all depends on how well the IQA team has done its job.

SUMMARY

At the completion of the physical, or "touring" part of the audit, and before the closing meeting, the IQA team meets to establish the quality management system's levels of compliance and performance. Compliance is established by considering the various nonconformities, looking for trends or systematic problems. Conformance refers to how well the process, product, or service meets the specifications. This evaluation results in a certain number of findings that identify and describe systematic causes.

Performance refers to the effectiveness and efficiency of the quality system. Effectiveness measures the extent to which planned activities are realized and planned results achieved. Efficiency measures the relation between results achieved and resources used. Each can be described with metrics and provide a basis for determining system capability.

At the conclusion of its deliberations and analyses, the IQA team drafts a report of its assessment that will be presented to interested persons at the closing meeting.

REFERENCES

1.   Taguchi, Genichi; Elsayed A. Elsayed; and Thomas Hsiang. *Quality Engineering in Production Systems*. New York: McGraw-Hill, 1989.

Closing Meeting

The closing meeting is *almost* the premiere event of the audit because it is here that the results of all the hard work are presented for general discussion. This is what it all comes down to. The auditors announce their findings and recommendations relative to correction, prevention, and improvement; the auditees examine this testimony, consider alternatives, and state their positions. Then the two parties iron out differences and agree to a schedule of action. The closing meeting is so important—and sometimes dramatic—that some auditors may walk away from it thinking the audit is over. However, like the commencement exercise at college, the closing meeting is not the end but the beginning of the all-important follow-up period, the post-audit activity. The closing meeting is critical and we shall spend some effort discussing how to conduct it.

As with the opening meeting, there is a purpose, an appropriate attendance, a structure, and action items associated with a closing meeting. There is a post-audit schedule to establish, which is concerned with accomplishing the follow-up corrective actions, and implementing preventive actions and improvement schemes. The closing meeting itself must be scheduled, but this is a trivial problem—you schedule it after conducting the audit and before the audit team disbands. The really important scheduling items are the post-audit activity deadlines, and this takes negotiation.

But the closing meeting's most important element lies in the lead auditor's ability to facilitate, for the grand purpose of the audit can be made or broken here. Some audits are easy, some are not, but they can all be successful with good leadership.

PURPOSES OF A CLOSING MEETING

The first purpose of a closing meeting is to review the nonconformities found by the internal quality audit (IQA) team. This review includes identifying each nonconformity, typing it as major or minor, and determining whether its root cause is a system, product, or service problem. This analysis leads to the possibility of agreement on how to resolve the problem. The problem belongs to the process owner—the system expert—but the IQA function, usually quality assurance, must agree that the corrective action suggested will solve the problem. Thus, the review of nonconformities is a group effort between the IQA team and the auditees.

The question naturally arises: If neither the auditor nor the quality assurance department is an expert in the audited processes, how can they know if a proffered resolution will solve the problem? In general, they don't. Sometimes the solution is obvious, and sometimes it requires great insight into the workings of the processes themselves. If system expertise is critical, then the wisest course for auditors is to let the auditees dictate both the proper solution of a finding and the time to repair it, then depend upon a reassessment to verify that the system is returned to compliance. This alternative may lead to a prolonged repair time, but there is little choice in the matter. In any case, we must presume goodwill—the auditee wants to solve the problem as quickly and surely as possible.

Nevertheless, there are certain kinds of problems that the auditors may be better at solving than the process owners. Systematic problems very often occur from a lack of integration or coordination between two processes or functions. For ex-

Figure 6.1 The purposes of a closing meeting

1. Review nonconformances
2. Agree on corrective actions
3. Examine possible preventive actions
4. Negotiate a corrective schedule
5. Identify correction liaisons
6. Discuss improvement ideas
7. Negotiate an improvement schedule
8. Identify report recipients

ample, credit-card billings work under three distinct schedules: transaction date, posting date, and billing date. These dates must be integrated cohesively because the customer will be charged for late payment. Auditors often find the occurrences of ineffective integration and coordination more easily than do the people assigned to a process because the latter are bound by ardor to the departmental or functional divisions, sometimes known as the "rice bowl syndrome."

Once agreement is reached on the nature of a nonconformity and its necessary corrective action, the audited process owner, the lead manager, and the quality assurance manager agree on a correction schedule. Production schedules can't be adversely impacted, but on the other hand, too long a delay in correcting the problem will lead to a deteriorating quality system and, more importantly, a deteriorating business. Presumably, the quality system contributes to business success or there would be little point to it. So corrective actions should be taken sooner rather than later.

A corrective action must be shown to have solved the problem. This usually takes more than a few hours or a few days, so that there must be quality assurance review of the resolution process. In other words, there will be a liaison between the person taking the corrective action and the quality assurance person responsible for verifying that the problem is solved. The liaisons are identified in the closing meeting.

Preventive actions should be considered also because they lead to improvement. Every nonconformity should stimulate a discussion on preventive action. Two questions should arise automatically: Why did this problem occur? Could it have been prevented in the first place? Whether the problem is systematic or random, it may have been preventable. Closing meetings, because of the variety of skills and knowledge represented, are ideal places for asking why something happened. It often takes a breadth of knowledge to answer why, and another breadth to determine how to prevent a reoccurrence. The closing meeting's structure lends itself to brainstorming, one of the major methods of approaching prevention as well as improvement. Prevention and improvement represent important strategies to IQA teams at closing meetings—they should never be satisfied with simply identifying a corrective action to a finding. Always consider how the occurrence might have been prevented and the system improved.

SCHEDULE OF THE CLOSING MEETING

The scheduling of the closing meeting was briefly discussed earlier, but we will expand on it here for convenience. This meeting takes place after the physical conduct of the audit is complete, and after the IQA team completes its preparation debrief. However, there is a caveat: "after" should not extend too long. An audit's momentum can fall off quickly as auditors depart from the activity areas and normal business resumes.

The closing meeting should be scheduled the same day of the audit, if possible. If the audit is not finished until late in the afternoon and several hours are projected for the IQA team's private debriefing, then it may not be feasible to schedule the closing meeting during the evening, even if the boss approves of the idea. People have had a long day. Good dispositions are essential for a successful closing meeting. Schedule it as the first piece of business the following day.

ATTENDEES

The attendance at the closing meeting differs from that of the opening meeting. The quality assurance manager should be there because the post-audit period is the responsibility of the quality assurance function. The IQA team is the agent of quality assurance during the audit, but in the post-audit period, quality assurance decides whether a corrective action is sufficient.[1] The quality assurance function is well-suited to determine trends and other systematic problems because it possesses the corporate memory on audit history—the outcomes of previous audits.

The IQA team members must attend the closing meeting because the person who has initiated a nonconformance report (NCR) is the one who presents it. The American Society for Quality recommends that the top management staff be there, as they are the ones with the authority to make any necessary changes in the system.[2] Some quality experts recommend that the audited process supervisors and lower-level stakeholders should *not* attend a closing meeting. However, the nature of internal audits is such that the company may deem it wise to include them. The potential for bruised egos and hurt feelings goes up, the greater the attendance, but also, with increasing attendance, the collective knowledge increases on how best to resolve problems. We have noted several times that the greatest portion of expertise required for prevention and improvement resides with the process owners and operators, not with the audit team.

Finally, the liaisons necessary for successful corrective and preventive follow-through will be established at this meeting, so it is important that these persons identify each other. The liaisons may take two forms: directly and through quality assurance. With direct liaisons each audited person communicates the corrective action progress directly to the auditor who initiated the NCR. The advantage to this arrangement is that it is first-party—the people most knowledgeable about a problem are handling it. The disadvantage is that the auditor is back at work during the post-audit period; the IQA audit team no longer exists, nor does its authority.

The alternate approach for liaison is that all correspondence on corrective and preventive action is channeled through the quality assurance function, and the quality assurance manager decides whether a particular step or action should be reviewed by the NCR originators. This process is preferred because the quality assurance office then acts as the control for the resolution of all problems and is aware of the overall audit status at all times.

STRUCTURE OF THE CLOSING MEETING

Despite the presence of the quality assurance manager and the highest-level audited process manager, the IQA team leader chairs the closing meeting. The team leader thanks the audited personnel for their cooperation, presents the meeting agenda, paces the review of nonconformities, using the team members as NCR initiators to present their respective nonconformance reports, and presents the evidence for findings. In this process it's a good idea to reiterate the relevant clauses of the standard against which each noncompliance or finding is identified.

The team leader presents an overall summary before the detailed review, inviting all persons to discuss their concerns as the meeting progresses. The sequence of each discussion should be: identifying the nature of the nonconformity or finding, identifying the probable root cause, defining a corrective action and schedule for this action, and defining a preventive action if appropriate. The basis of these discussions concern the following three questions:

■ Will this action correct the system?
■ Will this action improve the system?
■ Could the event have been prevented?

Whereas the duration of an opening meeting is relatively brief, e.g., less than an hour, there should be no arbitrary time limit on the closing meeting. One of the reasons for limiting attendance to exempt personnel is to accommodate an extended closing meeting if necessary. The chronology of audits is such that usually the closing meeting occurs toward the end of the day, and could run into overtime. If this is foreseen due to the findings' complexity, or if nonexempt personnel may be needed to help formulate solutions, then it may be well to schedule the closing meeting for the next morning. Alternatively, nonexempt personnel could be released from the closing meeting at the end of the business day, and brainstorming about prevention and improvement could take place the next day among the audited staff. This is a second-best scenario because the absence of the IQA team removes an important catalyst in the discussions.

The team leader ends the closing meeting by handing out copies of the NCRs and a copy of the draft audit report. The team leader verifies the overt agreement among all parties on the actions to be taken for correction, prevention, and improvement. The team leader should also ensure that every action is assigned to someone, and that assigned person acknowledges his or her understanding of the responsibility.

The team leader may also present a disclaimer, a tactic used in third-party audits, pointing out that the audit's structure was based on a sampling process. This may seem unimportant in an internal audit, but it is still worth clarifying to the audited persons that system verification was done by sampling. A discovery of none or a few nonconformities does not guarantee an effective and efficient quality system. Constant vigilance about quality is the only policy to guarantee an effective and efficient quality system.

ACTION ITEMS

Two distinct classes of action items are relevant to a closing meeting: the action items to be accomplished during the meeting itself, and the post-audit action items. An outline for action items appropriate to the former is suggested by the purposes of the closing meeting. Refer again to Figure 6.1. Each of these entries constitutes an action item to be accomplished during the closing meeting. The thought, skill, detail, and analyses that are required to conduct these action items is profound, but their sequence is mechanical—take them one at a time and perform them. When they are completed, however long that takes, the closing meeting is finished, and not before.

The post-audit actions for follow-up include the audit's objectives—why you did the audit in the first place. When you have completed all the steps indicated in Figure 6.1, you will have a list of defined actions that must be completed to implement correction, prevention, and improvement. These defined actions constitute the post-audit actions. What you fail to include probably won't get done as a result of this audit, so you want to be patient and comprehensive.

Each action must be unambiguously assigned to a person. This is an important assignment of accountability. That person may then reassign the action as a subordinate's responsibility, but he or she remains accountable. It isn't enough to assign action items to an organization because this opens the door to ambiguity: "I didn't know *I* was supposed to do it; I thought Shirley was going to do it." The reality is that, at any level, organizations don't do anything. *People* do things.

Whether there are major or minor nonconformities or no nonconformities at all, the company wants to improve its quality system, and the audit has served as a catalyst for improvement ideas. Even for a quality system that is in complete compliance with the standard, the closing meeting is the time and place where improvement ideas are advanced.

THE LEAD AUDITOR AS FACILITATOR

In the best of circumstances, auditors and auditees enter amiably into the closing meeting, each satisfied that the audit went well, a few issues were discovered, some ideas for corrective and preventive action are in the back of everyone's mind, and the chances for system improvement are good. The atmosphere is one of cooperation and mutual appreciation of a job well done.

But you, the auditor, should be prepared for something less than the best of circumstances. Not the worst, by any means. The worst is an atmosphere of distrust, concealment, deception, and real anger. This will rarely happen in an internal audit. What is more likely is that the audit team may have discovered a few problems of which the auditees were totally unsuspecting and unprepared, and because of which, a few egos are bruised. Professionals will rise above all this, and a sharp audit team leader can generate and maintain an atmosphere of professionalism. Nevertheless, some of the auditees may harbor some resentment; a few may be in a state of shock.

Yes, shock. In general, a responsible person—manager, supervisor, or operator—believes his or her operation hums along on eight cylinders and is completely unprepared for a devastating assessment, if such is the outcome. Most humans do not absorb information well when they are stunned. This is one reason why it's necessary to follow the closing meeting with a well-written formal report, in which all of the findings are repeated that were discussed during the meeting.

Much of what is said in a closing meeting will not be heard or will not be understood by persons in a state of disbelief. Anticipating this, the IQA team leader should devote extra effort to define and clarify the findings, and to direct the group toward a positive and reasonable discourse. Understanding how this is done is important for the IQA team members because they must be alert to what is going on, and because they may one day be lead auditors.

Facilitating

The term "to facilitate" comes from the Latin word *facilis*, which means "easy to do," and is a derivative of the Latin verb *facere*, "to do." Many people these days use the word *facilitator* in place of "leader." The words do not quite mean the same thing, but there is considerable overlap. For example, the U.S. Army defines leadership as the process of influencing others to accomplish the mission by providing purpose, direction, and motivation.[3]

Facilitators do this, too, but they do more—facilitators make things easier. This doesn't mean that the job will be easy; the task of a closing meeting is often very difficult. But by using tact and diplomacy, the facilitator makes human interaction easier. The working environment of the closing meeting is not one of hail-fellow-well-met. There is anxiety and a few ruffled feathers. The closing meeting is absolutely the wrong place to be arbitrary and dogmatic.

It is also the wrong place to be wishy-washy. There will be technical people in a closing meeting. According to J. E. Gibson, technical people tend to be judgmental and self-confident.[4] Mastering technical issues encourages these characteristics. There will also be managers and other self-starters in attendance. In other words, a leadership vacuum will be filled quickly, and if it's not the IQA team leader, it will be someone else, with perhaps a private but contrary agenda.

Diplomacy means influencing others through negotiation and avoiding confrontation. Lead auditors who have negotiating skills will be able to lay the groundwork for understanding and improvement. "In business," as the old saying goes, "you don't get what you deserve—you get what you negotiate."[5]

The Team Concept

For many years, I was involved in the U.S. Navy ship repair business. One of the characteristics of ship repair is the multiplicity of distinct teams involved in repairing a single ship. You have the prime contractor, subcontractors, the ship's crew, and Navy civilian teams. The trick is to get them all working together as a single team.

And so it is with the closing meeting. Effectively, you have two groups, the IQA team and the audited personnel. At the outset of the meeting, they will regard themselves as us vs. them, not withstanding the fact that they all work for the same company. This is human nature and the rice bowl syndrome at work. The trick is to get them to work together, which is entirely possible in an internal audit, and entirely necessary, given the audit objectives. The lead auditor must adopt this task as a personal objective.

The conditions for a team effort are there. Attendees of the closing meeting have much to do during and after the meeting itself. Their task is complex, and the path to resolution is unclear. They will require creativity in their actions and must have a high commitment to the audit's objectives. Implementing their plans for correction, prevention, and improvement will require mutual cooperation and cross-functional skills. Ronald L. Snee, et al., point out that the team concept is an effective way to meet these conditions.[6] Moreover, the notion of teamwork can extend beyond the meeting and the day without losing effectiveness.

As the facilitator, the lead auditor conducts the closing meeting with a firm understanding of group dynamics. People behave in different ways when in groups; to get the best from each, you must be aware of these behaviors. We have already spoken of anxiety and ruffled feelings—these may not be obvious, so you must be on the lookout for them. In addition, if you choose to use brainstorming as a strategy, you should be aware that some people are intimidated by group activity. They may have excellent ideas and offer nothing. Part of this reticence may be due to a fear of ridicule, so it's up to the lead auditor to encourage an open atmosphere and to tolerate no criticism. Everyone should feel free to advance ideas and understand that, whereas some ideas are better than others, all are worthy of consideration.

Free speech is encouraged in several ways. First, the lead auditor keeps the conversation focused on the agenda. This is done mainly to control the meeting so that objectives are reached in a minimum amount of time, but it also encourages participation because everyone knows which agenda item the meeting is addressing. Nothing is so embarrassing to a person, perhaps somewhat timid anyway, than to finally get up the nerve to voice an opinion, only to find that the group is talking about something else. Stick with the agenda. Free speech is encouraged by allowing people to speak without interruption, while ensuring they stay on the subject and remain focused. It's also encouraged by observing who remains silent and explicitly asking that person for his or her views.

In a small meeting, which may include brainstorming, the lead auditor should tolerate a certain amount of side chatter. Some people may wish to test an idea on the person next to them before they put it out for public scrutiny. The way to control this is to keep the volume down so that it doesn't interfere with the primary speaker, and equally important, so that it doesn't preclude the "ad libbers" from hearing an important idea.

Helene Uhlfelder discusses several critical traits of group dynamics, all of them unseen, but which can make or break a team spirit.[7] We have already discussed a few, but there are two that are particularly germane here. The first concerns conflict resolution. There is sure to be conflict during an audit critique, and you can either ignore it or find a way to express it. When conflict isn't permitted, frustration results, along with unsatisfactory or unintended resolutions—or no resolution at all. Teams must find an acceptable way to resolve conflicts. Avoidance is not an appropriate tactic because it fosters resentment.

Probably the best way to resolve conflicts is the way the U.S. Congress resolves them—you bring them out in the open and debate the pros and cons. The lead auditor's role is to open all subjects for discussion pertaining to the agenda, then keep the heat down. If a manager or supervisor appears to prohibit a subordinate from some particular contribution, it will be necessary to file the incident away until an opportune moment, then approach him or her quietly and ask what's going on. There are several reasons for this. First, the idea may be a good one; indeed, it might be *the* solution. It won't be the first time management has refused a solution to a problem without explanation. Second, you can't build team spirit in the presence of exclusion, and if a person isn't permitted to voice his or her opinion, you can forget about that person joining your team.

Uhlfelder also talks about trust.[8] It is a critical trait of groups—you can't create a team unless the members trust one another. This trait is particularly important to closing meetings because mutual trust is not automatically there. Two distinct groups are meeting, and the groundwork for welding them into one team, although critical to the closing meeting, actually begins at the beginning of the audit. Auditors strive to build trust with auditees through professional conduct, honesty, and competence.

The closing meeting concludes when the necessary corrective and preventive actions and improvement initiatives are identified, assigned to persons for resolution, and an agreed-upon schedule and liaisons for feedback established. The lead auditor arranges for a distribution of the final report, thanks the auditees for their cooperation, and then the IQA team departs.

SUMMARY

The purpose of the closing meeting is to provide a forum for discussion by both parties—auditors and auditees—on the merits of the observations, the nature of the nonconformities, and corrective and preventive actions required to bring the quality system to the desired level of effectiveness. The opportunity for improvement initiatives naturally occurs in the aftermath of this type of discussion and is one of the major objectives of the closing meeting.

With mutual concurrence derived from the closing meeting, an audit report and a corrective action plan are exchanged between parties. The plan is implemented, and its effectiveness verified by quality assurance. When the audit report's requirements are met and the quality system is operating at the level made possible by the audit, the audit can be formally closed.

REFERENCES

1. Miller, Mark R. "A Common Sense Approach to Corrective Action Systems." *Quality Progress*, Feb. 1995, p. 152.

2. ANSI/ISO/ASQC. *Q10011-1994. Guidelines for Auditing Quality Systems.* Milwaukee: American Society for Quality, 1994.

3. Department of the Army Pamphlet 350–58, "Leader Development for America's Army." Department of the Army, 13 Oct., 1994.

4. Gibson, John E. *How to Do Systems Analysis.* Workbook. Charlottesville: School of Engineering, The University of Virginia, 1990.

5. Karrass Institute, Beverly Hills, CA, 2000. Quotation of Dr. Chester L. Karrass, founder.

6. Snee, Ronald D.; Kevin H. Kelleher; J. G. Myers; and Sue Reynard. "Improving Team Effectiveness." *Quality Progress*, May 1998, pp. 43–48.

7. Uhlfelder, Helene. "Ten Critical Traits of Group Dynamics." *Quality Progress*, April 1997, pp. 69–72.

8. Ibid.

The Post-Audit Phase

A well-planned operation and a good book have this in common: an opening, a main body, and a closing. A good audit follows this sequence. You start with a plan, move to opening procedures, and then conduct the audit onsite. The audit has closing procedures, too. There is more to it than simply telling your customers what you found, then walking away. A formal audit report must still be written and distributed, and the process of tracking post-audit activities completed. At the end of the closing meeting, the audit may be only half finished. Indeed, the American Society for Quality often refers to the closing meeting as the *exit meeting*, to get away from the suggestion that the audit is somehow closed.

The post-audit phase is characterized by four primary activities: (1) writing and distributing a formal report, (2) conducting the follow-up activities of corrective and preventive actions and improvements, (3) evaluating the effectiveness and efficiency of the improvements, and (4) closeout.

THE AUDIT REPORT

The draft report presented by the internal quality audit (IQA) team leader at the closing meeting becomes the formal and final copy of the audit report from the quality assurance office. The final report should be signed off by the IQA team leader, as well as the quality assurance manager, issued as soon as possible after the audit, and distributed as agreed upon during the closing meeting. The IQA team leader's signature serves as a validation that the report represents the audit. The signature of the quality assurance manager indicates accountability for the audit, for the follow-through, and for the quality records.

Purpose of the Audit Report

The audit report summarizes the audit's analyses and conclusions, reiterating the strengths of the quality system as well as its nonconformities. It should *not* reiterate recommendations for corrective and preventive action that were agreed upon at the closing meeting. These responsibilities are the purview of the audited lead manager. Presumably, the manager will take the action agreed upon at the closing meeting, but this commitment must be made in writing by the manager, not by quality assurance.

Let's assume that the proceedings of the closing meeting were conducted in good faith by all and appeared to be fruitful. Nevertheless, the quality assurance function is accountable for the conduct of the audit; the audited lead manager is responsible for rectifying nonconformities. They can and should help each other, but their respective accountabilities cannot be abdicated. There are many good reasons why a specific tactic for correction, prevention, or improvement, agreed to at the closing meeting, might be changed or abandoned by the audited process owners. The time spent on these considerations during the closing meeting is valuable in providing a forum for thought, whether or not the results are definitive.

The audit report provides the audited lead manager with a written appraisal of the audit. This is important for several reasons. First, as we discussed previously, closing meetings can be traumatic. The audited persons almost never expect the nonconformities they receive, and the assault on their expectations sometimes impairs their ability to understand exactly what is being said. The written document presents concise and accurate statements of nonconformities and findings that can be studied and explored by a team representing the audited group.

The audit report also serves as the basis for research into corrective and preventive actions to be taken above and beyond the considerations of the closing meeting. The report explains the discrepancies in detail, which can stimulate another brainstorming session of audited persons about approaches to definitive solutions. An audit can serve as a source for impartial decision making because it is unbiased and objective.

The audit report provides a gauge not only for improving effectiveness, but for efficiency, too. Management of the audited operations can use the written report in a self-assessment of cost improvement. For example, one company that shall remain nameless makes high-quality, expensive fabric. Material that fails a quality inspection on the first level is sold as remnants at a considerable markdown in price. The material that fails inspection at a second level is sold by the pound as rags, at a few cents per pound. An internal audit at this company found there was no policy for valuing the re-graded material, apparently because management believed the dominance of the price of the good material over the lesser outweighed the cost of determining this value. And because no one knew how much was lost, there was little interest in improving the system.

Another company makes products using sheet steel. Again, a quality audit found that waste steel was discarded without measurement, although it was thrown out by the barrel. It would have been a simple matter to weigh the barrels.

To my knowledge, these circumstances have not changed, but under a policy of adherence to the standard, measures of efficiency are required (Section 8.2). In the case of the fabric maker, the problem could be addressed in two steps. An estimate of material loss could be made effectively and at low cost by simply weighing the material used for remnants and for rags. The weight of the high-cost fabric is already known because it is sold by weight. If it turned out that the loss was significant with respect to the total, then the second step would be to estimate the cost of improving the system to reduce wear and tear on material in process.

ANSI/ASQ Q10011 lists the contents that an audit report should have.[1] They are shown in Figure 7.1, and we shall discuss them point by point because they address a formal, system-level quality audit. It should be understood that some of the elements might be somewhat brief in a partial audit report, but all the elements should be included, irrespective of the audit type.

The scope and basis of the audit must be stated in the audit report because a good report is a stand-alone document. You shouldn't have to read the audit plan in order to understand the audit report.

Figure 7.1 The audit report

- Scope and basis of the audit
- Iteration of key details of audit plan
- Reference documents
- Observations of nonconformances
- IQA judgment on standard compliance
- System effectiveness
- Report distribution

Standard guidelines call for the full details of the audit plan, as well as a list of audit team members and other players involved in the audit, audit dates and identification of the processes to be audited. Clearly, this guideline can be pared down for the report of a partial audit. For example, why list the audited processes twice? If you list them in a paragraph of the audit report that is an iteration of the audit plan, don't list them again. Also, as Figure 7.1 shows, a list of key details of the audit plan should be sufficient. The audit plan may run to 10 or 15 pages. It's not necessary to repeat all that detail.

The reference documents that were used during the audit should be listed in the audit report. It may be necessary to cite them or to refer to them in the nonconformities. The references should appear near the beginning of the audit report, listed and itemized either by letter or by number. Then anywhere in the report where it is necessary to refer to a reference, you can refer to it by its index. It is easier to write "per Reference A" than the reference's entire title, for example, "per ANSI/ISO/ASQC. Q10011:1994. Guidelines for Auditing Quality Systems."

The auditors' observations and findings in their assessment are obviously a necessary part of the audit report. They are one of its main purposes. You shouldn't skimp on this narration but reiterate exactly the description found in the nonconformance reports (NCRs).

Tying Compliance and Effectiveness Together

The IQA team must compare the audited quality system's compliance against the standard and judge the system's ability to achieve quality objectives. This is called system effectiveness because achieving objectives is what a quality system is supposed to do. There are four ideas here: findings, compliance, objectives, and effectiveness. They are tied together by the auditors' judgment, and this responsibility goes well beyond a simple statement verifying compliance or its opposite. When you express findings in terms of quality objectives, you make it easier to determine the route to improvement. Talking about objectives is easy—you discuss the process in terms of how well it does what it is supposed to do.

Suppose, for example, that you have identified several nonconformities in purchasing. You can list them individually, which improves nothing. You can state that the purchasing process is noncompliant, which improves nothing. Or you can do your analysis, find that purchased parts frequently arrive late, and because of this, production backlog has increased. You learned in the pre-audit period that one of the purchasing group's objectives is to support production schedules. By framing your findings in this way, you show professional judgment and help guide the direction that improvement should take, without specifying how it must be done.

This requires thinking on your part, and understanding the objectives of the process, but when you think about it, this type of assessment is what a formative audit is all about. For example, we agree that presenting an audited customer with a laundry list of nonconformities is a useless way to close an audit, by any standard. The modern view is to evaluate those nonconformities at some level of aggregation, analyzing them for some commonality, and then derive findings that express them at a systems level. We discussed findings in chapter 5, and it was clear that findings are much more helpful to corrective improvement than a simple list of defects.

Expressing an assessment in terms of quality objectives follows the same philosophy. It presents the top-down view of performance—not whether the process is working, but how well it is working. This provides auditees with a baseline, which is the beginning of improvement. If the assessment is accompanied by numerical data from measurements of some type, as discussed in chapter 5, it provides a quantitative, as well as qualitative, view of system performance.

As an example, certified public accountants sometimes provide a numerical assessment of the controls in a financial system, based upon a commonly accepted empirical relationship between acceptable deviation rates and the reliance of a control.

The audit report should document its distribution. This is a list of persons, by job title, who will receive a copy of the report. The distribution should be determined and agreed upon at the closing meeting and is controlled due to the inclusion of confidential and proprietary data.

POST-AUDIT EVENTS

Figure 7.2 depicts a flowchart of follow-up actions that can lead to an improved quality system. There are three basic steps to this process. The first is the corrective or preventive action itself. The second is verification by quality assurance that the steps have proven effective. The final is closeout of the audit.

The post-audit process is driven by the audit report discussed in the previous section. This formal report should reinforce the initial draft report written by the IQA team leader for the closing meeting, and should repeat it exactly in the particulars of observations and findings. Some companies may consider using the draft report as a final report, but this is usually not a good idea because the draft doesn't include the results of the cooperative discussions of the closing meeting. It's worthwhile always to provide a considered, final audit report from quality assurance, even for small-sized audits. These can harbor a king-sized nonconformity.

Corrective and Preventive Action

The audit plan serves as the basis for a corrective action plan. Nonconformities were outlined during the closing meeting, but the major ones may be pervasive and require a full-scale plan to eliminate them, including schedule, action, and proof of effectiveness. The persons responsible for resolving the problems will generate a corrective action plan and coordinate with quality assurance to carry it out. Some companies use a *corrective action report* as an effective tool for this plan, but a well-designed nonconformance report can serve the same purpose, perhaps accompanied with an attachment if the corrective action is extensive.

Figure 7.2 shows a direct connection between auditor and auditee. This depiction is symbolic, as the actual connection will depend upon company policy. Certainly, the auditor who initiated the NCR has the best sense of it, but it's also true that if you have numerous auditors communicating with numerous auditees, the post-audit phase can quickly become incoherent. One auditor may say one thing while the lead auditor is saying something else, and the quality assurance manager

Figure 7.2 Flowchart of the post-audit process

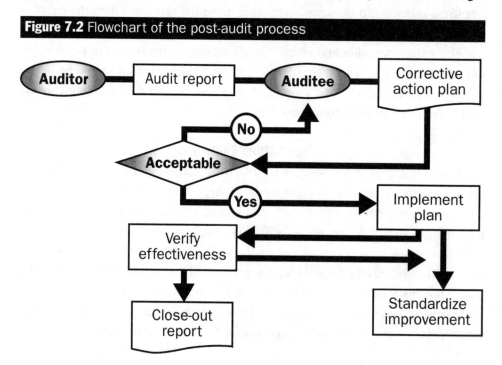

saying yet a third thing. Therefore, though such a procedure seems somewhat bureaucratic, it's best if this connection is channeled through the quality assurance department because it represents the controlling authority for audit follow-through.

Quality assurance personnel review the corrective action plan and, if it's acceptable, inform the auditees so that they may proceed. The review of this plan should include the originators of the NCRs that are driving the plan, for two reasons. First, the writers of the nonconformities deserve the courtesy and respect shown by keeping them abreast of problem resolution. The quality assurance manager may be tempted to exclude auditors from the post-audit phase, but, in my judgment, this policy belittles the role that auditors play in the quality system and diminishes their sense of contribution. Auditors, as everyone else, want to know that their work is taken seriously. Second, having observed the nonconformity, auditors may have a particular insight into the potential effectiveness of a corrective action.

Verification

The auditee implements the corrective action plan and, during the ensuing weeks or months, gathers evidence of its effectiveness. For example, if the NCR was written for failure to evaluate suppliers, this finding might have several dimensions: lack of policy, lack of procedure, or lack of implementation. The corrective action plan must address them all, which will take some time. Yes, the company can state a policy and write a procedure in one day. But the company can evaluate its subcontractors only as they perform, which is tied to the pace of contract awards and work volume. As the evaluations flow into quality assurance, at some point quality assurance acknowledges that the evaluation procedure is established, working, and effective, and the corrective action is verified.

Standardization

Every nonconformity has the potential to be systematic. That is why root-cause analysis of the process is needed for each one. If a procedure (in the sense of a physical process) is changed as a result of a corrective or preventive action, then the new procedure must be standardized. This usually means that a *written* procedure, and an associated policy, if appropriate, accompanies the new implementation. The old saying, "The job isn't over till the paperwork is done" applies here, otherwise you have an incoherent quality system in which the quality manual says one thing and the physical system is doing something else. In simple terms, "standardization" simply means that all the steps are taken to ensure that the improved system becomes the norm for quality performance.

Figure 7.3 Closeout of the audit

1. Audit report descriptive of the audit
2. Corrective action plan responsive to audit report
3. Effectiveness of implementation is verified
4. Close the audit

AUDIT CLOSEOUT

The critical activities of the post-audit period are the acceptance of the audit report by the audited process owners (auditees), the acceptance of the corrective action plan by the quality assurance function (auditor), implementation of the plan by the auditees, and verification of the effectiveness of the corrective and preventive actions by the auditor. Clearly, an internal quality audit is a process of mutual action and agreement by two parties. It's necessary that the quality system meets or exceeds the requirements of the standard and is effective. At the conclusion of these critical activities, the audit is officially closed.

This notion is contrary to Q10011, which states in paragraph 6.0, "The audit is completed upon submission of the audit report to the client."[2] This may be true in a third-party audit because the auditing party must keep an objective distance from the client quality system and its management. But in an internal audit, everyone is on the same team. They all have the same survival stake in the company's success. You might say that a golf swing is complete when the club hits the ball, but every golfer knows the importance of follow-through.

For our purposes, the audit is complete and ready for closeout when the nonconformities have been corrected and the audited quality system is operating at the level of expectations determined by both parties at the closing meeting. This would include achieving the targeted levels of the measures of performance as discussed in chapter 5, relative to the system's effectiveness and efficiency. Getting the system to that level is the purpose, and the promise, of the formative audit.

The inclusion of performance measures and their achievement represents a major distinction between internal and external audits. The objectives of a third-party audit are usually rather modest, oriented to simple compliance to the standard. The objectives of the internal audit are as grand as the executive management wants to make them. As we'll discover in subsequent chapters, the internal quality audit can be a major management tool for quality system improvement.

This chapter concludes part one, which is devoted to auditing techniques and forms. In part two, we shall discuss the structure and general requirements of ISO

9001:2000 and ways in which they can be audited. With part one as a background, the standard's requirements are readily understandable, both in their meaning and in how to audit them. In studying part two, many of the nuances of auditing techniques become clear. Parts one and two tie together in a closed-loop feedback system of learning to conduct internal quality audits.

SUMMARY

The post-audit phase is characterized by four primary activities: (1) writing and distributing a formal report, (2) conducting the follow-up activities of corrective and preventive actions and improvements, (3) evaluating effectiveness and efficiency of the improvements, and (4) closeout.

The audit report is the audit's major document, summarizing the analyses and conclusions of the audit, and reiterating the strengths and weaknesses of the quality system. It serves as the basis for research into corrective and preventive actions to be taken above and beyond the considerations of the closing meeting. Explaining the discrepancies in detail, the audit report can stimulate brainstorming sessions into approaches to definitive solutions.

Using the audit report as a basis, the auditee generates and implements a corrective action plan. The implementation of this plan, and its resulting effectiveness, are verified by quality assurance. When the requirements of the audit report are met and the quality system is operating at the level made possible by the audit, then the audit is formally closed.

The quality assurance office will close out a nonconformance report upon verification that the corrective or preventive action has been implemented and demonstrated to be effective. Depending upon the individual company, the closeout procedure may also require that standardization of the improvements has been verified.

REFERENCES

1. ANSI/ISO/ASQC. *Q10011-1994. Guidelines for Auditing Quality Systems.* Milwaukee: American Society for Quality, 1994.
2. Ibid.

Quality Management Standards

Auditing is a professional endeavor with its own philosophy, methods, and code of conduct. In any profession there are core strategies; one of the basic strategies of quality auditing is comparing the audited system to some standard to verify the system's conformity or effectiveness relative to the standard. The kind of system we are concerned with is a *quality management system*, which is literally a system established within a company to manage the quality of what it does—its performance, products, and services. Many standards of good business practices can be used as a basis for comparison, but the most universally accepted standard for quality management systems is the ISO 9000 series.

Thus, to be a competent quality auditor, it's absolutely necessary to be familiar with a reference standard—the more familiar the better, and the standard chosen in this book is ISO 9000:2000. In keeping with a systems perspective, our approach to this standard will be from the top down, the big picture of what it's all about. In my experience, the systems perspective is the best way to learn something in such a way as to see opportunities for improvement.

In this chapter, we begin with a discussion on the quality system perspective, describing how it has changed during the years since World War II. Then we examine the ISO 9000:2000 series and the principles that distinguish it from earlier versions of the standard: customer focus, continual improvement, the quality management system approach, and the process approach. Finally, we discuss ISO 9001:2000 in terms of its five primary responsibilities: the quality system itself; management; resources; product realization; and measurement, analysis, and improvement.

THE QUALITY SYSTEM PERSPECTIVE

For centuries, a product's quality was ensured by inspection, using a product standard as reference. This practice is still widely used today. Manufacturers routinely use a sampled inspection scheme called "acceptance testing" to verify the quality of incoming material and finished product. The U.S. Navy uses a very extensive inspection program to verify the repair of its ships in shipyards across the country.

Yet, product inspection has certain limitations. The first is obvious. A defect found in a final product or delivered service is after the fact—it has already occurred. Ideally, it would be better to prevent the faulty occurrence in the first place. In order to shift from corrective to preventive action, you have to address the processes that created the product or service.

The second limitation on the inspection-correction philosophy lies in the sheer magnitude of modern production and service enterprises. Large-scale production and service activities today require not only great numbers of direct processes, but also great numbers of support processes, too. It makes sense that all of them function in some optimal way to ensure product and service quality.

Early Quality Systems

During and after World War II, quality systems were developed that consisted of an inspection scheme augmented by a quality assurance program that acted *ex cathedra* over business operations. A classic example of this system, used for more than 50 years throughout the defense industry, was defined by the standards Mil-Q-45208 and Mil-Q-9858, which pertained to inspection systems and quality assurance systems, respectively. Mil-Q-9858 had certain similarities to ISO 9001, requiring procedures for contract review, documentation control, and manufacturing control. Its greatest disadvantage was its setup; it was burdened with the old notion that quality systems are simply broad inspection schemes. Organizationally distinct, the quality assurance function was often perceived as them vs. us by the functions within a company that produced or provided service. This distinction was due to a mistaken, and in some ways tragic, view that "quality" was done by quality assurance; everyone else worked. For years it never seemed to occur to many people that quality had nothing to do with a quality department—it was simply how well they did their jobs from the customer's viewpoint.

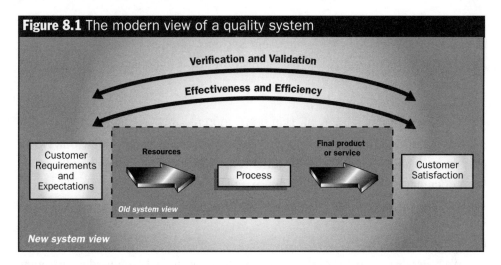

Figure 8.1 The modern view of a quality system

Verification and Validation

Effectiveness and Efficiency

Customer Requirements and Expectations

Resources

Process

Final product or service

Customer Satisfaction

Old system view

New system view

Quality Systems Today

Today, a quality system is no longer seen as a distinct function. Every person is responsible for the quality of his or her own work, and the quality assurance group, which may consist of only a quality system manager and a few assistants, supplement the production and service activities to ensure an effective quality system. Also, the quality system is viewed differently than in the past. It's regarded as the entire operation of the company, acting according to the principles of quality.

The modern view of the *scope* of the quality system has changed also, in terms of its inputs and outputs. In the introduction, we adopted Rudolph Kalman's definition of a system as a process with inputs, outputs, a state, and a state transition function.[1] This means that a system defined without inputs and outputs has no meaning—you must include inputs and outputs when you define your system, for they are inherent to it. For years, inputs to a production and service system were regarded as materials, and the outputs as the final product. However, this view is broadened greatly by ISO 9001:2000. The inputs are the customer requirements, and the output is customer satisfaction. The new perspective forces a refocus of the quality system from inspection to customer. Moreover, the focus is on present and future customers, so that an equal emphasis is placed on the need of processes for continual improvement of the quality system.

ISO 9000: QUALITY MANAGEMENT SYSTEM STANDARD

The term "ISO 9000" is properly used in two ways: As a reference to the ISO 9000:2000 series of standards for quality management systems, and also as the first standard in the set, which includes:

- ISO 9000:2000 Quality Management Systems—Fundamentals and vocabulary
- ISO 9001:2000 Quality Management Systems—Requirements
- ISO 9004:2000 Quality Management Systems—Guidelines for performance improvement

The focus of this book is on ISO 9001:2000 because we are concerned with internal quality auditing and need a reference of requirements to audit from. However, in its details ISO 9001 simply reflects the notions of quality embedded in all three documents, so a review of the newer and more emphasized ideas will provide the background needed to correctly interpret the requirements.

Customer Focus

We reiterate an earlier point that a company is necessarily oriented to customer focus by treating customer requirements, present and future, as inputs to the quality system, and customer satisfaction, present and future, as system outputs. It's easy to consider customer requirements as a measurable input because they must be translated into measurable specifications. On the other hand, customer satisfaction seems vague. Yet, it, too, can be measured, and an ISO 9001:2000-compliant company must do so, *and* meet or exceed customer expectations. Customer focus is auditable, as we'll demonstrate in chapter 11.

Continual Improvement

The notion of continual improvement is one of W. Edwards Deming's 14 points for management and has been emphasized so strongly over the years that it risks becoming a cliché.[2] You can find it in many corporate mission statements or quality policies. However, a statement such as "We at Ajax Co. believe in continual improvement of our goods and services," although auditable, has little meaning if the idea itself is not implemented. This is why ISO 9001:2000 requires that companies make continual improvement a permanent objective. This initiative is so important and basic to an effective quality management system that its implementation must be audited.

The problem for auditors is that "improvement" is a relative term. Moreover, it's a feel-good term. Notions that make you feel good are nice but hard to measure. The auditor's task is to verify the effectiveness of controls, and to do this, measurements must be made. However, when improvement is defined in terms of process capability, then it becomes meaningful and measurable. Improvement can be implemented with correction and prevention structures, and by finding a better way to do things. These structures are easily recognizable.

Understanding what continual improvement is and how it can be measured is essential to the quality auditor. For this reason, the next chapter is devoted to a discussion of the definitions, analysis, and processes of continual improvement.

Quality Management Systems Approach

Concisely put, the quality management system approach means implementing a set of good business practices arranged according to the Deming cycle of plan, do, check, act. This sequence enhances customer satisfaction and continual improvement through a continuum of verification and validation with respect to customer references. The first step is to determine the customer's needs and expectations. Then policies and objectives are established that are coherent to these needs. This phase sets the baseline for defining implementing processes and responsibilities needed to attain the objectives. Planning for optimal resource utilization is done in accordance with the customer's requirements, including cost and scheduling.

Once the system is in motion—plans, policies, processes, and responsibilities—the company then measures its progress and performance relative to its objectives according to previously determined measures of effectiveness. Correction and prevention methods are developed and employed to keep the system on track and to make improvements. The effectiveness of improvements is also measured in a continuum of the Deming cycle: You *plan* some action, and then *do* it. You *check* the results against the objectives, then *act* on the system to improve it.

Process Approach

Traditionally, businesses used a functional organization in their operations, which is visualized by the well-known organization chart. The chief executive officer or general manager was at the top. In descending order, various function's levels were defined by departments and subgroups within them: planning, purchasing, comptroller, production, engineering, sales, quality assurance, and so forth. The people heading these functions were called, reasonably enough, "functional managers." Being human, each functional manager, possessing a charter, went about institutionalizing his or her function in terms of responsibilities and authority—his or her turf.

The problem with this functional structure, as Joseph M. Juran points out, is that although the structure creates well-defined vertical responsibilities, things do not get done vertically—they get done horizontally.[3] This creates the potential for less effectiveness because "turf" tends to be defined so as to isolate one's responsibilities from another's, enabling cracks in the horizontal structure.

Recognizing efficiency loss and a drop in effectiveness, many companies have drawn up operations flowcharts (always a good idea) and have organized accordingly. This is called the process approach to organization. This approach is used in defining the core requirements of ISO 9001:2000

ISO 9001:2000

ISO 9001:2000 is structured as a process approach by defining four core requirements as processes within a quality management system, as depicted in Figure 8.2. The elements in this flowchart are management responsibility; resource management; product realization; and measurement, analysis, and improvement. These pertain to an organization's various processes that may affect quality and are expressed in terms of the top level of management. In application, they are necessarily approached at a more detailed level. Figure 8.3 provides a more detailed description of the meaning of these core requirements in terms of measurable responsibilities. Some of the detailed requirements will be familiar to experienced auditors; others can be intuitively grasped—human resources, for example, seem pretty easy to understand. As we will see in succeeding chapters, a few requirements introduce completely new measures to the quality auditor.

The fact that ISO 9001:2000 requirements are defined at various levels of aggregation can be useful to the auditor. For example, if an auditor discovers a nonconformity, one of the decisions he or she must make about it is exactly to which

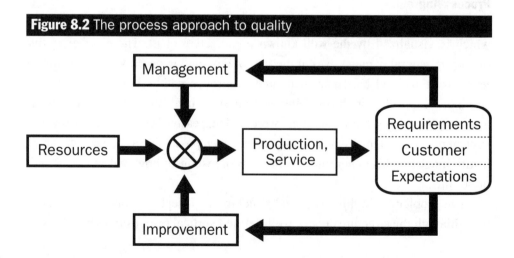

Figure 8.2 The process approach to quality

requirement or requirements the nonconformity pertains. This can be a needle-in-the-haystack effort, but in keeping with our belief that the auditor should keep the big picture in mind, it's helpful to consider nonconformity in the light of levels or areas of responsibility. Usually, nonconformities are visible from the bottom, but

Figure 8.3 Quality management system requirements of ISO 9004:2000

4.0 Quality management system
    4.1 Managing systems and processes
    4.2 Documentation requirements
    4.3 Use of quality management principles

5.0 Management responsibility
    5.1 General guidance
    5.2 Needs and expectations of interested parties
    5.3 Quality policy
    5.4 Planning
    5.5 Responsibility, authority, and communication
    5.6 Management review

6.0 Resource management
    6.1 General guidance
    6.2 People
    6.3 Infrastructure
    6.4 Work environment
    6.5 Information
    6.6 Suppliers and partnerships
    6.7 Natural resources
    6.8 Financial resources

7.0 Product realization
    7.1 General guidance
    7.2 Processes related to interested parties
    7.3 Design and development
    7.4 Purchasing
    7.5 Production and service provision
    7.6 Control of measurement and monitoring devices

8.0 Measurement, analysis, and improvement
    8.1 General guidance
    8.2 Measurement and monitoring
    8.3 Control of nonconformity
    8.4 Analysis of data
    8.5 Improvement

findings are visible from the top. When the nonconformities cluster within an area of responsibility, a finding may be suggested. The reader will recall from an earlier chapter that a finding is a grave conclusion derived from a pattern of nonconformities.

Fundamentally, ISO 9001:2000 requires that the factors governing quality of product be under control and that the process be documented. Implementation details are left to individual organizations on the grounds that each company has its own way of doing business. The standard's scope is defined by its requirements applicable to a particular organization, and so depends upon the breadth of the organization's operations. An organization that provides no service or does no design, for example, will have less breadth of operations than one that does, and thus will have fewer ISO 9001:2000 requirements upon it. This flexibility is known as *exclusion*. Processes defined in the standard, but which don't exist in the company, or that do exist but will not affect customer satisfaction with the product or service, are excused from compliance.

Many quality experts have long criticized the ISO 9000 series of standards on the grounds that they are not tough enough—they do not even ensure quality. They *do* establish stability, but if you are producing garbage, the fact that you are doing so with a stable process is cold comfort. These experts say that what is needed isn't a process management model but a performance excellence model such as the Malcolm Baldrige National Quality Award.

According to Jack West, chairman of the U.S. Technical Advisory Group 176 and lead U.S. delegate to the ISO, you need both.[4] ISO 9001 will give you process stability. ISO 9004, formerly a set of guidelines, is rewritten in the 2000 revision to serve as a performance excellence model that will make your business a world-class competitor. West calls the two standards a "consistent pair" that will enhance market success. Indeed, the company that wants to be ISO 9001-compliant really must restructure its quality system to satisfy both standards. Therefore, in this book we integrate the requirements and guidelines of ISO 9001:2000 and ISO 9004:2000, because we *do* stress performance measurement in the audit.

SUMMARY

Today's notion of quality means meeting or exceeding customer expectations. Product makers and service providers meet this challenge by relying on quality management systems. The ISO 9000 series is the most widely used model of this system and is structured in a series of processes according to the Deming cycle of plan, do, check, and act, which enhances customer satisfaction through continual improvement.

This summary concludes our general discussion on standards. Having discussed the basic structure of the ISO 9001:2000 quality management system, we will in subsequent chapters examine each core requirement. However, the new requirements cannot be fully appreciated without a solid understanding of continual improvement. Hence, we will momentarily digress from the requirements and, in the next chapter, discuss the meaning of continual improvement.

REFERENCES

1. Kalman, Rudolph E.; Peter L. Falb; and Michael A. Arbib. *Topics in Mathematical System Theory.* New York: McGraw-Hill, 1969.
2. Deming, W. Edwards. *Out of the Crisis.* Cambridge, Mass.: Massachusetts Institute of Technology, Center for Advanced Engineering Study, 1986.
3. Juran, Joseph. M. *Juran on Quality by Design.* New York: Free Press, 1992.
4. West, Jack; Joseph Tsiakais; and Charles Cianfrani. "Standards Outlook: The Big Picture." *Quality Progress*, January 2000, pp. 106–110.

Continual Improvement

When we speak of improvement, we refer to improving products, services, or processes in order to improve quality. Hence, we should start out by defining quality, and the definition provided by ISO 9000:2000 is very good because it is measurable and auditable: "Quality is the degree to which a set of inherent characteristics fulfills requirements."

Continual improvement refers to the ongoing pursuit of improving the characteristics of a product or service that the customer cares about. We call them "quality characteristics." The value that the customer wants a quality characteristic to have is called the "target value." For example, a customer who wants a dress with a color of navy blue does not want sky blue. For her, color is the quality characteristic, and navy blue is the target value.

VARIATION: THE ENEMY OF QUALITY

Products and services are made by processes, and because no process is perfect, its output will vary in its quality characteristics. Walter A. Shewhart concluded that during the production of goods and services, "measured quality is subject to a certain amount of variation as a result of chance."[1] (In fact, Shewhart was discussing the variation in manufactured product, but in subsequent years, others, such as W. Edwards Deming[2] and Joseph M. Juran[3] have made similar arguments for variation in services also.) Because the variation is off target value by definition, then variation is the enemy of quality. This is an extremely important idea, worth keeping in mind.

An Intuitive View of Improvement

The quality characteristic of a product or service can vary in two ways: (1) The output value will deviate from the target value, so that the mean value of the total production will differ from the target value, (2) The amount by which the output values deviate from the target value may be great or small or take on any values in between. This property is called "variance." Figure 9.1 presents two different views of variation. The graph on the right displays variation in terms of the process distribution of product or service. The graph on the left displays variation as quality loss resulting from differences between output and target values.

The graph on the right shows process random variation as a normal (i.e., bell-shaped) curve. Not all production or service processes vary normally, but for purposes of demonstration we will assume a normal distribution centered at some mean value. Figure 9.1 shows that the mean value is not on target but lies to the left (usually taken as lower in value). It's clear from this drawing that the process can be improved in two ways: we can make improvements to the process to increase the mean value so it's closer to the target or we can make improvements to the process to reduce production variation so that although individual values vary, they stay closer to target—making the normal curve "skinnier."

The graph on the left shows a Taguchi quality-loss curve, centered between its upper and lower specification limits. Because it's known that any production or

Figure 9.1 Quality profiles of product and process

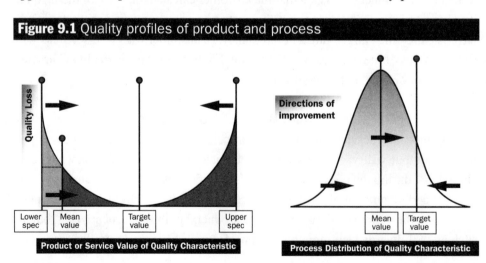

service scheme will vary, product or service designers determine in advance just how great a deviation the customer may accept. These limits are called "specification limits" in production and often called "tolerable limits" in service. The limits are shown as a vertical bar on either side of the target value. All values within the limits are regarded as acceptable. Furthermore, in the United States, the prevailing view is that any value lying between the limits is *equally* acceptable.

Genichi Taguchi et al. dispute that view, saying that variation is a "loss to society."[4] All products eventually break or wear out and must be repaired or replaced. The closer the value is to target, the longer the product will last, and so values close to target represent high quality. On the other hand, there is a *quadratic* decrease in quality as the value departs from target. Not only are values lower in quality, but they decrease rapidly in quality as they near the limits.

In the graph on the left side of Figure 9.1, the mean value is arbitrarily closer to the lower specification limit than to the upper. Specification limits usually are determined as equally permissible deviations from the target, so that the target value is, by definition, centered between the limits. Obviously, the mean value of a quality characteristic that differs from the target is necessarily closer to one limit than the other. Because of the closer limit's proximity, it takes less variation to drive output values out of acceptability than would be the case if the value were centered. This reflects on the capability of the productive process.

Stability

Every process has three properties: stability, capability, and improvability. Simply put, a process is stable if it maintains constant mean and variance. As Shewhart points out, some stable system of chance causes is inherent in any particular scheme of production and inspection[5]. In other words, a process can be designed so that it is stable in operation. The way to prove stability is to monitor the values of the quality characteristics, evaluating them over time for stable parameters. This is exactly what control charting does. As an auditor, you can easily verify process stability if such charts are available.

In the bell-shaped graph on the right in Figure 9.1, the horizontal axis is often indexed in terms of the Greek letter sigma, σ, which is the commonly accepted designation for standard deviation. 1σ is defined as the projection on the horizontal axis of the point of inflection of the bell curve. The area under the curve between the $\pm 1\sigma$ is about 68 percent of the total area of a normal curve, which means that about 68 percent of all normally distributed values will fall within the $\pm 1\sigma$ of the mean value. By similar reasoning, about 95 percent of values will fall within $\pm$ 2σ of the mean value, and 99.73 percent, or nearly all of the values will fall within $\pm 3\sigma$ of the mean value.

Process variation is often expressed in terms of standard deviations and a decision must be made on how much deviation should be considered inherent to stable operation. Historically, management has defined deviations up to $\pm 3\sigma$ as the variability of a stable process. Variation within this range of values is regarded as due to chance causes. Variation beyond this range indicates that some external factor is acting on the system, therefore the process is unstable and an investigation is required.

The effect of this decision is that 99.73 percent of product variation is due to the inherent randomness of a stable process. Why not define stability as only $\pm 2\sigma$, or about 95 percent of product variation? This rule would seem to define a more stable process because it requires more of the product quality values to be nearer to the average. However, it would also increase the false alarm rate, triggering a search for trouble when there is none. Conversely, why not define $\pm 4\sigma$, or 99.994 percent of product variation as stable? This rule would fail to trigger a search for trouble in the system when it really exists because it attributes greater variation to chance causes. As an economic matter then, industry commonly defines stable process variation as $\pm 3\sigma$. Thus, we can talk about process variation in terms of standard deviations. Notice that we have said nothing about specification limits. The process has no idea of "specs;" it just does its thing. Variability of $\pm 3\sigma$ is a measure of the stability of a process, but it doesn't tell us how good the process is.

Capability

Capability is defined as the ratio of acceptable variation to process variation. Acceptable variation lies between the specification limits. Process variation is the variation inherent in the production or service process. These ideas are indicated in Figure 9.2, where the Cp, is the index, or measure, of process capability.

As a demonstration, Figure 9.2 shows the specification limits and the process variation of a hypothetical process on the same graph to give an indication of how much of a product is beyond acceptable values. In the graph at left, the bell curve is almost entirely within specs. (No normal curve is *entirely* within any specs because the tails of the curve extend out to $\pm$ infinity. There is always a probability, however small, that a quality characteristic will exceed specs.) In the left graph, it appears that at least 99.73 percent of the product is within specs. Before you can interpret what this means, you need some common unit with which to measure both process variation and the specification limits. For ease of reference, we will no longer distinguish between manufacturing and service and simply refer to all design limits, specification or tolerable, as acceptable limits.

Acceptable limits are also expressed in terms of the process standard deviation, σ, because if you are going to take a ratio of acceptable limits to process variation, you need common units of measurement. This is why you must first establish stability before you can determine capability. An unstable process has no capability. It is always possible that a particular measurement will be within acceptable limits, but if the process is unstable you cannot predict how often this may happen, so computing capability is meaningless.

Expressing the acceptable limits in terms of the process standard deviation is easy to do. Suppose that the mean value of a quality characteristic is 5.0 units and that its standard deviation is 0.5 units. Suppose, too, that the mean value is on target, and that the designers have specified a target value and tolerances as 5.0 ± 1.0. Thus, the lower limit is 4 units; the upper limit is 6 units. Any value in between is acceptable. Now since either limit is 1 unit and since $\sigma = 0.5$, the limits of acceptance can be expressed as ± 2σ. We see immediately that although the process average is centered on target, its variance is too great. The acceptable limits extend only to ± 2σ, but the process variation extends to ± 3σ. This example is shown in the graph on the right, where about 5 percent of product variation is beyond the acceptable limits.

Now let's determine the process capability. We take the ratio of the acceptable variation to the process variation. Process variation is expressed as ± 3σ, the histori-

Figure 9.2 Two demonstrations of process capability

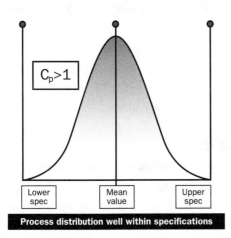

Process distribution well within specifications

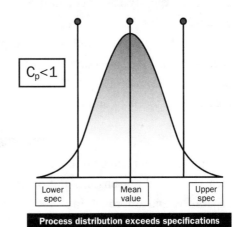

Process distribution exceeds specifications

cal baseline of production stability. In the preceding example, the acceptable limits were found to be $\pm 2\sigma$. Therefore the ratio is 2/3. Thus, the capability index of this process is $Cp = 0.67$. A capability index of $Cp < 1$ is not a good performance. Conversely, in the graph at left in Figure 9.2, clearly, at least $\pm 3\sigma$ of the process variation are within the limits. Hence, the capability index of that process is $Cp \geq 1$.

Capability is an effective, quantitative index of process performance. It is measured with real data. Nevertheless, although we can come up with a hard number, what exactly does the capability index tell us? Is $Cp < 1$ bad? Yes. More than 20 years ago the average for Japanese industry was 1.33. Then is $Cp > 1$ good? Not necessarily. An index of unity (3σ) represents 2,700 nonconformities per million; an index of 1.33 (4σ) represents 63 per million. Many companies today, for example Motorola (a manufacturer) and GE Financial Services (a service company) are striving for an index of 2 (6σ) or better.

In the examples of Figure 9.2, the process mean value is the same as the target value, and is centered between the acceptable limits. Usually, the mean value will differ from target and will be closer to one limit than to the other. Naturally, this affects capability. Just as a chain is no stronger than its weakest link, a process capability is no better than the nearest limit. If the mean value is nearer to one limit than to another, you measure the capability of the process relative to this nearest limit. In this case, the notation for capability changes from Cp to Cpk where Cpk is the index used to show that the process is not centered.

Conclusions

The loss of quality can always be expressed as a deviation from the value of the characteristic that the customer wanted. By measuring this deviation, we can establish a quality baseline and use it as a reference to improve the system. The capability index provides a technically rigorous and honest appraisal of the effectiveness of any production or service process. The sole prerequisite is that the process be stable. The index also provides a measure for process and product improvement. The corollary to this idea is that process improvement can always be measured in terms of an increase in the process capability index.

IMPROVABILITY

Improvement can be defined as an increase in capability. This is an important idea for several reasons. First, it orders the three properties of a system: stability, capability, and improvability. The auditor must first verify stability because an unstable system has no capability. Second, the auditor verifies the capability of a process in order to have a reference for improvement. Third, the auditor evaluates improvement initiatives in terms of an increase in the capability index.

Another reason to define improvement in terms of capability is that it removes improvement from the realm of imagination and makes it measurable. Of course, there are circumstances in which it is practical to evaluate improvements subjectively. For example, installing flowers and greenery in a work area will make the place more pleasant to work in, and positive comments from the work force are a sufficiently qualitative measurement.

And yet, it is often worthwhile to quantify even subjective measurements, and this is done all the time. For example, you take a poll of customers in a fast food restaurant, or in a bank or other service facility, and you ask them to rank, on a scale of 0–10, the quality of the service they have received. Measurement techniques are beyond the scope of this book, but keep in mind that auditors are obliged to observe where measurements are made and to take the results into their considerations on effectiveness.

Once you understand the concepts of stability, capability, and improvement in terms of things that can be measured, the next question follows: what process can be used to bring about improvement? In chapter 14 we'll discuss three specific processes for improvement: correction, prevention, and finding a better way. At this point, let's look at a general process for improvement that will satisfy any implementation plan.

THE CONTINUAL IMPROVEMENT PROCESS

When you improve something, you are effectively redesigning it. It seems reasonable, then, that a process for improvement would be similar in form to a design process. This is a comforting idea because whether you are talking about software, experimental design, or optimal design, they all follow a remarkably similar approach.

Determine the Improvement Goal

Consider Figure 9.3. The first step is to determine what you want to improve. The idea of improving something almost always originates with an individual, but the project's feasibility and scope is almost always fleshed out in a group. Therefore, the first step includes creating a team appropriate to the original idea. Usually, this team is composed of subject-matter experts, the subject being the entity under consideration—product, service, or process. The initial meeting should be a brainstorming session because you want to encourage a free rein on ideas.

You start to develop goals by generalizing the problem. This allows you to break out of the box, to avoid arriving at a solution before you have considered alternatives. Let's say you work in a billing office and have noticed the volume of business has steadily increased, such that your office is falling farther and farther behind in getting the statements out. At a weekly meeting, you present the problem as one of insufficient staff to process the statements, recommending that a staff increase would improve the system. What you have really done is to confuse the problem with one of its solutions. By generalizing the problem, you can correctly identify it—the problem is that statements are late.

The team should compose two scenarios of the problem: a descriptive scenario, i.e., the way things are, and a normative scenario, i.e., the way things ought to be. Writing out descriptive and normative scenarios not only helps you define and delineate the problem, but it will also provide the first assessment of whether you have the right combination of skills to determine the improvement. Quite often, a team of subject-matter experts proves to contain a necessary but insufficient variety of skills. Suppose that you want to improve a product. You certainly want people on the team who are familiar with it and similar competing products, and you will want process experts, too. But you may also need help from sales and marketing (the voice of the customer) and from purchasing (the cost people). In our example of the billing office, a diversity of expertise is more likely to introduce solutions outside the box, such as a complete change from paperwork to electronic billing.

Establish the Criteria

Goals are usually associated with criteria of some sort: constraints, quality characteristics, costs, and materials, as well as performance criteria. For example, if the goal is to reduce queue time in a supermarket, there's going to be a trade-off

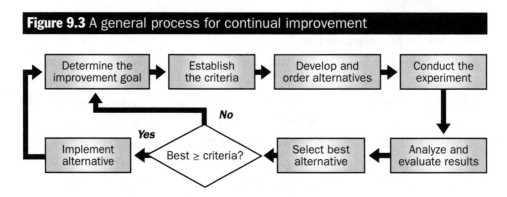

Figure 9.3 A general process for continual improvement

in cost to the obvious solution of simply opening more registers. For example, Wal-Mart of Charlottesville, Virginia, deals with trade-off by adopting a queue length policy: If there are more than three customers in line, another register is opened until all registers are open.

Constraints can include technology, cost, materials, space, or other considerations associated with the goal and that will eliminate adopting some alternatives. For example, the U.S. Navy has long wanted radar with the ability to detect target altitude. A prototype was built that could sense altitude with an array of infrared sensors that were gold-plated and kept at cryogenic temperatures. The cost was prohibitive and the Navy had to wait seven more years before a new, more cost-effective technology was available.

Develop and Order Alternatives

Once the goal, associated constraints, and other criteria are identified, the team is prepared to consider alternatives to get there. Again, thinking outside the box should be encouraged. By this I refer to solutions that are different in kind, rather than merely degree. Referring again to the billing office that couldn't keep pace with its work volume, hiring more people or reducing the number of entries on each billing are solutions of degree; the nature of the solution remains paper that must be transmitted through the mail. Adopting an electronic payment system is a difference in kind.

Thinking outside the box sometimes is associated with the notions of "radical redesign" and "dramatic improvement" that are popular in the reengineering philosophy. These concepts are excellent considerations and appropriate to any brainstorming session, but they should not be confused with improvement. Sometimes they are, and sometimes not. Masaaki Imai makes a strong case for incremental improvement, saying that it contributes to the low-cost solutions of *kaizen*.[6]

When alternatives have been generated and weighed against the criteria, some won't fit and will be abandoned. Those that do are the candidate solutions. They are ordered according to some preference, then tested and compared in regard to selected measures of performance. The tests and measures chosen for the experiment are part of the process of developing alternatives. For example, if test results are expected to have a random component, then statistical methods will be needed. In validating the development process, the auditor is concerned with whether the need for, and use of, statistical methods is included in the considerations.

Implementation

The best alternative is assessed as to whether it meets or exceeds the criteria defined for the goal. If not, the team will reiterate some part of the process, including the possibility of starting all over again. In light of what they have learned, they may have to re-examine the goal. If the best improvement meets or exceeds the criteria, it's implemented into the system, then the new system is evaluated in an ongoing process, for the potential for *new* improvement. In this way, the process becomes one of continual improvement, which is the goal of the quality system.

SUMMARY

Variation is the enemy of quality. Quality loss can always be expressed as a deviation from the value of the characteristic that the customer wanted. The capability index measures this variation and provides an index of the effectiveness of any production or service process. The index also provides a baseline for improvement. Process improvement can be measured in terms of an increase in the process capability index.

Continual improvement is a fundamental requirement of an ISO 9001 quality management system. It can be implemented as a process of actions as shown in Figure 9.3. This general process is applicable to correction, prevention, and finding a better way to do things. The internal auditor will look for this implementation in his or her assessment of the company's improvement process.

REFERENCES

1. Shewhart, Walter. A. *Economic Control of Quality of Manufactured Product.* Princeton, NJ: Van Nostrand, 1931.
2. Deming, W. Edwards. *Out of the Crisis.* Cambridge, MA: Massachusetts Institute of Technology, Center for Advanced Engineering Study, 1986.
3. Juran, Joseph. M. *Juran on Quality by Design.* New York: Free Press, 1992.
4. Taguchi, Genichi; Elsayed A. Elsayed; and Thomas Hsiang. *Quality Engineering in Production Systems.* New York: McGraw-Hill, 1989.
5. Shewhart, Walter. A. *Economic Control of Quality of Manufactured Product.* Princeton, NJ: Van Nostrand, 1931.
6. Imai, Masaaki. *Gemba Kaizen.* New York: McGraw-Hill. 1997.

CHAPTER 10

Quality Management System

One of the most important objectives of an internal quality audit is to measure the effectiveness of the organization's quality management system. Executive management has the overriding responsibility of establishing and maintaining the system regarding quality policy, goals, resources, processes, and effective performance, including monitoring and measuring process effectiveness and efficiency.

Figure 10.1 shows how ISO 9001:2000 delineates this responsibility into three distinct areas: 4.1 General requirements, 4.2 Documentation requirements, and 4.3 Quality management principles. Experience has shown that if executive management isn't active in these three areas, then they don't get done, and the quality system is ineffective. Let's look at them one at a time, first in terms of their meaning, then as auditable characteristics.

GENERAL REQUIREMENTS

The fundamental responsibility of an organization with respect to quality is to define the management system used to ensure and safeguard quality. This task begins by identifying all of the company's processes that will be a part of its quality system and their application within it. This assembly should be integrated and coordinated to achieve system objectives. The processes must be organized in a process approach and supported with necessary resources. Finally, quality system performance must be continually measured for effectiveness and efficiency, and active improvement structures developed.

The quality management system is profound in its application, extending to all levels of company activity that affect the quality of product and service. Yet, it also includes the participation of customers and suppliers, and so is very broad in its scope. At this point, you are justified in wondering if anything as all-inclusive in its reach and high-minded in its goals can even be auditable. The answer is that nothing is auditable until it's implemented, and once it's implemented, it is always auditable.

Section 4.1 of the standard sketches the quality system requirements, but with the exception of documentation, implementing the system is effected in other sections. In other words, when you have audited all the requirements described in Section 4.2 and in sections 5 through 8, you have audited the quality system. Therefore, we shall proceed immediately to the standard's documentation requirements.

DOCUMENTATION REQUIREMENTS

Past versions of ISO 9000 often were criticized because of their heavy emphasis on documentation. According to Jeanne Ketola and Kathy Roberts, the 2000 revision has reduced this requirement to just a few areas: control of documents and quality

Figure 10.1 The requirements of the quality management system

records; internal audit records; and the records of nonconforming product, correction, and prevention.[1] However, in order to achieve control, there must be structure, and the structure of documentation is defined in the company's quality manual.

The Quality Manual

In the general scheme of ISO 9001, a quality system consists of two parts: the documented part and the implemented part. The documented part, the quality manual, includes or refers to all those documents—policies, plans, procedures, and instructions—that affect the quality of the product or service. The manual need not be a formal volume or set of volumes but an assembly of printed matter and software programs. All these documents must be defined and controlled to ensure that current documents are available where and when needed, and to keep documentation from getting out of hand.

The entire assembly of documents can be considered the quality manual; indeed, the standard refers to it as all documentation used to specify the quality system. However, many companies assemble a variety of documents and software as their total quality documentation and present a small policy document that they call the "quality manual." This policy document is justified as a quality manual as long as it formally refers to the total quality system documentation.

This view is reflected in Figure 10.2 as a tiered documentation structure. The tier one quality manual contains policies and responsibilities related to ISO 9001's requirements. It expresses top management's written commitment to quality. It also contains the list of tier two quality documents with associated revision lists and defines the manual's distribution list. The manual also may contain a few company-level procedures, such as steering committee procedures.

Departmental procedures explain the responsibilities, provide the department's organization chart, and describe the input and output interfaces of its processes. Also, just as the quality manual provided an index of tier two documentation, so also the department procedures provide an index of the department's tier three procedures.

A work instruction, sometimes called a standard operating procedure, is a document that describes, step by step, how a task is to be done. To avoid confusion on this matter, a work instruction should be distinguished from a "job description," which is a document describing what tasks a given employee performs. The job description describes *what* an employee does; the work instruction describes *how* to do it. The description is located on-site and tells how to set up the machine or equipment with respect to a given job order. For example, a work instruction for a lathe doesn't describe how to do machining; it describes how to set the machine up. Similarly, running a test on a centrifugal chiller requires highly skilled electronic technicians. Despite their skill, the tests also require work instructions that describe test station setup for the particular kind of chiller under test: loop temperature ranges, pump pressure ranges, and so on. The purpose of the work instruction is to establish the conformance between the machine's or equipment's range of operation and the specifications on the job order.

Not every task requires a work instruction. As an auditor, you can determine whether a task requires a work instruction by asking two questions: (1) If the task is done incorrectly, will it affect the quality of the product? (2) Are the task's instructions self-evident to a new employee? Yes to the first question means that a work instruction is required. Yes to the second means that a work instruction probably isn't needed, except possibly to provide data. For example, engineers don't need work instructions to design things. The task is self-evident based upon their qualifications.

Auditing the Quality Manual

A great deal of latitude is given companies in defining and designing the quality manual. You can nitpick a manual forever, but this approach isn't constructive. As an

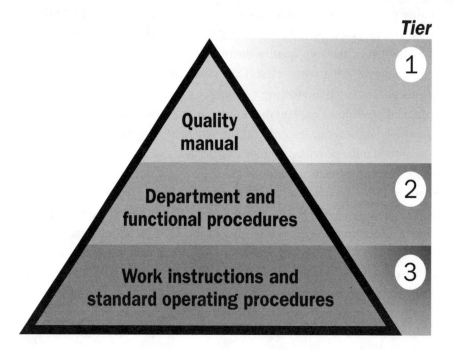

Figure 10.2 Quality documentation arrayed in tiers

Tier

1

Quality manual

2

Department and functional procedures

3

Work instructions and standard operating procedures

internal quality auditor, you should be concerned with only three matters: Does the manual cover the quality system? Is it controlled? Can people get it when they need it?

Given the quality manual's scope, an auditor may seem overwhelmed by its sheer volume, but the naturally tiered structure of operational documentation helps you to get a grasp on it. Start at the top and examine documents on a sampling basis. As the pyramid of Figure 10.2 suggests, the number of documents increases greatly as you descend the tiers, but the total is united by an index system. The policy manual will index tier two documentation. Each department procedure will index its own tier three documentation. Choose a sampling method *before* you examine the indices, then select documents randomly within the constraints of the audit scope.

Verify that the appropriate content is complete, as described in preceding paragraphs. Your company is *not* obliged to follow ISO 9001's format in its quality manual format; indeed, those that followed the format of the 1994 version of the standard will be out of order with ISO 9001:2000's format, which is radically different. Admittedly, a format that follows the format of the current version of the standard makes the desk audit easier, but the manual's usefulness to those who use it is the primary concern.

ISO 9001:2000 requires auditors to verify exclusions, which are declarations in the policy manual that certain standard requirements do not apply to the company's operations. For example, in the past, a company that had no design function would seek compliance to ISO 9002. This standard no longer exists, so now such a company must comply with ISO 9001:2000 but may exclude design requirements in its quality manual. Exclusion applies also to processes that the company does have, but which it claims have no pertinence to the quality of the products or services that it provides to customers.

Auditing Document Control

The standard requires distribution control of all documents and data related to quality, with associated procedures describing the method of control. Quality documents are those that attest to the quality level of product and process performance, and include specifications, procedures, drawings, blueprints, and many types of records. To avoid nitpicking, the auditor must understand the purpose of document control and keep the big picture in mind.

The purpose of document control is to ensure that current and correct documents are available where and when needed, and that they are used. From this definition, we can construct the controls necessary for quality documents:

- Identification
- Collection
- Indexing
- Disposition
- Amendment

Identification refers to the document title and revision date. Every quality document is assigned an "owner" who is responsible for its control. The owner and users identify each document by a name and control number. Documents and data may be in hard copy form or stored in a computer.

Collection means the orderly and accountable distribution of documents. For each document, owner and users determine the minimum number of copies needed for effective use and where each copy is to be kept. Only controlled copies are to be used, and copies must be easily available to users.

Indexing means keeping a master list of current documents, each having a current date, revision number, and approval signature to ensure document validity. As we described earlier, the master list of tier two documents resides in the policy or quality manual. The master list of tier three documents resides in the tier two document associated with it. For example, the index of work instructions within a department will reside in the departmental procedures book.

Disposition is the issue of new or revised documents and removal of obsolete ones. You must verify that a policy and procedure exists for the removal of obsolete documents, and then ensure during your onsite visits that only current documents are in use in the various work areas. You may know from your own experience that old documents are not always discarded, and if they have an operator's notes in them, they may be deliberately saved. The presence of an outdated document at a workstation is a nonconformity.

Amendment refers to making changes to controlled documents, for which there must be a procedure. This procedure should describe: (1) how changes are identified within the document, (2) how and when current revisions are identified, and (3) the number of revisions before a document is reissued. Some documents, such as test reports and purchase orders, seldom change and there are those that often change and so have revision levels—for example, drawings, procedures, and specifications. The process for revision is: (1) identify the level on the document, (2) review and approve changes to documents at the same level, (3) identify the nature of the change, (4) maintain a master list, and (5) reissue the document after a practical number of revisions.

Examples of documents that require control are drawings, specifications, blueprints, test procedures, inspection instructions, work instructions, operation forms (when filled out), quality manuals, operational procedures, and quality assurance procedures. Each company can choose which documents it wishes to control, but there must be a policy and a procedure to describe it.

Auditing Quality Records

Quality records are those that demonstrate conformance to the specifications and effectiveness of the quality system. How do you distinguish between documents and records? Eugenia K. Brumm answers the question simply: A document exists before the fact; a record exists after the fact.[2] A document is a written or graphical description of a policy, procedure, or instruction of an activity. A record contains data and information resulting from that activity. Each company may choose to define its own quality records. Examples might be the reviews of executive management, design, or contracts; test and inspection results; calibration records; supplier evaluations; and last but not least, audit reports.

The quality records should be defined in the quality manual, together with the responsible storekeeper and retention times. The company will determine some logical period of retention that is appropriate to its business, but this period must be stated. In many cases the retention period is indicated by the storage purpose, for example, to ensure that product quality was verified at the time of delivery. Consequently, in such a case, the warranty period suggests the retention time.

Finally, storage must be secure and environmentally sound to protect records from abuse and deterioration. Software is the best storage option because such data are easy to retrieve, and ease of retrieval is an audit concern.

USING QUALITY MANAGEMENT PRINCIPLES

A standard is an agreement between participants to conduct their activities in a certain way. This simple truth is not always clear, and from time to time we hear from a Savonarola of the quality world who advocates "really tough standards." Such persons fail to understand that a truly tough set of rules would find few participants and so could not be a standard. Nevertheless, through the years certain management practices have become generally recognized as good ideas and have achieved the status of principles.

These principles are enumerated in Section 4.3 of the standard as eight well-recognized practices used by managers to ensure a successful quality system. We have already mentioned three of them: customer focus, the process approach, and continual improvement. These, and others, such as leadership and mutually ben-eficial supplier relationships, will be expanded upon in the next four chapters on quality system implementation. Again, principles are not auditable, but their imple-mentation is.

IMPROVEMENT IN DOCUMENTATION

Everyone wants to lighten the burden of documentation. Generally, this has been taken to mean a reduction in the amount of paperwork necessary to conduct business. Intuitively, we understand that we need documents of some sort, such as records, but reducing the amount of documentation seems to be a reasonable im-provement strategy. In recent years, for example, there has been much discussion of a paperless information system as the ultimate goal of any organization.

In fact, you need to think carefully about improving a documentation system lest you suffer too much of a good thing. Documentation is closely associated with information—ISO 9000 defines a document as information and its supporting medium—and a reduction in one can lead to a reduction in the other, which may be no improvement at all.

There are downsides to the paperless goal. For example, the U.S. Navy has long sought a paperless information system to relieve its burden of logistical and technical documentation and is near the point where it can document almost all its ships and shore bases on a computer network. Its entire technical publication rep-ertory could be eliminated. Yet, the sailors themselves have resisted this effort because in many cases they work in confined areas where the technical manuals are needed onsite. The inconvenience of having to troubleshoot a problem at one place, while going to another place to refer to a technical computer readout is self-defeating and cumbersome.

The paperless organization implies that all information is available as a com-puterized record. The Internet carries this idea to its penultimate development and provides a good glimpse of information saturation. Hence, we begin to understand that although being paperless has its virtues, it also carries constraints and limita-tions, and so a more profound notion of improvement in documentation systems must be developed.

It should be clear that improving documentation is a complex issue. You start by determining how your company defines improvement, and what its objectives are. As an auditor, you should examine your company's approach to the following issues regarding the improvement of its documentation system:

■ The definition of documentation
■ Delineating documentation and information
■ Effective information media
■ Efficient records
■ Easy access to information

On the first issue, most readers will agree that paper is not the only documentation medium, which now generally includes software. Although spatially conservative, software can be every bit as invasive and saturating as paper. Whatever the medium, your company should have as its goals the effective provision of information when and where it's needed, an efficient and effective system of keeping records, and media that permit easy access to information.

Indeed, as an auditor, you can't separate the requirements on documentation and information, even though the first responsibility falls within Section 4.2 and the second within Section 6.5. This is one of those occasions when you are most effective and efficient in your audit by conducting simultaneous assessments.

SUMMARY

The quality management system is supported by a documentation system that attests to its quality policies and objectives, includes a quality manual with a system of procedures and instructions, maintains required quality records, and provides information necessary to the effective and efficient operation of all processes in the quality system. This documentation system includes bootstrap and feedback structures to ensure that the information is current and available to users and interested parties everywhere in the system.

REFERENCES

1. Ketola, Jeanne, and Kathy Roberts. "ISO 9000:2000 Update." *Quality Digest*, Oct. 2000, pp. 33–36.
2. Brumm, Eugenia K. "Managing Records for ISO 9000 Compliance." *Quality Progress*, Jan. 1995, pp. 73–77.

CHAPTER 11

Management Responsibility

Top management is required to play an active and leading role in the company's quality system. One of the objectives of an internal quality audit is to measure this role's effectiveness. At first blush, the measures seem rather esoteric—they provide vision and leadership, create an environment conducive to employee involvement and development, communicate direction, identify the processes that add value or influence effectiveness, and so on. However, as Peter Drucker once described it, "Sooner or later strategy and the big picture must degenerate to work."[1] When the management role gets down to work, you can measure it. If it never gets down to work, you can measure that, too.

Figure 11.1 shows how ISO 9001:2000 delineates this responsibility into six distinct areas: 5.1 Management commitment; 5.2 Customer focus; 5.3 Quality policy; 5.4 Planning; 5.5 Responsibility, authority, and communication; and 5.6 Management review. Let's look at these responsibilities one at a time, first in terms of their meaning, then as auditable characteristics.

MANAGEMENT COMMITMENT

Commitment refers to the dedication a company puts into developing and improving its quality system in four areas: communications, policies and objectives, management reviews, and availability of resources. It might seem that commitment is too vague a notion to be audited or that it can be demonstrated by a declaration of commitment in the quality manual. Neither is true. Real commitment is measurable when it results in physical implementations: processes, resources, and time dedicated to some quality objective. We'll discuss communication here, and look at the other factors of commitment later in the chapter.

Communication

The top management decisions related to quality must be communicated to those concerned. The communication's sole purpose is to transmit information, so the implementing information, database, and knowledge systems are all evidence of commitment through communication. We tend to think of exotic images such as cyberspace and embedded computer systems when we think of information systems, and given the volume of necessary and available information, such systems are often necessary. However, all means of transmitting ideas can be effective and

Figure 11.1 Top management's responsibility in the quality system

are part of a total communication system. Top management that is communications-wise will use a wide variety of media to propagate such quality issues as customer requirements, regulatory and legal issues, and technical and cognitive matters that help people do their jobs better. Communications systems will be set up internally to facilitate transferring information from workstation to workstation and will be set up externally in order to stay close to the customer.

Auditing Communications

The existence of current and topical means of communication throughout a facility or network is *prima facie* evidence of good communication. Internet connections; local area networks; written, oral, video, and sound media; bulletin boards; documents; and even forms all provide information, and hence are evidence of communication. Although most forms of written information will not be controlled, a company that wants effective communication will ensure that notices are current and that old ones are removed. A bulletin board covered with notices is seldom read. In any medium, information saturation is evidence of a poor communication system.

Topical communications are informative—workstations, for example, may have posted charts of progress or performance. Again, these notices should be current and shouldn't saturate the display area. It's not unusual to see run charts or control charts or an assembly of performance indices posted periodically near the process. For example, Toyota believes in visible management, and one manifestation of that policy is a current and prominent status report at each process. The posted data may be quite brief. At TABC Inc., a division of Toyota in Long Beach, California, you may see a single chart of direct run ratios on the production line

A simple form can be an important communication. We don't often think of a job order as a means of communication, but this is exactly what it is. Although just a form, when it is filled out a well-designed job order contains all the necessary information, such as the product specifications and required materials, to make the product. When auditors discover an improperly filled out or poorly designed job order, they are gathering evidence at several levels. A nonconforming document is the most obvious level, but if similar evidence accumulates, the auditors may also be discovering a problem at a much higher level—a lack of management commitment.

Good communication within the company, at any level, is indicated by employees being aware of company policies and objectives, and by adequate information of customer requirements. As an auditor conducting interviews, a good tactic is simply to ask people if they are getting the information they need when they need it.

CUSTOMER FOCUS

In chapter 8, we viewed the classical customer-performer process as a closed-loop sequence of events: determine the customer requirements, convert the requirements to a product or service, and meet or exceed customer expectations with the results. In other words, the process begins and ends with the customer. An organization is customer-focused when its operations are oriented toward meeting or exceeding those expectations. The auditor needs evidence of customer focus in terms of observable and measurable activities. Before discussing the nature of this evidence, we must distinguish between customer requirements and customer expectations.

At the initial customer-performer contact, the customer may not know exactly what he or she wants. Until this notion is firmly established, the performer cannot know whether he or she can meet the need. Sometimes an off-the-shelf item is sufficient, and sometimes not. For example, you go to an automobile dealer with the intention of buying a "fully loaded" blue Ford Explorer. The vendor has a fully loaded Explorer, but it's white. The salesperson is willing to order a blue one for you, but says that the delivery time is six weeks. You either adjust your expectations or you order what you want and wait.

In complex negotiations, both the customer and the performer will assemble teams to define the requirements. For example, when Boeing Corp. negotiates with an airline to discuss the design of a new airplane or the reconfiguration of an existing one, many skills are needed on both sides. The airline's team may include pilots, maintenance personnel, and experts from service and marketing. Boeing's team may include purchasing experts and a wide variety of engineers: manufacturing, airframe, materials, and industrial. During the process, both customer and performer will mature—the former in expectations, the latter in understanding of what must be done.

If the performance period is lengthy, as with building an aircraft or repairing a ship, there will be further negotiations and changes in expectations. The cost or availability of materials may change, or schedules may slip. These kinds of things aren't necessarily the performer's fault and may have nothing to do with quality per se. For example, a labor strike or severe storm damage may cause a delay in delivery. Quality gets involved in the recovery process and in keeping the customer informed so that his or her expectations can adjust to the circumstances. If the delay is acceptable to the customer, expectations are adjusted, and customer satisfaction is still possible. If a delay is unacceptable, then customer satisfaction is not going to be achieved.

Customer Satisfaction and Expectations

Expectations are related to satisfaction in this way: If the product or service fails to meet the customer's expectations, then there will be no satisfaction. If the product or service meets or exceeds customer expectations, then the customer will be satisfied, perhaps greatly. Everything hinges on expectations, which can vary during the performance period, even when this period is brief and the product is off-the-shelf. For example, you go to the store to buy Tylenol. Unfortunately, they're out of it, but the pharmacist convinces you that Dristan will solve your problem. The pharmacist has changed your expectations by modifying your requirements. You go home, take the medicine, and it works. You are highly satisfied because your real expectation was not so much to get Tylenol as to get rid of your headache.

The purpose of this discussion is to show that the whole matter of customer requirements, satisfaction, and expectations is quite complex. Whether the job is a simple purchase of a headache remedy or the multimillion-dollar construction of an airport, customer expectations are variable. Customer focus requires the ongoing commitment of executive management, and the processes and procedures for implementing this focus are auditable.

Defining the Customer

We normally think of the customer as the person who buys the product or uses the service. This view is correct but too limited to ensure companywide quality. The broader view considers both internal and external customers. In a production or service process, the person downstream from your workstation is considered your customer. A project may have a variety of customers: stakeholders, decision makers, and sponsors, none of them users of the product or service, but all with a vital interest in its quality. It is appropriate for an auditor to include as a regular question on the interview checklist, "Who is your customer?"

Auditing Customer Focus: The Paper Trail

The customer-focused company will have processes and procedures in place to help the customer track progress and hone expectations. They include a dynamic contract review process that is ongoing during the performance period, and processes for communicating directly with the customer before, during, and after the performance: sales, job, and delivery orders; service calls and records; change orders; and specification and design reviews. In short, customer focus creates a paper trail. The auditor can assess the degree of customer focus by examining this trail.

A small business provides a simple example of the customer-focused paper trail. Acme Technology of Crozet, Virginia, manufactures mobile shelving systems. The company sells off-the-shelf systems but will also manufacture systems to order. Acme operates efficiently to remain competitive, so its relationship with its customers is easily traced. Three pieces of paper tell the whole story. The first is the sales order, which describes the customer requirements. It is filled out by direct communication with the customer, perhaps over several discussions. The second is the job order, which describes the specifications. The design conferences necessary to translate customer requirements to specifications are implied in the job order, which documents and then follows the required materials through the fabrication and assembly process. The third document is the delivery and installation order, which releases the product from the factory and accompanies it to the customer. After installation of the system, the delivery order is signed by the customer in acknowledgment that the contract is completed.

Does this simple paper trail imply customer focus? It does if the requirements truly reflect the customer's expectations, if the specifications truly reflect the requirements, and if the work is done well and on time. An auditor can verify these conditions through observing the processes themselves. In determining whether a company is focused on the customer, an auditor should do what auditors have always done—ask questions! Let management explain its customer focus. The auditor can hypothesize a sales situation: A customer wants to purchase something. How does the company respond? Take it through from beginning to end, gathering evidence that supports the description. The continuity and volume of evidence demonstrates the extent of customer focus.

QUALITY POLICY

Policies are action statements derived from the mission statement. They must lead to achievable goals. Every organization has its own policies, but Joseph M. Juran lists some common characteristics of good policies: meet the needs of customers; equal or exceed competitive quality; conduct programs of improvement throughout the year; extend to all areas of the business.[2] A sample quality policy might read: "It is the policy of James Fauret Inc. to provide our customers with products and services that meet or exceed their expectations in terms of quality and cost."

Executive management is responsible for developing and implementing a quality policy. The literal interpretation of this statement is that a company needs a policy regarding quality, but a policy as such is too narrow to lead to capable systems. In an important sense, "policy" and "quality policy" are redundant terms. Every policy should reflect the principles of quality.

Auditing the Quality Policy

The auditor may well wonder how anything as esoteric as a quality policy can be measured. It cannot, per se. However, quality policy is implemented by assigning supporting and coherent policies at all levels of the organization's activities. It's *these* policies whose existence and implementation can be measured. The auditor can ensure an integration of corporate and quality policies by verifying that all of the quality system's requirements are supported by policies. General and special policies create a holistic structure throughout the quality system.

Special Policies

Many processes affect the quality of products or services. Most of them will require some sort of policy. A purchasing process, for example, requires a policy of contractor evaluation; an operations process requires policies on equipment maintenance and various measurements; a handling and storage process requires a zoning policy for the kinds of storage that product and inventory will undergo. Many processes correspond to specific requirements of the standard, so it's convenient to define a special policy as one that is identified with a given requirement of ISO 9001.

The standard doesn't indicate which processes or sub-processes require policies, nor how many. It's only through experience that an auditor gains insight as to where and when special policies are needed. Unfortunately, internal auditors will see the same quality system time after time, so if some process requires a governing policy and there is none, this won't become apparent until failure occurs and a problem review indicates that a policy on the matter would have prevented the problem. This is getting experience the hard way.

The best way to determine where special policies are needed is by regularly convening a review board of some type, composed of management and technical people. The combination of bottom-up and top-down review puts authority, direction, and technical insight together so that effective policy-making can be achieved. For example, equipment needs to be maintained on a regular basis and top management may be quite naïve about this. On the other hand, maintenance often means shutting down the production line, which requires an authority that only management has.

Figure 11.2 Some subjects for general policy

Subject	Brief Description
Benchmarking	Self-assessment against a standard
Continuous improvement	Systematic *kaizen* iteration
Empowerment	Participation of bottom-up expertise
Environmental issues	ISO 14001 purview
Market research	Anticipation of customer requirements
Quality costs	Prevention and failure cost analysis
Safety	Healthful working environment
Statistical quality control	Capability analysis throughout the company

General Policies

There are also *general* policies that pertain to many or all of the organization's operations. Figure 11.2 provides some categories of general policy. These are always made at the highest executive level because they tend to apply companywide. The decision to adopt a policy on employee empowerment, for example, must be preceded by an understanding of exactly what is meant by that term. Policies on safety or the environment will usually be established top-down.

Even a policy on using statistical measurement requires a decision on the extent of its use. Consider, for example, the issue of statistical quality control (SQC). The traditional view is that it refers to methods of variation reduction in manufactured product. But variation occurs in all corporate activity, not just manufacturing, and this, too, can be reduced by SQC techniques.

However, this idea is easier said than done. The people associated with the manufacturing process usually are familiar with statistical methods and don't need to be sold on them. It will take top management to get all the other departments to measure their variation because they may not be familiar with statistical methods. Also, in the interest of fairness, it's best to make similar kinds of measurements throughout the company, where possible. A central-decision authority can ensure that all processes measure capability in terms of their own parameters.

Both specific and general policies are auditable. It's easier to audit specific policies because the need for them is suggested by simply observing operations. If there seems to be some nonconforming product stored in a shipping area, the first question that arises is, "What is the policy for this area?" In terms of minor and major nonconformities, it's one thing to violate a policy or procedure; it's far graver if there is no policy or procedure to begin with.

General policies often cannot be inferred. The best tactic for an auditor is, as usual, to ask questions. For example, if the company has a policy on employee empowerment, you simply ask management what it means and how it's implemented. Then you examine the processes and procedures to gather the evidence of this empowerment.

PLANNING

In French, the management of a business is called *la direction*, a term that reflects very accurately what it is that management is supposed to do. "Direction" carries a notion of the future. The job of management is to lead the organization into the future, and that task begins with thinking about where the company should go and how best to get there.

At the highest level, a company's direction is indicated in a mission statement, which is always formulated from the customer's perspective. Mission statements tend to include "blue sky" goals such as: "to build a profitable, continuously improving company through ongoing development of products in order to exceed customer expectations." A company has only one mission statement, and it applies universally. It's everyone's mission. The mission is never attained but is always just over the horizon. It's pursued forever, providing direction for the company. It gives focus and influences decisions.

At the working level, where the auditor labors, the customer establishes the direction. Meeting customer requirements becomes the company's objective, and a plan is needed to get there. Plans are auditable, but you must be careful not to measure something just because it's easy to do so. Every plan is written down and so becomes a document, and the existence of documents is verifiable. However, just because a plan exists doesn't mean that it adds value to the quality system. A plan also has important components, which when put into action provide its meaning. The auditor should be interested in the plan's components, not its existence.

The Components of a Plan

I once worked for a company where it seemed that all we did was write plans. We wrote plans for plans. To my knowledge, no one has ever read these plans, much less carried them out. The existence of a plan doesn't mean that there is any effective planning going on. The written plan is necessary but insufficient evidence of quality planning. Yet, a quality auditor must verify that a planning process exists, and that it is effective. To make a valid judgment about this important requirement, the auditor should understand the plan's components and all the evidence that supports it. We discussed these components in chapter 2, relative to the audit plan. They are: why, where, how, who, what, and when. Let's re-examine them in the context of planning as a process.

The planning process is described by a series of logical steps. You must know *why* you need a plan in the first place. You want to do something or go somewhere. It follows that you must know *where* to go, figure out *how* to get the job done, *what* you will need in terms of resources, *who* will need to help you, and *when* you want to do it. To summarize, quality planning follows this process:

Why	Customer requirements and satisfaction (i.e., the objective)
Where	The performance site
How	The processes used to achieve the objective
Who	The performing team
What	Resources required to achieve the objective
When	Performance period

These components are auditable. When implemented, they infer a dynamic plan and so provide evidence of planning. They are better evidence than the written document itself.

Auditing the Planning Process

The auditor approaches the task of verifying the planning responsibility in two ways. First, you ask about it. You may be provided a written plan as evidence, and it's worth your while to scan it, for a well-written plan is *prima facie* evidence that at least the auditees know how to plan. You look for the above components, effectively described. For example, a plan may be written as a proposal, replete with statements such as "we will leap over tall buildings in a single bound," where the "we" is editorial. A good plan specifies who the "we" is, not by name, usually, but by title. This is called accountability. Without it, the plan is pie in the sky. With equal honesty, the plan specifies what will happen, when and where it will happen, and how it will be done.

The second way to verify planning is by inference, which is both a valid and preferable alternative to reading plans all day. As you go about the audit examining policies, procedures, and processes, check to see if the components of a plan are evident; if people appear to know what they are doing and why; and if resources and skills are available; if products and services are on time. If so, then you can be confident that the auditees have planned their operations.

RESPONSIBILITY, AUTHORITY, COMMUNICATION

The emphasis of management today is on performance—strategic planning, leadership, knowledge management, and customer focus. However, there is an administrative side to the managerial role that seems rather mundane, which is the task of assigning responsibilities, delegating authority, setting up systems of internal communications, and establishing documentation systems. Mundane or not, these tasks must be approached with the same management commitment as that required of the more visible processes of production and service, whose success is in proportion to the quality of administrative support. We have already discussed the auditable features of communication and documentation, so our focus here is on the remaining administrative tasks.

Responsibility and Authority

We often use the terms "responsibility" and "authority" without considering what they really mean. You can define them as you wish, but within an organization committed to quality, it's important to consider them as controls to achieve quality objectives. In this sense, *responsibility* is the assignment to a person of a well-defined task, and the measurement of the performance of that task. By defining and assigning the task precisely, we refer to the congruity of the job requirements and the performer's qualifications, as well as to the clarity of task.

Authority is the provision of the resources required to achieve the task. These include human, material, capital resources, and time. We usually think of authority as a spoken mandate bestowed by a superior, but the mandate is worthless without the necessary resources, and thus the resources are the real authority. One of the major criticisms of matrix management is that the project manager depends on line managers to provide resources. They in turn operate on their own schedule. Without resources, the project manager lacks the authority to do the job.

Auditing Responsibility and Authority

When people have well-defined tasks and understand their scope and purpose, this is evidence of quality responsibility. When they have the resources they need to accomplish their tasks, this is evidence of quality authority. Quality auditors must verify that persons performing a task are qualified to do the job effectively. As you go about your audit, observing and interviewing people and examining training records, you indirectly verify their responsibility. If they understand the job requirements and are qualified to do them and if they are aware of their interfaces with other processes and how to integrate their effort with the total, then management has achieved its responsibility in this regard. If people are provided the resources they need in a timely manner, then management has provided the necessary authority.

An inadequate distribution of resources implies a lack of sufficient authority, and vice versa. Perhaps authority can't be measured easily but insufficient resources can, and one reflects the other. When you verify responsibility and authority in terms of job qualifications and availability of resources, you are verifying several areas of ISO 9001's requirements. You verify product realization, but you also gather evidence of certain management responsibilities. Responsibility and authority reflect on management commitment and acceptable administration.

Management Representative

The company's quality management system is the responsibility of executive management. Beyond the participation of management at all levels in operating this system, ISO 9001 requires that a management representative (MR) be designated from among the managerial ranks. This person is responsible for the day-to-day management and operation of the quality system and for verifying its adherence to the standard. The MR must have sufficient authority to change or modify the system as necessary.

The company quality assurance officer is usually assigned as the MR. Indeed, for a company with a quality assurance department, it would be quite awkward if the MR were anyone else. On the other hand, ISO 9001 is flexible about this; the MR responsibility can be a corollary duty, as long as the requisite authority applies. Small companies often have no quality assurance department, assigning quality control to the employees themselves and assigning quality assurance overview as a corollary duty to a member of its executive management.

ISO 9001:2000 permits more latitude than earlier versions and allows for more than one MR. Although this may satisfy some companies, in my view it's a bad idea. It opens the door to redundant management, in which different people, unaware of the other's thinking, rule in opposite ways on the same issue. You can prevent redundancy by "divvying up the pie," assigning certain quality responsibilities to one person and the remainder to others, but then you admit a possibility just as bad as redundancy—things falling between the cracks. In my experience there is no such thing as a seamless organization. Foresight is finite, but events are not. Management will assign the various quality responsibilities to accommodate foreseeable events, but sooner or later an unforeseen event will occur for which there is no authority or responsibility, and the problem can be damaging before it is resolved.

On the face of it, auditing the MR function seems to present a challenge because all findings are routed through this person. The MR may forward the report to top management as a matter of conscience or because it advances his or her own agenda, or the MR may filter the report. In my experience, MRs have been entirely professional, using audit teams as their eyes and ears, and have appreciated their efforts, including their critiques. In the end, the MR is highly motivated to support the internal quality audit (IQA) team; if not, the better members may not return. Internal auditing is usually a volunteer duty, and good people don't like to waste their time.

Internal Communication

ISO 9001 requires effective communications at all levels within a company. An effective communication system is one of the best indications of management commitment to quality because it enables the exercise of leadership. For example, a U.S. Navy surface combat ship uses many communication systems aboard. One of them is used by the commanding officer to distribute information to all ship personnel. This is analogous to the communication system used by top management to communicate their concerns throughout the facility. Among the other systems, the ship has one called internal communications. It's used for horizontal transmissions—peer group to peer group.

Your job as auditor is to verify the existence of effective, two-way communication between:

- Top management and all personnel at all levels, or vertical communications
- Business unit to business unit, or horizontal communications

Consider the term "internal communications" as broadly as possible. Such systems should include offsite company personnel and even suppliers if they are part of the quality system. "Internal" refers to within the entire system, not just to within the facility.

MANAGEMENT REVIEW

Continual improvement requires periodic review of the quality system by top management. This review includes the results of an internal quality audit, which indicates the minimum frequency with which this review should take place. The review also indicates how effective the system is in achieving objectives, systematically handling problems, and integrating new technology or people into the system. In addition, ISO 9001 considers the results of management review a quality record, which must be retained.

Although ISO 9001 doesn't specify the attendance at management review meetings, it's easy to determine whom they should include. Improvement of the quality system means change, and change requires the concurrence of the affected line managers if it's to be effective. If there is apprehension among line managers, a referee—i.e., the CEO—may be required. In short, for most medium-size companies an appropriate representation at the quality system management review would include the MR, department heads, and the general manager or president. Some issues will profit from the presence of key personnel; it never hurts to have bottom-up input as a reality check.

Auditing Management Review

You want to audit a management review as you would any other area within the organization. The three essential components of any meeting are the agenda, attendance, and action items. The agenda should include audit results; customer feedback; performance analyses of products, services, and processes; the status of corrective and preventive actions as well as action items from previous meetings; and recommendations for improvement.

The attendance should reflect responsibility and authority relative to the agenda and action items. This assessment may not always be obvious to an auditor, but with experience, you will gain a good idea of who should be at a particular meeting if it is to be effective. For example, if one of the agenda items involves production bottlenecks, and the production boss is absent, not much is going to be done with this action item.

The term "action item" is more dynamic and responsible than "output" because it carries with it a sense that someone is assigned to see that the work gets done. In fact, that is exactly what an action item is; there is always an assignment "to take for action," hence the name. Outputs that have no responsible person assigned to accomplish them are simply smoke. Always examine outputs to verify that they have been assigned or you will see the same item on the output of the next meeting.

Outputs will differ in their specifics, depending on the agenda, but in an effective quality system their nature will always be the same: improving the quality system and its processes, improving the products or services relative to customer requirements, and assigning resources needed to achieve the quality system objectives.

IMPROVEMENTS IN MANAGEMENT RESPONSIBILITY

In Figure 9.3, we saw that the first step in a process of continual improvement is to determine the goals, and the first step in doing this is to establish an expert team. The expert team in management responsibility is top management, and their most effective tool is the management review process. Indeed, *all* of the steps of Figure 9.3 are achieved or authorized in management review. Therefore, certain characteristics of the management review process will enhance the prospects for continual improvement of management performance:

- Easy access of ideas to the agenda
- Attendance and participation of all key personnel
- Conduct of the management review forum in the pattern of the continual improvement process
- Conduct of action items in the pattern of the continual improvement process

Easy access means that new ideas and key people are encouraged to provide input to the review board. The key people might be customers, consultants, employees, or other business or community leaders. New ideas may be expressed through any effective medium and pertain to incremental or radical improvement. Attendance of key personnel is a tacit recognition that a variety of skills and knowledge are needed to solve most problems, and that the bottom-up view is equally as important as the top-down view. This characteristic of management review meetings is a corollary to employee empowerment. Conducting the forum in a process of improvement offers an assurance that the outputs will be improvement steps, per the requirement of ISO 9004. And finally, conducting the action items, whether they are simple or complex, in this same pattern will enhance their correct implementation.

MANAGERIAL NONCONFORMANCE

When I first began to work for IBM, I noticed that managers had no desks, only a table and a credenza. One day I asked my division manager why this was so, and his answer has stayed with me all these years. "Bill," he said, "I have no desk because there is no need. Managers at IBM don't get paid to work; they get paid to think." What has this to do with auditing? It means that the auditor will rarely find a nonconformity directly attributable to a manager. Because they don't *do* anything, they can't do anything wrong. But managers *do* make bad decisions that end up as the common causes of nonconformance. W. Edwards Deming estimates that 94 percent of common causes are attributable to management.[3] Joseph M. Juran puts the figure at 80 percent, but in either case, the contribution to bad quality made by managers is significant.[4] However, the nature of this contribution, i.e., bad decisions, is usually detected by inference rather than direct measurement. Management responsibility is almost always described by findings.

The role of executive management in all aspects of the company is strategic. Managers are responsible for determining the direction the company will go and enacting the policies and general procedures to get there. This responsibility includes a continual review of the quality system. This system is not quality assurance but rather running the entire operation of the company according to quality principles. All this is accomplished with respect to the needs and preferences of present and future customers if the company wants to stay in business. Therefore, management style is properly anticipative rather than reactive.

For this reason, many management responsibilities are lofty goals. Yet, they are auditable once you understand how they are manifested. Managers assign responsibility and authority. These assignments can be verified by auditing routine records. Responsibility means defining and assigning a task to a person and measuring performance. Authority is the provision of the resources required to achieve the task.

This theme is repeated in all aspects of an audit. For example, top management is tasked to provide communications systems. The auditor is tasked to determine whether the communication is effective within a company; evidence that it is effective is also evidence of the proper exercise of management responsibility.

There is an important idea here. By the nature of their job, auditors look at detail—a job order, a training record, a departmental procedure, a work instruction. The auditor's strategy should be to interpret the evidence as systematically as possible. Suppose the IQA team gets together at its private debriefing, and in reviewing their NCRs, one auditor finds a nonconforming delivery order, another finds an untrained person doing a task, still another finds a job held up because of inadequate provision of parts. The nonconformities will be written up as applicable to specific ISO 9001 requirements and the responsible departments and process owners will be so informed.

However, the IQA team must arrive at a finding, if such exists. At first glance, this array of nonconformities seems to have little in common, but at a higher level, it indicates that there are problems in exercising administrative management responsibility. As evidence accumulates to support this notion, you have a major finding. It can't be blamed on the little guy; this goes right into the lap of top management.

SUMMARY

Executive management must take an active leadership role in the company's quality system by establishing a formal system that is documented and implemented throughout the company, and includes management overview and commitment. This system will be supported by quality policies and objectives, and by integrating improvement initiatives into the company's processes. The quality system also will include procedures for determining the present and future needs and expectations of its customers.

As part of its active and demonstrated commitment to quality, top management will ensure free and active two-way communications, both vertically and horizontally, within the system; empower a management representative with incumbent authority to maintain a dynamic and effective quality system; and establish and maintain regular management review of system performance effectiveness.

REFERENCES

1. Tomasko, Robert M. *Rethinking the Corporation*. New York: AMACOM, 1993.
2. Juran, Joseph. M. *Juran on Quality by Design*. New York: Free Press, 1992.
3. Deming, W. Edwards. *Out of the Crisis*. Cambridge, MA: Massachusetts Institute of Technology, Center for Advanced Engineering Study, 1986.
4. Juran, Joseph. M. *Juran on Quality by Design*. New York: Free Press, 1992.

chapter 12

Resource Management

It takes resources to produce things or provide services; how those resources are used defines the effectiveness of the processes using them and, therefore, the quality of the products or services. Thus, resource management is seen as a proper subject for quality management. The usual categories of resources include human, capital, and material, but within ISO 9001's context, these are expanded upon in order to relate them more closely to the process approach.

Resource management is a major field of study in business graduate schools. Some of the methods used to manage resources include material requirements planning (MRP), just-in-time (JIT) inventory and production, information management, and forecasting. Some strategies, such as JIT, have been regarded as quality initiatives for many years, so it seems reasonable that quality auditors would have some purview over resource management.

The problem is that resource management is closely tied to company cash flow and has ever been regarded as the singular prerogative of management. For example, the implementation of MRP and JIT techniques differs greatly depending upon the business one is engaged in, the local market conditions, and management's sagacity. For any given set of conditions, there are good, bad, and terrible ways to manage resources, but many management methods are difficult to evaluate except in their bottom-line effect—net profit over the long term. It's also true that most quality auditors don't have MBAs. Nevertheless, the expanded view of resource management in ISO 9001:2000 is one of the areas about which quality auditors must learn. Fortunately, most of the resource management metrics are well known and easily understood and measured.

Figure 12.1 shows how ISO 9001:2000 delineates resource management. The ISO 9004:2000 guidelines describes the elements in richer detail than does ISO 9001:2000, so we shall rely more on the guidelines than we have in previous chapters. For example, ISO 9001:2000 addresses 6.1 Provision of resources, 6.2 Human resources, 6.3 Infrastructure, and 6.4: Work environment. ISO 9004:2000 adds 6.5 Information, 6.6 Suppliers and partnerships, 6.7 Natural resources, and 6.8 Financial resources. ISO 9004:2000 thus contributes to a much better understanding of how resources are managed.

PROVISION OF RESOURCES

The strategic goal of resource management is the timely provision of resources necessary to implement and improve the quality system and to address customer satisfaction. Thus, resource management maintains the same perspective as man-

Figure 12.1 Resource management in the quality system

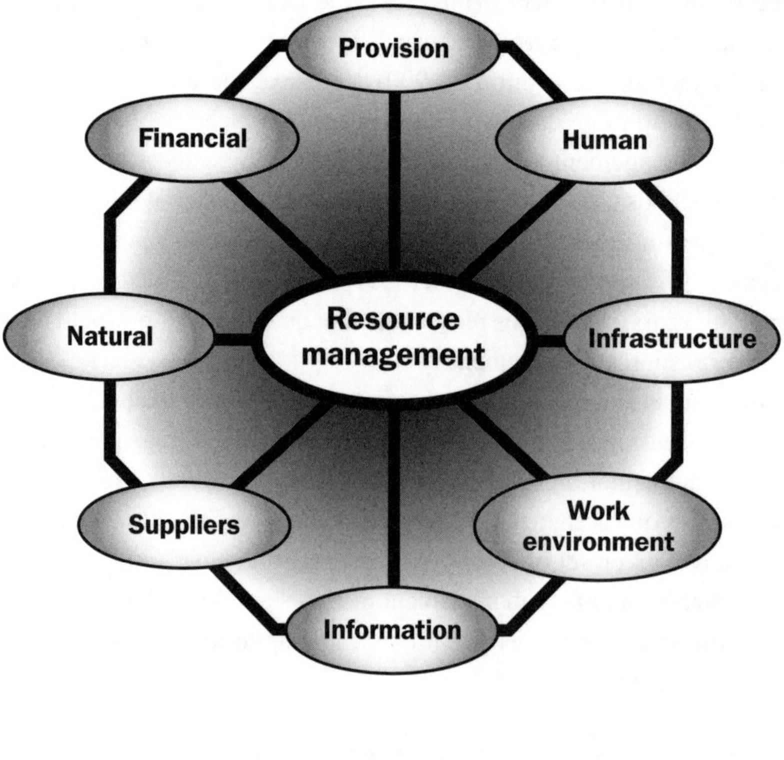

agement responsibility: The quality system includes a company's entire operations and processes, and customer focus remains a critical factor. Provision of resources will be sufficiently flexible to accommodate various factors:

- Tangible and intangible (e.g., intellectual property) assets
- Line and project organizations; production and support processes
- Requirements for encouraging continual improvement
- Planning for future resources

Supply and Demand

Provision of resources means meeting the needs of the company's various activities in terms of supplies, parts, and raw materials. It's what we usually think of when we talk about resource management, although the standard shows this very important viewpoint as rather narrow. At this point, the auditor should understand that the provision of resources is quite complex. It's often connected to inventory, and so is a matter of supply and demand.

Although it might seem that having a large inventory prepares a company for any eventuality, modern ideas of production control recognize that maintaining inventory has costs associated with it, the greatest being the tie-up of corporate funds in untimely or unneeded supply. Indeed, JIT inventory is one of the quality strategies used to reduce this undesirable expense. Ideally, an organization with a JIT inventory system would carry no inventory at all; its suppliers would provide resources on the day they were needed. Few companies enjoy such tight control over their suppliers, so inventory control usually amounts to a pragmatic compromise by management between JIT's ideal and the practicality of having at least some materiel in store. (No, *materiel* is not misspelled—it's a military term for material, raw or finished, that is used to get the job done. In one word it describes all the things we are talking about, so we'll borrow it.)

Production can occur in two modes. In a *push production* scheme, supply governs the production rate, and inventories are large. You usually see this mode when seasonal demands are anticipated, or when the company foresees an impending external force, such as a labor strike, weather severity, or oil embargo, affecting the production rate for the anticipated market. In a *pull production* scheme, the inventory is established by the rate of regular market demand, with a customer associated with each production.

There is some redundancy between 6.1 Provision of resources and 7.4 Purchasing. Both sections are concerned with the hardware and software required for producing and servicing, both are concerned with suppliers, and both are concerned with the flow of raw materials and purchased products. For the purposes of this book, we'll regard raw materials and purchased products as resources to be managed until they are put into production or service—when they fall under the purview of product realization. Thus, inventory is properly the concern of resource management.

Auditing Resource Dynamics

There are three auditable aspects to the provision of resources. The first is the use of material management methods, such as MRP, *kanban*, forecasts, bills of materials, and a host of other techniques. This is *prima facie* evidence of resource management at the first level. The second has to do with whether the production and service activities are receiving the correct materiel when they need it. This is *prima facie* evidence of resource management at the second level—the bottom line. Generally, the auditor will make this observation while monitoring production operations by asking operators about their supply support.

The third aspect of resource provision is inventory, whose policies, procedures, and metrics are well identified. A JIT policy is viewed in some quarters as the ultimate in quality performance, whereas in others it is impractical. For example, shipyards store large amounts of materiel as a prerequisite for the unpredictable capture rate that characterizes the industry. In contrast, one of my clients is autonomous in everything but its inventory, which is mandated by its parent headquarters and so must store larger inventory than it can use in any given time period.

In-process inventory is one of the indicators of how well resources are managed in a manufacturing plant. Most auditors have at one time or another observed unfinished parts stacked on the production floor. Those trained in quality methods might well deplore in-process inventory as wasting space and capital, and a poor business practice. On the other hand, it also characterizes a push-production strategy, deliberately chosen by management.

The appropriate action for a quality auditor is to inquire about the company's inventory policies, observe the procedures, including materiel management schemes such as MRP, and ask what metrics the company uses to measure its inventory policies' effectiveness. One such metric is "inventory turnover rate," which indicates how long inventory is in-house before it is used. When total inventory is expressed in dollars, and compared to sales, you get a measure of inventory policy effectiveness. Suppose the ratio were one-third; you might say then that it costs you $1 to make $3 simply because of inventory.

Another metric is parts lead-time, which reflects both machine setup time and in-process inventory delays. Parts lead-time might properly be a measure of product realization, which raises a point for auditors. The audit's basis guides you in what to look for, but many processes can be ascribed to one ISO 9001 requirement or another, depending on your company's structure.

HUMAN RESOURCES

In most companies, the people who work there are the most important asset. A quality-focused company doesn't waste materiel or capital resources; neither does it waste its people. Accordingly, ISO 9001 is concerned with the *effective* involvement of personnel in the quality system. Evidence of effective involvement is reflected in training programs, assignments of objectives and responsibility, employee empowerment, awards systems, the work environment, and employee satisfaction. All of these factors are auditable, some more easily than others, but from a chronological point of view, the first factor is training, so let's start there.

Training

ISO 9001:2000 requires that personnel be assigned responsibility on the basis of competence, defined by appropriate levels of education, training, skill, and experience. Jeanne Ketola and Kathy Roberts point out that this criterion is a double-edged sword for auditors because it goes beyond the standard's earlier version.[1] No longer is it sufficient to train employees for jobs; they must be competent, too. It's easy to verify if people are trained—just look at the training record. However, it's quite difficult to evaluate competence, which concerns both the employee's competence and the training program's.

ISO 9001 doesn't specify the type or how much training employees need. These factors are industry-specific and must remain a managerial prerogative. As a result, the extent and breadth of training programs vary greatly. Many companies will train employees for a specific skill but may be reluctant to offer career-long programs. Jon Breka and Laura Rubach point out that it's often difficult to show the connection between training costs and gains made.[2] In that sense, training suffers the same dilemma as quality itself: Intuitively, we tend to believe that it's good, but we can't directly trace its effect to the bottom line. Hence, some companies don't put significant investment into their training programs. I've worked with companies in certain technical industries that had *no* training budget. When they needed a particular skill, they hired it. When it was no longer needed, it was released.

Such companies don't meet ISO 9001's training requirements, which go beyond current job assignments and offer opportunities for professional development. Conformable training programs must respond to demands in strategic and operational plans and objectives—the top-down approach to learning that we talked about in chapter 8.

Specifically, training should lead to competence in technical, managerial, and social skills; knowledge of customer needs and expectations; and in standards and documentation related to one's responsibilities. It should increase awareness in the company's policies, objectives, process structure, and improvement initiatives, and should encourage creativity and innovation.

The company is free to determine training policies and procedures according to its own needs, but the training system must be defined and formalized into a program. Training can be continually effective through education, on-the-job training (OJT), symposia, home study, seminars, and any form of information input that increases one's abilities in a measurable and documented way. The most elemental training is that needed to qualify for the job. This might be as simple as presenting proof of a high school education plus some OJT. From this point, the employee's career continues on through advancement or job change. There may be changes to the equipment or system with which the employee works, which will require additional advanced or upgraded training, with associated record keeping and performance evaluation.

An effective training program can be maintained on a very modest scale. ISO 9001:2000 doesn't require a company to maintain a training department or even a full-time training program manager. Instead, training requirements are identified and agreed upon in a joint employee-supervisor review. Training is obtained through any of the options previously cited: OJT, classroom, and symposia, and training records are kept in each employee's records file by the personnel department. In-house instructors can be company experts or external consultants. Off-site training can be obtained through professional commercial houses or at the local community college or university.

Auditing Training

Usually, an auditor can't evaluate the issue of competency, but the auditor can ask the company how it ensures that its training programs achieve their objectives, and how it ensures that employees perform competently. The usual process follows a logical sequence of steps that results in capable performance for most people. This process is quite often similar to the following: (1) determine the training needs for achieving conformity of product or service; (2) provide the necessary training; (3) evaluate the training's effectiveness by evaluating subsequent job performance on a continual basis; and (4) maintain records of education, training, experience, and qualifications. If these steps are met, and if managers and supervisors attest to their employees' and training programs' competence, then the auditor will accept this as *prima facie* evidence of competence.

The auditor will examine training records and observe work performance, and this should be done through sampling. It's better to do a comprehensive audit of a relatively few records than to skip hastily over many, because you want to identify and verify each step of the training process. Randomly select a few people, and audit their training history and performance evaluations. Interview the employees to determine the level of input they have in their own training programs and to validate the effect of their training programs on their careers.

An individual's training history should agree with his or her work history, reflecting a policy of training personnel for assignments related to quality. The training's scope will include topics in the standards and regulations applicable to the work and of the company quality initiatives. You reinforce your reading of the training histories with interviews, asking, for example, if the person has confidence that the training he or she has received is sufficient and appropriate for the job.

To verify the employee's understanding of the quality system, you ask how he or she puts improvement ideas into the system and how customer needs and expectations relate to what the employee does. At the least, the audited employee should understand how the job order reflects the customer requirements. Anticipating the future, you ask how the training program prepares him or her for advancement. You've verified the company training program when you have evidence that all components of the program are in place, the persons examined are trained and appear competent in their tasks, and records of training and education are maintained.

INFRASTRUCTURE

Infrastructure refers to the company facility and everything in it: work and storage spaces, tools, equipment, hardware, software, transport, and support services as well as the hotel services (water, electricity, and climate control) that many of us think of as associated with *facility*. In fact, there is some redundancy between 6.3 Infrastructure and 7.5 Production and service provision. Both requirements are concerned with the hardware and software necessary for producing and servicing. This redundancy isn't meant to delineate materiel but to emphasize the process approach to quality—the plant has a physical presence *and* it also does something.

In the context of resource management, the infrastructure responsibility is directed to caring for and maintaining company property—hardware, software, transportation, buildings—all the materiel needed to support the company mission.

Defining the Infrastructure

When you apply the process approach to the facility, you go beyond simply doing an inventory of everything the company owns. In principle, each item has an associated cost, objective, function, performance criteria, availability, maintainability, operability, security, and renewal. This isn't an extraordinary idea—you do the same thing to everything you buy, albeit less formally. Common sense prevails here. Materiel includes paper and pencils as well as $250,000 electronic measuring devices and $3 million stamping machines.

A company will define major infrastructure—the materiel for which reliability and maintenance records will be kept, materiel amortized for renewal, and materiel used in production and service processes, and for which performance effectiveness will be tracked.

Auditing the Infrastructure

With regard to company infrastructure, the auditor is concerned with three areas: maintenance, performance effectiveness, and environmental issues. You look for records that are evidence of systematic maintenance: schedules, repair, and replacement. Calibration would seem appropriate here also but tends to be regarded as an issue of product realization because it primarily concerns the production processes' effectiveness. Whether a nonconformity in calibration should be written against resource management or product realization is a moot point, but it would probably be directed more quickly to the appropriate person if it were addressed in product realization. You should also look for maintenance records on software, including repair, upgrades, down time—all the things that happen to hardware happen to software also.

Effectiveness records probably will be maintained by personnel in the production and service processes and so are best addressed in product realization. Effectiveness is a concern of resource management to the extent that the acquisition of materiel reflects operational needs. You should ask how the company determines what hardware and software it purchases, verify policies and procedures on the matter, and inquire if reliability and availability measurements are maintained.

Auditable environmental issues include conservation, pollution, waste, and recycling. Of these, the easiest to audit is pollution—leaks and spillage are obvious and should be regarded as unacceptable by everyone. However, conservation, waste, and recycling quite often are the result of conscious managerial decision. This doesn't mean you should ignore what appears to be waste or that you shouldn't suggest recycling of material or conserving energy where it seems appropriate; on the contrary, a conscientious auditor should do just that. If management is willing to accept a certain amount of waste, let them explain it to you.

WORK ENVIRONMENT

Environment has come to mean different things, depending on a company's concerns. Popularly, it means the natural environment. To the systems engineer, the environment is anything exterior to the system. Throughout most of labor's history, it meant the *working* environment—literally, the microclimate one worked in—lighting, heating, and cooling.

Defining the Work Environment

Today, the environment is the working environment and more. The notion is greatly expanded to include safety issues and even creativity in providing methodologies and opportunities to encourage innovation and new ideas. It also includes ergonomics and special facilities for personnel who need them. ISO 9001 sums it up as "factors that influence motivation, satisfaction, and the performance of people, potentially enhancing the performance of the organization." One might say that a good work environment offers an *atmosphere for creativity*.

Auditing the Work Environment

In a sense, you do this every day. You are, after all, an employee. If you look forward to coming to work, if you find your job challenging and your surroundings acceptable, then you have implicitly evaluated your work environment positively. You *feel* satisfied. As an auditor, you must find out how others feel, and try to measure it, if possible.

Things that can be measured include the environment's physical factors: heat, noise, light, hygiene (bathroom facilities), humidity, cleanliness, vibration, pollution, and airflow. You should inquire about policies and procedures on the physical properties that pertain to your facility—most of them do—and also, as you tour the plant, verify the environment's adherence to the procedures.

Noise and cleanliness issues are relatively new concerns, and some of the older plants may not be up to par on these standards. Cleanliness may not seem a quality issue to Americans, but it's so regarded by the Japanese, and is an important factor in *kaizen*[3]. This was brought home to me forcefully during my visit to Toyota's TABC division in California—I had never seen so clean a manufacturing plant. Apart from the contribution a clean environment may make to a creative atmosphere, it certainly makes the place safer. Without a cleanliness policy, it's only too possible to head down a steep slope of slovenliness until you cross the threshold into a hazardous environment. If you find an unclean or noisy situation, or any unpleasant environmental condition in your facility, write it up. Maybe it won't be against policy, but to paraphrase an old Chinese proverb, improvement begins with a single step.

Observable things include safety issues and special facilities for those who need them. You should examine the company's safety programs, policies, and procedures, and interview the safety officer, if your company has one, to determine what is done on a daily basis to ensure safe conditions and how improvement initiatives are encouraged. You also want to keep an eye out for unsafe conditions in your travels about the facility. Unsafe conditions very often catch the eye. Sometimes conditions are safe, but violations are frequent. A person from the front office steps out onto the factory floor—only for just a moment—and leaves his safety glasses on his desk. Perhaps you see someone in a clean area without a hair covering or in a hardhat area without proper head protection. All such observations should be recorded, as an accumulation of them is evidence of a lack of safety discipline.

Things that promote creativity are a little harder to audit. For example, some companies pipe in music, but the jury is out on whether this is a good or bad idea. Most people find music relaxing, but some people can think while music is being played and some can't. Equipment and software can promote creativity; for example, special programs for creating Web pages offer a great flexibility in design. However, generally the auditor is not in a position to evaluate the worth of creative methodologies because such programs are usually very specialized—you must be an expert in the field to know if a particular methodology, equipment, or software program aids in creativity. In any case, the evidence often will come to you in the form of complaints such as, "If I had this kind of software program or that kind of measuring device, I could do thus and such."

Suppose that you get opinions from different people about how their creativity could be increased with the provision of certain assets. Would you write this up as a nonconformity? No, because creativity can't be mandated, and whether a particular asset could improve a person's originality is a matter for conjecture. It would be appropriate to write it up as an observation and candidate issue for discussion on quality system improvement.

INFORMATION

Some years ago the latest management fad was database management. Software programs to create databases became big business and still are. Then came information management. Many companies created a position of chief information officer (CIO), so as not to fall behind in this trend. Today, the rage is knowledge management. Are these games people play? Not really. Although we often see the three words used interchangeably, they can mean different things, depending on who is doing the defining and what nuances are used to distinguish them. Moreover, how you define them can make a difference in how they are stored, but this would be unique to each company. As an auditor, you should be familiar with the style of information management your company uses and with its vocabulary.

MANAGEMENT INFORMATION SYSTEMS

Given the attention that various kinds of management information systems (MIS) have received, you get the impression that it's all too esoteric for a layperson to understand. In fact, the systems are easy to understand but hard to implement. To understand this, let's first consider such a system's components. Market research, production scheduling, payroll, bill of materials file, the general ledger, personnel records, accounts receivable—these are just a few examples of information used on a daily basis in most companies. The purpose of MIS is to keep this information current and readily available to users. As you might expect, computers help us enormously in this task, but you also need a CIO. Users will want to control the information, but the CIO must control the system. For example, the CIO is responsible for *connectivity*, a system characteristic that refers to how well computers and computer-based devices communicate with one another.

The standard is concerned with information management as a process, so its requirements are outlines in the following checklist:

- Identifying information needs and sources
- Timely access to adequate information
- Using information to meet strategies and objectives
- Appropriate security and confidentiality

These factors are the auditable, necessary, and sufficient descriptions of information management.

Auditing Information

Unless the quality manual is very well written, you may have some trouble locating policies and procedures on information management. If so, begin with an interview of the CIO, if there is one. Appropriate questions can be generated from the previous checklist: "How do you identify what information you need?" "Where do you get it?" Continue until you are satisfied with security and confidentiality arrangements. This is also the person who can direct you to pertinent policies and procedures; how, when, where, and by whom information is stored; and what metrics are used as measures of effectiveness.

If there is no CIO, you can begin to suspect that the company policy is *chaqu'un pour soi*, or every man for himself. From the point of view of needs and sources, this policy is not too bad because most people know what they need to know and where to get it; at least they know as much as the CIO knows. Moreover, they probably want the information in order to meet strategic and objective requirements. In a *chaqu'un pour soi* policy, timely access, security, and confidentiality are sure to fall between the cracks. Moreover, *information sharing*, which is not in ISO 9001, is a valuable asset that is enhanced when information is managed and suffers when it isn't. Information sharing is important because often employees in one department can use information that another has gathered, if they know it exists and where it is stored.

Except in very small companies, the information officer's position is essential as either a primary or corollary duty. Using effectiveness measurement, the internal quality audit (IQA) team can work with the CIO in its evaluation and in generating ideas for improvement.

SUPPLIERS AND PARTNERSHIPS

At one time it was believed that the more suppliers a company had for a given material, the better price it could get because one bid against the other. Perhaps this was true, but often quality suffered as a result. The high quality of some purchased parts might be difficult to achieve, so that you don't necessarily want a low-bid product. One recent quality initiative breaks away from a low-bidder policy to one of sole-source suppliers and even "partnering." Sole-source suppliers receive a guaranteed contract from you in exchange for a guaranteed level of quality at a price reasonable to all parties. Partnering goes even farther. Here, a company engages a supplier in a special contract in which it requires the same stringent quality performance as in-house, but the company also shares information, technology and perhaps even resources.

An example of partnering is described by Michael Hammer and James Champy, in which Wal-Mart provides access to its MRP system directly to Procter and Gamble.[4] Effectively, P&G manages the Wal-Mart inventory of its P&G products. As another example, General Electric Power Systems shares its design facilities with partners, which it defines as a "long-term business relationship with suppliers, based on a mutual commitment to maximize total value to the customer."[5]

Requirements

The ISO 9001:2000 approach to suppliers calls for establishing relationships with suppliers and partners to improve communication and processes that create value. This includes:

- Optimizing the number of suppliers in some sense
- Establishing two-way communication at effective levels
- Cooperating with suppliers to validate their process capability
- Monitoring of the quality of supplier deliverables
- Encouraging continual improvement initiatives
- Involving suppliers and partners in one's own processes, as appropriate
- Involving suppliers in purchasing needs and in joint strategic developments
- Evaluating and rewarding suppliers and partners

Auditing the Supplier Relationship

In the earlier discussion on facilities, we saw that inventory, and particularly in-process inventory, could be audited with respect to resource management or with respect to product realization. As an internal auditor, you make your evaluation with respect to the basis that will get the best visibility. Here again, on the subject of suppliers, the same dichotomy applies. Suppliers are a resource. They are also part of your production and service operations and concern for their effectiveness is a matter of product realization. Most of the factors you can measure will be within those parameters.

Nevertheless, a checklist of requirements can be measured in a qualitative sense. You put them in your own checklist, and you ask appropriate questions, for example, "What is the policy for choosing suppliers?" "How is their work integrated with our own?" "How are suppliers evaluated?" Your company will have either good answers to these questions or poor ones. If the latter, then the IQA team can bring about an improvement in the system by bringing the standard requirements of resource management into open discussion at a management review.

NATURAL RESOURCES

ISO 9001's requirements on using natural resources is also concerned with their misuse. In the first case, some natural resources can be used for production or service, and companies are quick to identify them because there is monetary value in doing so. Examples would include using wells and springs, or natural ventilation or light, or even creating a picnic or recreation area for employees. Some companies go to great lengths, putting in ponds, Japanese gardens, even waterfalls. Invariably, such companies prove to be what James C. Collins and Jerry I. Porras call *visionary companies*, which build for the future.[6] They invest in their employees.

ISO 9001 also is concerned with a company's negative impact on natural resources: polluting rivers or air, generating noise, deforestation, and erosion, to name a few. How you audit this requirement depends entirely on your company's policies in this regard. It may acknowledge, for example, that because its noise levels are high or its smoke stacks pollute it has installed baffles or scrubbers. In this case, it has made measurements to verify the reductions. Measurements are auditable and improvable. You can start by asking about the policies and procedures and whether there are paths to improvement.

If the company has no policies in matters that the IQA team has identified as an issue with respect to the standard, then you bring it up as an audit observation. For example, your company has decided to double the size of the parking lot by clearing away trees and shrubs on land with a natural runoff. The final configuration appears to lead to erosion. The IQA team has the duty, under its standard mandate, to bring the matter to management's attention. Nothing can be improved until a problem is recognized.

FINANCIAL RESOURCES

At first glance, including finance as an area of interest to quality invites controversy. Most companies undergo financial audits as a matter of law. Indeed, many of the techniques used in quality audits come from certified public accountants (CPAs). Moreover, the same companies undergo internal financial audits, described by Barbara Apostolou and Francine Alleman:

> *An auditor performs tests of controls to see if they are functioning properly, measuring compliance with the control procedures in terms of deviation rates. Compliance in a given test means the control works—control is present. Noncompliance means that the control does not work—control is absent. A deviation exists. The*

judgment is made by comparing an estimate of the process devia-tion rate made from sampling, to an acceptable deviation rate de-termined during the planning of the audit.[7]

This sounds very similar to a quality compliance audit and suggests that an audit of the finance function by the IQA team would invite internecine sniping.

The Financial Requirement

Careful study of the standard requirement reveals that no redundancy of re-sponsibility is intended. From the quality viewpoint, *finance* refers to financing the quality system. It is a cost of quality initiative. Rather than audit the finance func-tion, ISO 9001 calls for auditing and analyzing the funding of resources. In par-ticular, the following concerns are checklisted:

- Plan, make available, and control the financial resources of the quality system
- Measure the effectiveness and efficiency of the cost of quality
- Examine results of measurements for purposes of improvement
- Include quality financial reports in management reviews

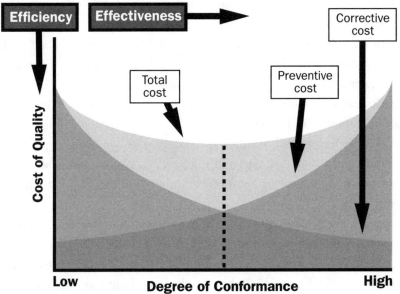

Figure 12.2 Degree of conformance related to the cost of quality

You can get an idea of how quality's cost is related to the production or service process by examining Figure 12.2. The degree of conformance is proportionate to process effectiveness. A high degree of conformance means the process is very effective. This implies that the correction cost is low—there isn't much to correct, but the cost of prevention is high. The high degree of conformance is achieved by expensive equipment or labor costs, or both. On the other hand, a low degree of conformance means that the company has put little effort into the process, so prevention is inexpensive, but because of poor performance, corrective costs are high.

The total cost of quality forms a bowl-shaped curve with a minimum where the correction and prevention curves cross over. This is the optimum trade-off cost for quality.

Auditing the Cost of Quality

The optimum point of costs shown in Figure 12.2 is not just theoretical but exists in some sense as the quality system's overall cost. Nevertheless, it is largely an abstraction. Yet, the notion of a trade-off between correction and prevention is useful because it satisfies intuition and implies that wisdom is required in maintaining an efficient quality system.

The auditor can begin by making inquiries developed from the checklist in the preceding section. Put the first bullet into a question for the audited manager. If this person has been tasked to measure the function's capability, then he or she will have already selected metrics and have made measurements—perhaps of process and product failure counts, equipment down time, material waste or rework, and other appropriate metrics. There are also external costs paid on behalf of the customer because of product failure, warranties, costs of sending repair persons on the road, and even costs in terms of a loss of customers.

An internal audit whose objective is improvement rather than inspection will offer an opportunity for the quality auditor to work with the audited manager in finding ways to lower costs or improve the degree of conformance, or both. Take another look at the total cost curve in Figure 12.2. If your company is operating below its optimum degree of conformance, then you can improve effectiveness *and* lower costs.

Moreover, even if the company is above its optimum degree of conformance, it's possible to improve effectiveness without increasing costs by improving efficiency. Recall that efficiency is a measure of the relation between results achieved and resources used. Figure 12.2 shows only the relationship of conformance to cost of quality, but conformance is related to efficiency also.

The internal quality audit provides a forum for discussion on improving efficiency as well as effectiveness. The very fact that auditors come from outside the audited function and are familiar with other processes enhances the opportunity for fresh ideas. Suppose, for example, you work in a fabric plant and run a knitting machine. You use a C-type control chart to track a "stitches per inch" metric, which measures the quality of the weave. You are assigned as a member of the IQA team to audit the dye shop and find that they seem to be having a problem with metal-content variability in the water provided by the city. The variation affects the Ph balance they need in the dyes. The dye shop would like to characterize the variation, both to demonstrate the problem to the city and determine how best to resolve the issue in-house. Because of your familiarity with control charts and other problem analysis tools such as cause-and-effect (Ishikawa) diagrams, you can make a contribution to their efficiency and effectiveness.

The essential character of an internal quality auditor is the opportunity for improvement. Conformance to requirements remains important, but it's less important than improvement.

IMPROVEMENT IN RESOURCE MANAGEMENT

You can approach resource management improvement from two directions: via the resource or the technique. From the resource standpoint, far and away the major resource is human and deserves continual consideration for improvement. We've discussed the basic issues of safety and a pleasant, creative environment, but at some point you reach the point of incremental or diminishing returns on these issues.

However, you never reach diminishing returns in training. People remain loyal and work hard as long as there is challenge and opportunity, and training provides a path to both. As an auditor, you might find it useful to ask all auditees how they find challenge and opportunity in their jobs, and whether the company training programs help them in this pursuit. People who are satisfied have attained a personal plateau comfortable to them and may say so. People who crave more may offer ideas on improving the training program through scheduling, costs, curricula, or other factors. These ideas then become the food for thought at the next improvement meeting.

There are many resource management techniques, and some of them, such as MRP II, can be quite expensive, Others, such as a computer-controlled inventory model, can be inexpensive. As a general rule you won't be in a position to evaluate these techniques, but you can evaluate resource management's measures of performance. In considering improvement initiatives, focus on these measures and let management suggest the initiatives. Your audit role is to act as the catalyst to maintain management's interest on continual improvement. You should have little difficulty with this, as resource management directly affects the bottom line and is frequently under management consideration. Specific areas for improvement may exist, and here you can count on the self-interest of affected managers to suggest initiatives.

NONCONFORMANCE IN RESOURCE MANAGEMENT

Management is rightly entitled to define how it manages resources. Jeanne Ketola and Kathy Roberts point out that the standard allows companies a great deal of latitude in defining their resource management systems.[8] With this prerogative goes the responsibility to measure effectiveness and efficiency. "Everyone is responsible for his or her own quality" is just as applicable to management as to employees. The auditor's responsibility is to inquire after these measurements and to use them in its overall assessment of resources management. However, if management does a poor job defining its systems, or offers a fainthearted evaluation of its asset utilization, then according to Ketola and Roberts, the onus is on the auditor to show that the system doesn't work.

For example, one of the requirements in human resource management is the issue of getting people involved in the system beyond some minimal performance of their tasks. Suppose the company decides that when people are deeply involved in what they do, they find job satisfaction. Conversely, if they are lackadaisical in their involvement, they will be unhappy and go elsewhere. Therefore, management adopts a metric of "personnel turnover rate" as a measure of its employees' involvement in the system. Suppose further that the turnover rate is 20 percent and that the company is satisfied with this.

There are three audit issues here: (1) the metric's validity, (2) the size of the rate, and (3) the acceptance of the rate. You might decide that the metric is valid as far as it goes; probably other metrics should be used also. You can't evaluate the turnover rate unless you know what the industry average is, and although you might question company acceptance, it will be difficult to challenge it. Your best strategy is to obtain the industry average but also work through the IQA for an improvement scheme for measuring employee involvement.

As another example, suppose that the in-process inventory in your plant seems very large most of the time. We mentioned earlier that this condition, although generally regarded as a poor quality practice, might be the result of management's deliberate decision to push production. In one plant I audited several years ago, management maintained high levels of in-process inventory because the union had asked them to do so, believing it indicated job security. How do you prove that the inventory is hurting the system? You can't by yourself, but if it really is, others will share your opinion. Those closer to the problem may well want to bring it up as an improvement issue, using the audit as leverage.

SUMMARY

The strategic goal of resource management is the timely provision of resources needed to implement and improve the quality system, and to address customer satisfaction. The standard establishes eight areas of resource management: provision, human resources, infrastructure, work environment, information, suppliers and partners, natural resources, and finance. The company is free to plan and implement whatever resource management systems it chooses, but these systems must include processes for measuring those systems' effectiveness and efficiency.

REFERENCES

1. Ketola, Jeanne, and Kathy Roberts. "Resource Management." *Quality Digest*, April 2000, pp. 30–34.
2. Breka, Jon, and Laura Rubach. "Corporate Quality Training Facilities." *Quality Progress*, Jan. 1995, pp. 27–30.
3. Imai, Masaaki. *Gemba Kaizen*. New York: McGraw-Hill, 1997.
4. Hammer, Michael, and James Champy. *Reengineering the Corporation*. New York: Harper Business, 1993.
5. Rader, Louis. "Partnering: A Conversation with Lou Rader." *Sourcing News*, General Electric Power Generation, Oct., 1990.
6. Collins, James C., and Jerry I. Porras. *Built to Last: Successful Habits of Visionary Companies*. New York: Harper Business, 1994.
7. Apostolou, Barbara, and Francine Alleman. *Internal Audit Sampling*, Altamonte Springs, FL: The Institute of Internal Auditors, 1991.
8. Ketola, Jeanne, and Kathy Roberts. "Resource Management." *Quality Digest*, April 2000, pp. 30–34.

Product Realization

In chapter 8, we found that in the quality management system approach, quality requirements dictate how an activity is performed, and quality objectives are measured against process output. Hence, a company is a dynamic enterprise of activities responding to the customer's needs and of processes operating to meet or exceed customer expectations. The totality of these activities and processes constitutes the quality system. *Product realization* refers to implementing and integrating this network of processes and activities, and the word "product" should be understood in the context of a product or service.

The requirements of earlier versions of ISO 9000 were concerned with implementing the many processes, but there were few criteria for putting them all together into a quality "system." To appreciate what this means, recall our discussion in the introduction about systems and subsystems. A company's processes that affect product or service quality are the subsystems of the quality system and must be integrated if the system is to be effective. In ISO 9001:2000, the task of system integration follows from the process approach, which is one of its characteristics.

The issue of what is and what is not part of the system is inherent to any process integration scheme. It follows that 7.0 Product realization is the section, and the *only* section, of ISO 9001 that permits exclusions. This is where auditors go to find out which company processes are excluded from ISO 9001's requirements, bearing in mind that processes that affect product or service quality must not be excluded. All processes that affect the company's ability to meet customer requirements are subject to all sections of the standard.

Figure 13.1 shows how ISO 9001:2000 delineates product realization into six major areas: 7.1 Planning of product realization, 7.2 Customer-related processes (termed "Processes related to interested parties" in ISO 9004), 7.3 Design and development, 7.4 Purchasing, 7.5 Production and service provision (abbreviated in the figure as Operations), and 7.6 Control of monitoring and measuring devices (abbreviated in the figure as Measurement devices). Readers familiar with earlier versions of ISO 9000 will recognize some of these areas as longtime quality system requirements, for example, purchasing, design and development, and control of measuring and monitoring devices.

The major areas of Figure 13.1 are defined in ISO 9001 (requirements) and expanded on in ISO 9004 (guidelines) in terms of performance improvement. For example, the guidelines provide a general exposition on planning, a necessary supplement for auditors who wish to broaden their understanding of the planning of processes. Similarly, the guidelines expand upon customer-related processes to include all interested parties.

Figure 13.1 Product realization in the quality system

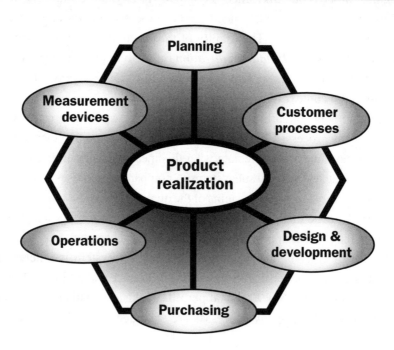

PLANNING OF PRODUCT REALIZATION

The requirement areas of product realization may create confusion because planning appears as a requirement in management responsibility and reappears as a requirement here. There is a subtle distinction, however. In product realization, planning refers to planning of processes, but in management responsibility it covers the process of planning—ensuring the planning is effective. We stressed in Chapter 11 that there is planning and *effective* planning, and the two are not the same. *Effective* planning contains necessary elements, is carried out (dormant plans have no effectiveness), and takes place in all areas—process, resource, training, auditing—across the breadth of quality activity. In short, process planners are responsible to plan effectively; management is responsible to see that effective planning gets done.

Process Planning

A good plan contains answers to why, what, how, who, where, and when. So, too, in a process plan. In realizing a product or service, you must identify:

■ The kinds of processes required and their objectives

■ The resources and documentation to support them

■ Activities for verifying and validating criteria for acceptability

■ The records necessary to provide confidence of conformity in processes, products, and services

We have discussed most of the above factors in previous chapters. In chapter 8, we saw that a system is defined in terms of its inputs and outputs, so to identify a process that can achieve a given objective you must also identify its inputs and outputs. As a rule of thumb, the inputs will reflect customer requirements, and the outputs will reflect customer expectations.

Verification and validation require some new considerations. With respect to planning a process, validation addresses the "why"; verification addresses the other components. B. W. Boehm describes them neatly:

Verification answers the question, "Are we doing things right?"

Validation answers the question, "Are we doing the right things?"[1]

Auditing the Planning of Processes

As we discussed in management responsibility, it's not necessary for auditors to review plans to verify effective planning. You can use inference because things never happen consistently by accident. A process that runs well was planned well.

If the process outputs meet or exceed customer expectations consistently, then these results are *prima facie* evidence of effective process planning. If, in addition, measures of performance (MOP) show that the process is stable, capable, and reliable, then this, too, is evidence of a well-planned process. The measures of effectiveness (MOE) also are evidence of process verification and validation procedures. You can verify documentation at the first level by a desk audit, and verify records and additional documentation onsite.

MOP and MOE often are used interchangeably, although there are those who distinguish between them. For example, you could say that stability is an MOP but not an MOE. We know that control charts indicate stability, but they don't tell us how good the process output is. In this book, we don't distinguish between MOP and MOE. We are interested in performance effectiveness, so it's important to choose the metrics that measure both. If it is necessary to establish stability before capability, so be it. Indirectly, then, stability is an MOE, too.

In ISO 9001:2000, reliability is one of the measures required in the process planning. Robert H. Lochner and Joseph E. Matar define reliability as quality over time, supporting the idea that it is a quality issue and its metrics measure quality characteristics.[2] If you are auditing a process or product, you should inquire about its reliability as evidence of good process planning.

ISO 9001 also requires evidence of the validation of effective planning. This covers a wide spectrum because it applies not only to the process output but also to its every aspect. For example, at the highest level of customer concern, is the process giving the customer what he or she wants? If the customer wants a blue Ford Explorer and the process is turning out green Explorers, the process is verified but is invalid.

Below this first level, methods and procedures used in the process must be validated. Suppose, for example, that the traffic department of your company uses a control chart to track delivery time and uses control limits based on normality. You suspect that the delivery time distribution is neither normal nor robust, and the limits may not be valid. Or suppose your company uses a sampling procedure to digitize sound for recordings, but the sampling rate is not appropriate to the major harmonics. Then this procedure is invalid from the customer's point of view. The music will be there, but it won't have the required quality.

Usually, auditors can't technically validate processes because they audit areas in which they aren't experts. They must rely on positive customer testimony, if it exists. If it doesn't exist, then process validity is in doubt. If some expressions of customer satisfaction are available, that will be shown to the auditors, who must then estimate whether the expressions are typical of the whole. This is why a formative audit is so important: You need the auditees' cooperation to arrive at a true assessment of effectiveness, which offers the only possibility for improvement.

CUSTOMER-RELATED PROCESSES

Most processes in a production or service activity are related to the customer if they affect the quality of product or service. However, to achieve added emphasis, ISO 9000 defines customer-related processes as those that deal *directly* with the customer. These processes are:

- Identifying customer requirements
- Reviewing customer requirements
- Customer communication

Customer requirements are those needs expressed by the customer that are relative to the product or service, its availability date, and support. The company also must identify needs that may not have been expressed by the customer but which are needed to accomplish the task, and it must identify regulatory and legal requirements. Because of the range of concerned persons suggested in these requirements, ISO 9004 refers to this section as "processes related to interested parties."

The three activities of identification, review, and communication can all be achieved in a single process—comprehensive contract review will do the job. For this reason, we'll focus on this particular process as an appropriate response to customer-related requirements.

Contract Review

The formal relationship between a customer and a performer begins with a contract. Moreover, if you agree to provide a product or service to a client, the contract between you defines its quality because of the way ISO 9000 defines quality: "the ability of a set of inherent characteristics of a product, system, or process to fulfill requirements of customers and other interested parties." Thus, a properly written contract, in which the requirements and inherent characteristics are expressed, is the very definition of what the customer is going to get. When supported by ongoing reviews with the customer participating, executing the contract will meet or exceed the customer's expectations. Of course, the expectations aren't in the contract, but if it becomes apparent that they aren't being met, the contract as written becomes inadequate. Recall that in the discussion of customer satisfaction in Chapter 11 we pointed out that everything hinges on expectations.

Peter Hybert defines contracting in a way that conforms strongly to the spirit of the ISO 9001:2000: "Contracting is the process by which customized systems are designed and delivered."[3] This view goes much farther than convention dictates. Most people will agree that the contract is not over until delivery, but Hybert is saying that *contracting* is not over until delivery. This is a very important notion because it carries with it the sense of an ongoing process, whereas the term "contract review" might suggest a single event in the execution of a contract. In keeping with ISO 9001's process approach, we are concerned with an effective contracting *process* that includes all the customer-related requirements.

Auditing the contracting process is easier if you know what the steps are and how they are connected. Figure 13.2 depicts the interrelated steps of an effective contracting process. The first step is identifying customer requirements, which usually starts with an initial meeting between customer and performer. At the same time, a notion of customer expectations is established. You must determine which function of your company is the primary interface agent with the customer. Companies differ on this. Sometimes the marketing department is the first point of contact, in others, the customer service department. For complex requirements, a team representing all concerned functions meets with the customer to identify needs

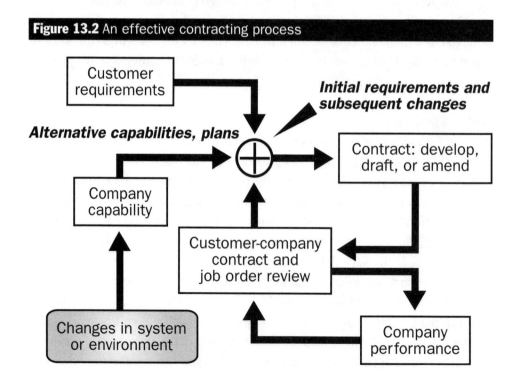

Figure 13.2 An effective contracting process

because any single company agent is limited in his or her ability to exactly understand the customer's requirements or how those needs may be met by the company's capability.

It's equally true that a single customer agent is limited in the ability to express exactly the requirements for all but the simplest products. If the product is a system of some sort, then the contract review team should consist of members representing both customer and performer. The performer's team will have members from marketing, sales and service, design, manufacturing, and purchasing. The customer's team will consist of the users of one or more of the capabilities that the system will provide. There are almost always multiple users for systems, for example, materials requirements planning systems, management information systems, communications systems, or a fleet of aircraft. A customer purchasing a passenger airplane will want people in the contract review process who represent its own marketing, service, technical support, and maintenance functions.

Once the customer requirements are identified, the next step is to review the company's capability to meet the requirements with its existing facilities or to determine if new processes are necessary and feasible. Assuming an initial agreement of expectations between customer and performer, a contract is then developed and an initial review takes place, including the job order if the customer requires it. In some cases, the contract contains the customer requirements and not the specifications. In other cases, the contract will contain both. In all cases the people in operations work from the job order. Thus, even if the customer is able to verify from the contract that the specifications meet the requirements, this doesn't verify the job order, which may contain more, fewer, or different specifications.

The contracting process is structured to maintain an agreement of expectations between the performer and the customer throughout the performance period. This is shown in Figure 13.2 as the system's feedback element. It lets the customer verify that requirements were recorded as they were transmitted, and that the specifications are a valid translation of the requirements. During the performance period it provides the customer and performer with an opportunity to review progress and resolve problems together. This helps the customer understand what must be done, the options available, and their cost. The customer's expectations may rise or fall as a result of the review, which enhances agreement and satisfaction at the end of the contract.

Figure 13.2 shows that after an agreement on the contract is reached and the company begins the various phases of work—design, development, and production—periodic contract reviews continue throughout the process. During these reviews, both the customer and the performer may request changes. Perhaps a material is no longer available or its price has increased, which changes the product's scope or cost. Perhaps the customer's requirements have changed. Joint review by customer and performer enhances opportunities for maintaining an agreement between them of customer expectations.

Auditing the Contracting Process

As an auditor, you should approach the notion of contract review as an ongoing process, for only in this context are all customer-related requirements satisfied. You should understand the elements of Figure 13.2 and how they are related. This system concept can help you in making up a checklist and asking the right questions, as well as in evaluating the effectiveness of the process.

Your audit of the company's contracting process will verify that:

■ An initial meeting with the customer establishes the product or service requirements, including those for delivery and support, if any.

■ Customer requirements are balanced against company capabilities and resources as well as against regulatory requirements.

■ After a contract is drafted, an initial joint review is conducted to ensure that the requirements are adequately defined and confirmed as well as documented in terms of specifications.

■ An ongoing process of periodic contract and performance review takes place in which the customer participates, either directly or through continual feedback.

■ Customer satisfaction with the final product or service is assessed and recorded.

These ideas should be incorporated into your checklist, but remember the broad picture—the standard requires that you verify processes related to interested parties, which means that your inquiry should look to appropriate representation. In other words, a joint review conducted by one or two persons may not ensure the customer's interests. ISO 9004 guidelines are concerned with identifying customer requirements, reviewing product requirements, and customer communication, but all interested parties must participate in the processes.

DESIGN AND DEVELOPMENT

Design and development refers to the planning, inputs and outputs, amendments, improvements, verification, and validation of the design of products, services, and processes. The design process includes life cycle, ergonomics, reliability, and maintainability issues, as well as the risk issues of safety, disposal, and the environment.

The Design Process

The design process tends to be similar in every industry. Software, hardware, product design, and system design all use a process as shown in Figure 13.3, which, with interconnecting feedback loops in every phase of activity, allows continual opportunity for evaluation and improvement. The basis of any design is a set of customer requirements, which are transformed into specifications. The process may include developing an initial design into various prototypes or configurations that are preliminary to a final design. In-process testing is often used in the development cycle of software programs or complex hardware systems. For example, an intermediate testing phase feeds back into an iterative design scheme because as you develop a design it may become apparent that you "can't get there from here," or that a different approach offers improvement.

Indeed, it may even be necessary to change the specifications. Because this is tantamount to changing the customer requirements, the customer can't be left out of this loop. The design process must allow for adaptability at any stage. This flexibility imposes two obligations on the design team. First, all interested persons, including the customer, should participate appropriately in the amendment considerations. Second, configuration management must be maintained. In the early stages of design, when requirements may be fuzzy, changes can be undisciplined. Without a paper trail it may be difficult to review why design changes were made. This loss of information can limit the effectiveness of design reviews and re-evaluating alternatives.

Figure 13.3 The design-and-development process

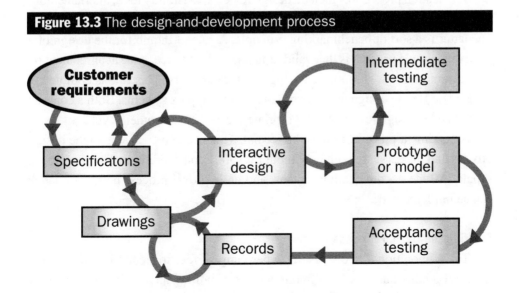

The design process requires horizontal and vertical interfaces. *Vertical* interfaces are those communications in a line organization related to a particular job order. *Horizontal* interfaces refer to the exchange of ideas, data, and information between appropriate groups while the design is in a particular phase. For example, early design meetings should include marketing, customer service, production, purchasing, and the customer. Purchasing people provide a reality check for materials costs and availability. Production people ensure the conformance of requirements to capability.

The design output must be documented, verified, and validated with respect to the design input requirements in each phase of the development cycle. Crucial characteristics of the design must also be identified at this point, such as safety, storage, weight, and other features required by law or critical to operation. Final design is often preceded by iterations of preliminaries. The design team can do what they wish with their intermediate designs, but final designs must be documented. They must also be reviewed for conformance, verification, and validation prior to release. This confirmation usually takes the form of well-designed acceptance criteria, which is as important as the product design itself.

Review meetings should be formal, documented, and include all the players concerned with the design. The outcome of these design reviews is considered a quality document. The scope of the design has a great deal to do with the review's magnitude. A large software program, for example, may take more than a year to write, and the design process would include many reviews and walks-through. ISO 9001 is concerned only that the process be formal and suitable.

Verification procedures include design reviews, feasibility tests, alternate models, and comparisons of a new design with a similar proven design, if available. The latter is a sort of benchmarking principle. A rule of thumb for the design of a relatively simple product is that validation takes place twice, once at agreement on contract and once at acceptance testing—before delivery. This rule is completely inadequate for the design of many products and complex systems. Both a contract review and a design review are appropriate for each development cycle.

Amendment procedures must be formal. This is a universal step in the design process and makes sense with or without ISO 9001 considerations. The procedures should include documentation, review, and an approval process before a change can be implemented.

Auditing the Design Process

The admonition, "Fools rush in where angels fear to tread" is often on the minds of quality auditors, who find themselves auditing an activity in which they aren't experts. Certainly, auditing a complex business unit is an intimidating prospect, and the design process is as complex as most. This is why an auditor is well advised to study and understand the process shown in Figure 13.3. You don't need to understand all the details of each block; on the contrary, the auditees will provide you with the details of their work. However, you must compose your checklist so as to ask the right questions, and understanding the flow diagram of Figure 13.3 helps you to do that. The following outline can help you in developing your list and in formulating your questions.

■ Customer requirements must be determined and translated into specifications. This includes the determination and timely availability of materials, skills, information (drawings, software, policies, procedures, technical manuals, safety issues, statutes, regulations, and environmental constraints), and other necessary resources.

■ A preliminary set of drawings represents the initial design, and the process is iterated in a development loop until an optimal design is achieved in terms of the final requirements. This loop includes developing prototypes or configurations, with verification and validation procedures leading to stages of assessment, amendment, and improvement.

■ Reviews are conducted of each development stage and include all interested persons to consider assessment issues. The reviews are open to discussion of improvements in design of the product, service, processes, or even specifications.

■ Acceptance testing is conducted of the final design configuration. This testing is designed to verify and validate the designed product or service.

■ Records are maintained of all review results and changes. These records are treated as quality documentation and include updated final drawings, specifications, and approvals. The customer is the primary approval agent of record.

PURCHASING

Products are made from materials or other products purchased from suppliers. Services include the materials or other products purchased from suppliers. Therefore, for any company, an effective purchasing process ensures that these materials and products conform to specifications and that they arrive on schedule. The basic purchasing process has three stages: requisition, receiving, and parts management, and the purchasing system's overall effectiveness depends upon how well each stage is organized, for they are interdependent.

An effective purchasing system includes its suppliers and forms a closed-loop system by a process of receipt verification. Whether all the functions and activities of the company's overall quality system are in-house, distributed, or even composed of other companies is immaterial. A company is responsible for the quality of its suppliers. They are part of the system.

Requisitions begin during planning, to meet projected schedules, or during operations, to meet unforeseen needs, growth, new work, or breakage. Management reviews these requisitions because company money is being spent. Buyers request quotes, review competitive pricing, and issue purchase orders. If delivery dates are close to need dates, the company may actively track the logistic process because a slip in delivery dates will affect operations.

The incoming material is verified against the purchase order for correctness, count, and condition. Correctness means that the receipt is validated against the requisition. Count means either a literal count of the number of units or a measurement of volume, capacity, weight, or other quantity. Condition means the received material is serviceable according to the specifications. Once the material is verified, the appropriate persons are notified, and the parts go to operations as needed, or to inventory.

The management of purchased parts is an ISO 9001 requirement, but whether it falls under Section 7.4 Purchasing or of Section 7.5 Production and service provision, depends on how the company chooses to define it. One point of view is that once the parts are received and verified, they are in the process, and therefore they concern operations. It's also true that the operations function requires materials planning. But so does the purchasing function. And quite often the purchased parts go into inventory at least briefly and are not immediately "on the floor." Some companies classify parts management as a purchasing function under the rationale that most inventory systems contain purchase triggers, so that inventory is simply one of the phases of the purchasing cycle.

Evaluation and Selection of Suppliers

Suppliers are selected based upon their ability to provide consistently acceptable products. The method of evaluation must be documented in a procedure, and records of the evaluations must be retained as quality records. A company can "grandfather" longtime suppliers, but once it has formalized its quality system, all suppliers must henceforth be continually evaluated, with their retention justifiable from a quality viewpoint. Most companies maintain a list of suppliers that have been approved in some way. In a few cases, the government requires that certain products—for example, powerful drugs or toxic chemicals—be purchased from licensed vendors. ISO 9001 doesn't explicitly require an approved vendor list, but it does require that a vendor selection process be maintained. The supplier evaluation need not be burdensome. Only a few metrics are needed, such as on-time delivery, correct product, good condition, correct count, and acceptable quality.

Verification of Purchased Product

Purchased product can be verified either at the supplier facility or upon arrival at the company facility, or both. The arrangement should be formal, described in documents of policy and procedures, and in the supplier's contract. Verification at the supplier facility places most of the weight of quality on the supplier. The company can accomplish this verification in two ways. Company buyers or quality experts can visit the supplier facility and conduct an audit of its inspection procedures. Alternatively, the company may accept, with the delivery of the purchased product, associated control chart results, other statistical evidence of product quality, third-party certification of test results, and conformance certifications from the supplier.

Product quality verification by the supplier does not relieve the company of its responsibility to provide acceptable product to its customers. Nevertheless, the company need not repeat the verification process in its own plant. Major corporations often use supplier verification if they have hundreds of suppliers, and the sheer volume of receipt inspection is inefficient or costly. If the company opts to inspect purchased products in its own facility, its inspection procedures must meet ISO 9001's requirements and there must be a formal procedure to notify the supplier of the outcome of such inspections.

Some customers may wish to verify a purchased product's quality for themselves, either at the company facility or the supplier facility. This option will of course be stipulated in the customer's contract with the company. The U.S. government is often such a customer. ISO 9001 makes it clear that inspection of purchased product by the customer absolves neither the supplier nor the company of its responsibility to the quality of its products.

Auditing the Purchasing Process

When auditing the requisition process, you want to verify that the purchasing documents include the technical data necessary to ensure that the delivered product is the same as the required product. The data will include an identification of product characteristics. For example, an order for a metal fitting will specify whether it is to be brass or steel, and if the latter, whether it is to be stainless, galvanized, or some other type.

Technical data establish the order's correctness relative to customer requirements. Typical data come from drawings, specifications, process requirements, and inspection instructions. These data ensure that the purchase order matches the customer requirements, and that the received materiel meets the specifications of the purchase order. Thus, there are both outgoing and incoming purchase procedures. The data are given to the supplier so that it, too, can meet the requirements.

You must know how your company classifies parts management. You will audit the process in any case, but in the event of a nonconformity, you must know what criterion against which to write the report. In fact, it's not unusual that a nonconformity can be ascribed to several ISO 9001 requirements. You should keep in mind that the formative audit's purpose is *constructive*—to improve a process. Therefore, you should address a nonconformity to the owner of the process, the person who has the authority to make the necessary improvement.

In composing your checklist, you'll want to include the following considerations:

■ The requisition process should include procedures for matching customer requirements to the purchase of parts and materials; a solicitation process of inquiry, quotation, and tender; a process for selecting and evaluating suppliers; timely order and delivery of resources; an effective purchase order format; and long-lead time parts ordering policies and procedures.

■ The receiving process should include: verifying and validating parts and materials against the purchase order and customer requirements, and evaluating suppliers in terms of effectiveness and efficiency.

■ The parts management process should include protecting and caring for received materiel, timely delivery to the end user, and an inventory mechanism with triggers for maintaining material of varying inventory turnover.

PRODUCTION AND SERVICE PROVISION

Manufacturers make products. Service industries and government agencies provide services. In every case the performer activates a system of processes that begins with resources and ends with a product or service that is sold directly to the customer. This system of basic processes is the meat and potatoes of what the performer does. In manufacturing, the meat and potatoes function is called "production." However, the word "operations" is a useful term for the same thing in any industry. For example, a hospital may not consider its primary care as production, but "operations" seems to fit. A bank conducts banking operations and even assigns an operations officer. The manufacturer, too, can use the term "operation" in place of "production" with no misunderstanding.

In this book, *operations* refer to those functions that directly provide a product or service to a customer. All the ISO 9001 requirements that apply to operations are discussed: the processes for handling incoming materials and purchased products, tracking materials through operations, controlling the operations, verifying conformance to requirements, disposing of nonconformities, and delivering product or service to the customer.

Operations Control

ISO 9001 requires that operations be planned and conducted under controlled conditions. These include:

- Establishing initial requirements for planning operations
- Making available information specifying customer requirements
- Using an adequately described job order and supporting work instructions
- Providing measuring equipment and employing monitoring processes
- Approving or rejecting deviations to specifications or schedule
- Employing processes for release, delivery, and post-delivery activities
- Developing procedures for changing schedules, objectives, specifications, or the process itself
- Changing an aspect of the process or its environment to maintain equilibrium or achieve improvement.

We assume that all operations are planned, but that isn't always true, and may not be done well when it is. Inadequate planning manifests itself in operations in many ways, but the two most common are bottlenecks and fire drills. Bottlenecks are caused by inadequate strategic planning or a failure to align supply and demand. Fire drills sometimes result from the unforeseeable but just as often occur because of inadequate tactical planning that creates disturbances in the day-to-day routine. There are other reasons for bottlenecks and fire drills, but these events catch the attention of an auditor, who is charged with inquiring about their causes.

On the other hand, using flowcharts, process layout diagrams, Gantt charts, PERT charts (program evaluation and review techniques), and materials requirements planning programs indicate that the planning function is understood and utilized. To the auditor, the use of formal planning techniques is a measure of operations' effectiveness. Smooth flow-through of processes, low in-process inventory, and using planning tools indicate good operations planning.

Documented procedures and work instructions provide control conditions because they define the production, installation, and servicing processes. They should be part of the departmental log and are easy to generate from flowcharts. Flowcharts are a key to good documentation because they describe the logical sequence of production and identify critical points in the process, factors to be measured, and the method of control. Flowcharts suggest policy by revealing potential operational problems. Finally, they show if the processes have feedback loops, which are characteristic of a controlled system. Other useful process control documents are effective job orders, inspection reports, test results, specifications, and standards.

Almost all operations require some type of equipment, from huge steel presses to desktop computers. Most companies provide the appropriate tools for a job, so that this requirement isn't a difficult one to achieve, and yet using the wrong tool or the right tool incorrectly is more common than you might think. Such events should attract the auditor's eye. There is a strong interaction between proper equipment and proper training, and process control is where it all comes together.

Equipment requires an effective maintenance program, which is an operations control because it grooms the equipment. Regular preventive maintenance and equipment alignment adds to its reliability. The program will include maintenance schedules and describe the nature and extent of the cleaning, lubricating, alignment, and other grooming concerns. The maintenance may be done by a team of personnel trained specifically for this process, or by external agents—for example, original equipment manufacturers. In one company reported by David A. Turbide, the operators themselves are trained and scheduled to maintain their own equipment.[4]

Maintenance periods, of course, will be integrated with operations because they usually represent down time. In keeping with the notion of measuring things, a good maintenance program improves reliability, and an optimum integration with operations improves availability. Reliability and availability are important indices of effectiveness in process control.

Proper equipment includes suitable working conditions, which usually means a safe, well-lighted area in which to work. Safety refers to the use of equipment, the area immediately surrounding the equipment's operational range, and waste discharge, particularly toxic waste. Safety is an element in process control because so many injuries occur from misusing equipment. Auditors have a certain degree of freedom in auditing safety in work areas or in areas of heavy equipment. You often find strict enforcement of policies on hard hats and safety glasses, and companies are usually strict in toxic waste cleanup. But where you may see a great deal of laxity is in the area of nontoxic liquid waste, grease spills, refuse, and just plain trash. A well-controlled process will have few accidents caused by things that shouldn't be there in the first place.

Operations control includes the provision and use of standards and codes, quality plans or procedures, and technical, operational, and maintenance manuals. These documents are references, and they must be provided, available, current, and used. These criteria aren't as easily met as you might suppose. Many companies will have been in operation for a long time, and the documents associated with a particular process sometimes get lost, become outdated, or are so dirty and ragged as to be unreadable. Auditors should verify that correct, current, and readable references are onsite.

Inspection and Test Status

During production, a product's status must be known relative to its conformance to inspection and test criteria so that only an acceptable product is delivered. Logically, you might expect this status to be in the purview of measurement, analysis, and improvement. However, as Jeanne Ketola and Kathy Roberts point out, it's good business practice to consider this status as an operations control.[5]

There must be no ambiguity about the quality of a product delivered to the customer. In the course of production, a product evolves, during which its quality is in transition. To preclude the accidental delivery of a nonconforming product, its inspection and test (I&T) status must be declared throughout the production process. The status is usually determined by inspection, and there are three categories: (1) not inspected, (2) inspected and rejected, and (3) inspected and accepted.

The I&T status of a product is usually easy to determine, except in the case of repair. A few examples will clarify the issue. To simplify things, let's define a "unit" as a product in some stage of its development. Units go through a series of value-added activities with inspection stations here and there in the sequence. As long as a unit is in the sequence, its status is inferred—it's either not inspected, or it has been inspected and accepted. The status of units in the production line is clear and need not be declared because they are in a well-defined sequence. (This example differs from receipt inspection, where incoming parts may lay around awaiting inspection and their status isn't clear at all unless declared.)

As long as a unit stays online, its status is known simply by its position in the sequence. But suppose that a unit fails inspection. It's then taken off line and sent to repair. Because it's off line, its position no longer indicates its status, so the status must be declared. The declaration can be in the form of a tag or label firmly attached.

A unit in the repair area is either in repair, awaiting repair, or on hold waiting for a part. During this time its status continues to be "inspected and rejected," and it should retain the label saying so. After it's repaired, the unit will move back to the production line according to the company's reinsertion policies.

Identification and Traceability

Where appropriate, a company will use suitable means to identify products and services throughout operations. What does "appropriate" mean? One answer is that it's appropriate if it's spelled out in the contract. A general notion is that if a purchased part used in a manufactured product contributes a unique quality characteristic to that product, then it should be identified.

Parts identification is necessary for three very important reasons. First, the company can verify that the appropriate part is available and being used throughout the production process. Also, the company must be able to identify quality failures by part or lot. The common way to identify a part is through a part number listed on the job order, which then accompanies the part through the production process.

The third reason is that an inventory system based on parts identity and scheduling permits evaluation of the dynamics of both logistics and operations. You can index inventory turnover, the first step in improvement. You can determine the cost of storage and in-process inventory. You can track raw materials to machine centers, finished parts to assembly areas, and final product held for delivery. You can determine, and perhaps improve, lead times and queue times. An essential part of inventory and production dynamics is continuous parts identification.

Traceability is the control of an identified product or service and is used if required by the contract or by the law. Kenneth L. Arnold points out that tracing has two parts, extending rearward to a point before receipt and forward to a point after delivery.[6] The ability to trace a product from its supplier through to the consumer is clearly necessary in the case where it is the active ingredient in a powerful drug. Tracing is often required by government regulation or industry protocol. Even when there is no regulation or protocol, a manufacturer might still want tracing if it envisions going back to the supplier, or forward to the customer *after* product delivery. This can come about as a result of customer complaints or of court actions related to product liability.

A simple example will show the importance of identification and tracing. Suppose that a lot of tuner circuits is installed in 300 television sets out of 10,000 sets manufactured in a given period. Later, it's found that this lot was poorly designed. Without being able to identify the lot, it might be necessary to recall all 10,000 sets rather than the suspected 300.

In this example, tracing the tuners reduced the problem's magnitude by a factor of 33. Tracing can involve enormous proportions in the automotive industry, where recalls may number in the tens of thousands. Even relatively small manufacturers can limit liability costs if they can trace parts. For example, a manufacturer of mobile shelving systems may rely on several sources for drive motors. If one of the brands develops a systematic fault in the field, then the ability to identify which of several hundred products contain the drive motor can significantly reduce travel as well as replacement costs.

Customer Property

Customer property refers to any product, part or parts, information, or intellectual property that is provided *by the customer* to be used in manufacturing a product to be delivered to that customer. Customer provision of property is quite common in some industries. For example, a company that replicates compact disks will receive tapes from its customers, replicate the music onto the disks, then return the tapes to the customer when it delivers the final product. In a somewhat different scenario, the U.S. government will deliver weapons systems to a shipyard to be installed on a newly constructed ship. Upon delivery, the customer receives the ship with its own property installed aboard. In each case, the tapes and weapons systems always belonged to their respective customers; they never at any time belonged to the performing organization.

There are two responsibilities to customer property: stewardship and quality control. As steward, the company is responsible for safeguarding the customer's property as inventory until it is put into production. At that time the material falls into the mainstream of the company's quality control processes. Safeguarding means the material must not only be protected from theft but also from the weather or damage on the floor or in the yard. The auditor will be concerned with written and implemented procedures on how this stewardship is achieved.

Because the quality of the customer property will affect the quality of the final products, the company is responsible for recording and reporting to the customer the event of lost, damaged, or delivered products unfit for use. This report is a quality record because the customer will deliver its product to the performer in good faith and assume that its responsibility has been fulfilled. If the product is somehow unfit, there may be grounds for contract dispute and customer grievance.

Customer property is received as any other material—through receipt inspection. The delivery date, condition, quantity, and fitness of the property are recorded and compared to contractual requirements. The property will then go to inventory until it is required in operations. It should be distinguished from other inventory by labels and location because it doesn't belong to the company. The holding area need not be unique—other material can be in the general storage area—but it should be sufficiently isolated so it is easily distinguished. Of course, it must be safe from damage or misuse.

The material is integrated into the final product according to the job order, but this final product may not be called for immediately. If not, it again returns for holding, and again it has a unique status. The auditor should be aware of a possible ambiguity here. If the customer property is integrated into a final product, as in the case of the weapon system installed on a ship, then the performer has added sufficient value that routine care of final product also ensures care of the customer property. On the other hand, in the case of CD replication, only the intellectual property was removed from the tapes, the latter remaining the physical property of the customer. Hence, the special care that the performer has defined in procedures must be in effect throughout the retention period of this property. At some point the final product will be called for delivery and will transit in accordance with the company's standard operating procedures.

Preservation of Product

If a company's operations are effective, the final product will have its maximum added value and will meet or exceed customer expectations. It is ready to go. Obviously, the company has a vested interest in preserving this state, so post-production activities are critical. These activities are handling, storage, packaging, and delivery.

Handling refers to the moving about of product within a facility, which may be a factory floor but could just as well be a bank loading dock or a hospital ward. Quite often the product is in lots and is heavy. Heavy things require care in lifting, even if a forklift is used. The container must be balanced on a pallet, which is lifted by a skilled forklift operator. Sometimes the product is kept in open boxes for a few hours or days, where it is exposed to damage risk.

When handling product, care must be used to prevent deterioration or damage. For example, problems in handling are sometimes caused by careless operation of forklifts. A forklift may graze a nearby product with its load or graze a nearby object while carrying a product. Or the operator may be careless in picking up and laying down product.

Accidents can be avoided in several ways. The first is to mark off areas that are not to be used as pathways. Isolation, quarantine, shipping, and reject areas should always be well marked, and an effective way to do this is with yellow nylon rope. The second is to ensure the best training for forklift operators. The third is to enact plant-floor traffic discipline. Only qualified operators should use forklifts, and traffic rules should be established and included in the operators' training. Auditors can verify all these considerations.

Storage refers to retaining product within the facility, either as incoming purchased parts or as outgoing finished product. Both incoming and outgoing processes must provide freedom from damage and deterioration. For example, things can be stored outside but must be protected from the elements if they are perishable or diminished in some way. Common sense pertains here. Automobiles are offloaded from a cargo ship in California and stored in an open field for a time. No problem; the automobile is made for this kind of exposure, and many customers will store them the same way. But things that tend to rust easily must be sheltered, and perishable goods must be refrigerated.

Purchased parts must be safely stored prior to use; finished product must be stored appropriately pending delivery. This is best accomplished by establishing storage areas, clearly delineated either by chamber or by yellow nylon rope, and by using appropriate packaging or cover. When product or parts are stored for a substantial period of time, their condition should be periodically checked. What does "substantial" mean? That decision is up to the company. Storage policies and procedures are required. Even a reject area should be protected from intrusion in order to preclude inadvertent use. Also, products should be labeled within the storage area. Different products can be stored in the same area if they have the same status: quarantine, accepted, rejected, ready for delivery, and so on. Color-coded labels can be used to delineate the status, according to written labeling procedures.

Packaging refers to ensuring the environmental security of the product. The specifications may define the packaging requirements, but if not, the responsibility remains. Procedures will designate the kind of material to be used and the extent of the packing required. If security is a customer requirement, then written policies and procedures are required that define security limits and describe the process. Packaging includes labeling, securely affixed, to identify the contents and provide destination, storage date, delivery date, and special characteristics.

Delivery has two components: traffic and protection. *Traffic* defines the method of transport of product and can take three forms: do it yourself, contract carrier, or common carrier. Of the three, the first provides the greatest control because all the factors are under the authority of the company—conveyances, drivers, loaders, routes, and schedules. However, doing it yourself requires a fleet of vehicles, with associated purchasing, maintenance, and full-time labor costs.

Contract carriers, such as moving companies, offer a door-to-door delivery service that you pay for only when you need it. The company has little control over traffic factors, but can negotiate schedules and freight rates. Or the company can use common carriers, which offer similar services. Common carriers don't guarantee door-to-door delivery but may off-load and on-load freight at various terminals. Traffic policies must be defined in the quality manual, and delivery procedures should spell out how a delivery is effected. There will be a paper trail of product tracking and signatories from shipping to customer that verify product quality upon arrival.

The contract may specify that the company must protect the product after final inspection and through delivery. If common carriers are used, the spirit of the requirement is met when the contract with the common carrier includes protection of the shipped product. In this case, the carrier is simply a supplier, subject to the evaluation and control required by the company of all its suppliers.

Post-Delivery Services

A company may agree in its contract with a customer to provide support services after delivering a product or service. Support services are not the same thing as customer services. Warren Blanding describes customer service as a process by which an agent of the company attempts to match customer requirements to company capability.[7] This is *pre-performance* service necessary to draw up a realizable contract. Support services, such as installation, in-service engineering, product support, and post-operative convalescent care at home, are *post-performance* services. Post-delivery services requirements don't apply to companies that exclude service from their contracts.

Examples of installation service are PBX communications systems and mobile storage systems. Copying machines represent an example of in-service engineering, and product support services might include replacing expendable items such as office supplies, printing inks and paper, and fuel supplies, or offering desktop computer technical support. When the product is extensive, heavy, or complex, installation is a major factor.

Generally, warranty work is not a service within the meaning of post-delivery services. A product that failed to perform as specified would fall in section 8.3 Control of nonconforming product. The process of nonconforming product control is internal in most companies. Their service departments are set up to support technical matters in the field, and warranty work is most efficiently handled through these agents. The important issue is service, not bureaucracy. If a company wants to handle both warranty work and support service through the same department, then it needs only to put the relevant responsibility, policies, and procedures in that department.

Sometimes companies don't offer a service in their contracts but provide it anyway as a matter of policy. Many mail order computer manufacturers and software houses provide warranties but also offer a telephone information service for an undefined period of time to help the customer get up to speed. The performing company is under no contractual obligation to provide this service, but wants to maintain a good relationship with the customer in the expectation of repeat or extended business. If a company provides a service, under contract or not, then its post-delivery services must be documented.

Scheduled service is provided for certain products that have extended term maintenance requirements, where the maintenance capability is either proprietary or too complex and costly for the customer to assume its responsibility. It may thus be cost-effective for the company to pay for maintenance service. This service will be stipulated in the contract, along with the maintenance schedule and other foreseeable issues such as expendable supplies that might be a byproduct of maintenance. A job order will be written up, and the service will be provided, usually by an agent in the field. After the job is completed, there will be some written acknowledgment of satisfactory performance as de facto evidence of product quality. It serves as a quality record.

On the other hand, random failures of the product, during or after the warranty period, will result in the customer's initiating the contact. This process should not be too complicated so as to discourage the customer. A telephone call, e-mail, or facsimile transmission should be all that is needed to initiate support service. The problem may be resolvable by a telephone call to a company expert familiar with the symptoms. Even so, the call will be logged in, a job order filled out, and a customer satisfaction acknowledgment received, perhaps by fax. The transaction is a quality record, attesting to restoration of a product from a degraded or nonfunctional mode. Also, the event will provide product reliability information and service quality data. Even easy problems provide insight into the integrity of the quality system.

The format of the report is important, too. After the service is performed, the company's field representative may submit a travel report, but this isn't an adequate quality record. There should be some document, if only a simple form, that specifies the work that was done and relates the customer's agreement in the form of a signature. This document is necessary because it may be a quality record. The service process must be defined in a written procedure, which can be brief but should describe alternate ways of handling customer calls and how problems may be addressed.

Monitoring and Measuring Devices

ISO 9001 requires documented procedures for the control, calibration, and maintenance of the inspection, measuring, and test equipment, including software used for measuring conformance to specifications of product or service. Every measurement made by the company requires a procedure that defines the measuring device used to make the measurement, and the metrics; parameter; and range, accuracy, precision, and sensitivity of the measurement. All of these factors define the measuring device's capability. Each measuring device must be calibrated, and its capability is a matter of the calibration record.

Parametric range means the measuring device must cover the range of the measured variable. *Accuracy* is the ability of the measurement to determine the true value of the characteristic being measured. *Precision* refers to the variability of the measurement and hence differs from accuracy. A voltmeter that repeats the same reading for the same measurement time after time is more precise than one whose reading varies. As the characteristic being measured also varies, it's possible to confuse the two. The measuring instrument's precision must be established by first measuring a known, fixed quantity. *Sensitivity* of the instrument refers to its ability to detect small differences in the measured unit.

The operation of any equipment is established by its manufacturer in making adjustments of variables, gains, and power within the unit. These adjustments establish the equipment's accuracy, scale factors, and linearity. With time, minute wear and drift occurs in the equipment, which must be readjusted to restore it to its required operational capability. This is called *calibration*. You usually don't wait for equipment to be obviously wrong but schedule calibration periodically. Many states, for example, require periodic calibration of devices used to measure some commodity such as gasoline pumps and grocery market and butcher shop scales.

Many companies use software programs designed to be calibration records. Every measurement is an operational pair—a measuring device and a thing measured. The calibration record contains an entry for each pair. You examine the entry and verify that a measuring device is in calibration and capable of making the measurement described in the entry. It is capable if it has the required parametric range.

Let's say you work for a dye shop and quality assurance is tasked to test the dyes' color fastness. One of the measurements is to see if a given color holds fast at 230° F. The device must have a range beyond this value, and it must be in calibration.

"In calibration" means that engineers from your company or from the original equipment manufacturer have determined an appropriate period for verifying and readjusting of the measuring device. The calibration entry states the date of the last calibration and the due date of the next one. If the day of your audit falls within this range, the device is in calibration.

Auditing Production and Service Operations

Generally, auditors will have a good idea about their company's products and services, for these things manifest the company mission. Except for the details, the auditor should feel quite comfortable in this examination. Nevertheless, auditors are obliged to learn a certain amount of operations specifics within the company because each process is unique.

■ Operationally, there is a logical and unbroken connection from the handling of incoming materials and purchased products, tracking materials through operations, verifying conformance to requirements, disposing of nonconformities, and the delivering of product or service to the customer. You could reasonably call all of this activity "operations," but as we have seen, ISO 9001 doesn't assign all of these processes to the same core requirements. For example, you can't dispose of nonconformities until you have verified nonconformance, and you can't verify nonconformance until you have made some sort of measurement. Hence, the processes of verifying and disposing of nonconformities are addressed in chapter 14, on measurement. Therefore, you want to consider adding the issues listed below to your checklist for production and service operations:

■ Planning processes are inferred from observations as well as effectiveness and efficiency measurements; objective evidence of installed and operating processes with associated documentation such as technical manuals and procedures; verification and validation procedures for customer requirements; policies and procedures for identifying and tracking.

■ Input processes are inferred from definitions and descriptions of required materials and purchased parts for products and services, defined acceptance criteria and verification procedures, up-to-date quality records of incoming materiel, and quarantine areas for rejected parts.

■ Throughput processes are inferred from equipment maintenance and calibration; availability of current work instructions; use of trained personnel; measurements of parameters such as cycle times, setup times, stability, and capability; clean work areas; safety notices where appropriate; documented procedures for installation and service; provision of codes and standards; and clear and comprehensive job orders.

■ Output processes are inferred from procedures and processes for product disposition; quarantine areas for nonconforming product; and policies, procedures, and processes for releasing and delivering product or service.

To audit I&T status procedures, you must know your company reinsertion policy. Suppose that a unit is removed from the production line because it failed some criterion at a test station. Depending on the nature of the unit, it is scrapped, re-graded, or repaired. Suppose that it is repaired, and then reinserted into the production line. Where should it be reinserted? Should it return through the test station where it failed or through the next value-adding workstation downstream from the test station? Some repair stations can perform the exact test, or a similar one, as that performed at the test station. Having been repaired and passed a similar test, the unit receives an "inspected and accepted" status and rejoins the production line at the next workstation following the test station in accordance with, say, Policy A.

Some repair stations have no test capability or perform a different kind of test than that done at the test station. The test station on the production line, for example, may conduct an operational or "light off" test on a unit coming from an upstream workstation, whereas the repair station may be set up to conduct only a continuity check of the repaired unit. In this case, the unit receives the status of "not inspected" and is reinserted into the production line to be retested at the test station where it had previously failed, in accordance with Policy B.

It's reasonable and economical to accept the position (i.e., location) of a unit on the production line as *prima facie* evidence of its condition. From feeder station to final assembly, the unit is in development. Prior to a test station, it bears the status of "not inspected" by that station. Following a test station, the unit's status becomes "inspected and rejected" or "inspected and accepted." The status is assumed and no declaration is necessary.

However, if the unit is taken off line at any time in its development cycle, its status must be declared. The declaration should be identified by both a printed record and by its placement on the floor. Printed records can be color-coded tags or labels, or a checkoff sheet and must be attached to the product in such a manner that it is not easily separated. Areas on the factory floor should be properly indicated as quarantine or reject areas and can be marked off by rope to fit the required space. The rope, supplemented by a "Rejects" or "Quarantine" sign identify the area where a product is not to be used in the production process. Then each product within the isolation area is likewise tagged or labeled, providing a redundant and fail-safe system of I&T status.

Auditing parts identification can be done at two levels. You can make a simple observation of the job order to verify if the parts are identified on it. The numbers won't mean anything to you, but at least you can verify that they are there, like a nametag on a fellow employee. A second way to audit this product is indirectly, through measurements that indicate the parts' identification process is in place and working—high-inventory turnover ratios and reduced lead and queue times. Many other factors contribute to these statistics, but a poor parts-identification process leads to poor values in these performance measurements.

According to ISO 9001, tracking is a factor in quality records. This means that a retention period must be assigned to the records of those products subject to this factor. Usually the law or industry custom will suggest a reasonable period for retaining tracking records. Durable goods often will have a very long retention time because the period of liability is long. However, liability isn't the only concern of a producer of goods and services. The company may also want to reproduce or improve the characteristics of a popular product or service, and sometimes it may take a long while to realize success in the market. The motion picture industry is a good example of this; some films become extremely popular a generation later.

There are many factors that affect retention time. The wisest course for an auditor is to look for a retention policy of some sort in the quality manual and, if it exists, accept the company's judgment as to whether it is appropriate.

Auditing customer property requires you to verify both stewardship and quality control procedures. Safeguarding is easy enough to verify; you ensure that procedures exist, then verify that the safeguarded areas are secure and properly marked. You must verify the receiving process, through receipt inspection, including the recording of delivery date, condition, quantity, and fitness of the property and comparison to contractual requirements. You will want to verify, too, that quality records are maintained of lost, damaged, or unsuitable property.

Handling, storage, packaging, and delivery processes are rather easily audited. For example, forklift efficiency is highly visible in terms of safe driving and properly picking up and laying down material. Storage areas should be well marked, adequate to their task, and secure from damage, theft, and environment. As an auditor, you will rely on observing and verifying procedures to assess the storage process.

Packaging procedures are best verified by comparing the activity to associated procedures. Simply observing the actual process won't be very enlightening unless you see safety violations. Similarly, delivery processes should be verified by examining the physical processes to the procedures. You want to visit the loading dock, of course, to observe how things are done and to verify safety issues. Traffic alternatives are a matter of policy, so you will want to familiarize yourself with policies and procedures for traffic, especially if contractual conditions are such that the delivery agent is effectively a supplier for the company. If so, then the same measures of performance apply to this agent as to any other supplier.

Calibration records are easy to audit, but you should remember to verify both whether a measuring device is in calibration and whether it is capable. Sometimes capability is not obvious because the readout scale of the device isn't visible. Most digital readouts fall in this category; they yield a reading only when making a measurement, and you have no idea of their range. In this case, you should ask about it. The operator will be happy to tell you if the device is not capable because he or she would love to have one that is and may see the audit as a chance to declare his or her point.

IMPROVEMENTS IN PRODUCT REALIZATION

Improvement in product realization is approached at two levels. The first and most familiar is at the subsystem level: improving the processes of planning, design, customer service, purchasing, operations, customer property, preservation, and measuring equipment. The second is at the system level: improving the "global" measures of product realization performance.

At the first, or process level, the improvement approach is straightforward and follows the format demonstrated in Figure 9.3. For example, the personnel in the purchasing function are its immediate experts and have developed MOP such as timeliness, correctness, condition, and count for deliveries, and they maintain supplier performance evaluations. Yet, some of these metrics are measured by other personnel in the receiving and operations functions. Open communication and feedback between these groups offers continual opportunity for assessment and improvement. This communication should be both instantaneous and periodic. There should be direct and immediate information exchange, for example, from receiving to purchasing, and between the latter and operations. Periodically, there should be a brainstorming session between these functions with the express objective of generating improvement ideas. The internal audit can serve as a catalyst for deriving an agenda for just such a session.

Similarly, some of the operations metrics are setup times, lot sizing and priorities, and queue times. These measures are best approached by the experts within the operations function, who can often directly associate a given sub-process to a given performance metric.

The system's effectiveness, or product realization level, is established by metrics that are meaningful to top management but might mean less to quality auditors. For example, inventory turnover and throughput are high-level performance measures of the entire production or service system, but these measurement statistics cannot be traced exactly to a particular subsystem. Brainstorming sessions and problem identification techniques, such as cause-and-effect (Ishikawa) diagrams, are quite essential in these circumstances. At this level, you need a wider diversity of skills in the sessions than might be the case at the subsystem level. Moreover, improvement strategies will require added time to measure and understand their effects because the connection between cause and effect is not direct and may well include interactions with other factors.

For example, throughput can be defined as the rate at which a production system generates money through sales and thus includes the company sales function as well as each subsystem within product realization. The company might decide to change to a more reliable supplier, but if there are bottleneck operations online, throughput might still not increase. Generally, to improve high-level performance we must heed the advice of Eliyahu M. Goldratt and J. Cox to optimize the whole system rather than to focus on optimizing each sub-process.[8] In fact, the authors claim that if each subsystem is optimized, the whole system won't be.

NONCONFORMANCE IN PRODUCT REALIZATION

In chapter 8 we defined the four core requirements of ISO 9001:2000. Of these, product realization is the one that lends itself most readily to traditional quality audit assessment. This is good news and bad news. The good news is that there is much to verify, and the areas of nonconformance are familiar. This is also the bad news because you can get mired down into a bottom-up assessment. The focus of a product realization audit should be on performance, just as it is in the other core requirements. In the next chapter we discuss some measures of performance that are appropriate to product realization. Armed with an understanding of these MOP, you audit this core requirement with a view to improve its capability.

SUMMARY

Product realization refers to the set of processes used to directly convert customer requirements into a deliverable product or service. Some of the processes deal directly with the customer, such as the custody of customer property and contract review. In others, customer needs are implied, such as operations and selection of suppliers.

There are a number of supporting processes to product realization, but the major ones are: contract review, in which customer requirements are identified to ensure the company is capable, and which is continued through the performance period to ensure the satisfaction of all customer expectations; design, in which the customer requirements are translated to specifications and the processes needed for fabrication, assembly, or service are identified; purchasing, to ensure that only top-quality materials and parts go into the product or service; operations, to ensure the stability and capability of the processes used to make the product or to provide the service; inspection and test status, to ensure that only acceptable product or service is delivered to the customer; handling and delivery, to ensure the quality of *delivered* product.

REFERENCES

1. Boehm, Barry W. "Verifying and Validating Software Requirements and Design Specifications." IEEE Transactions, *Software Engineering*, Jan. 1984, pp. 75–80.
2. Lochner, Robert H., and Joseph E. Matar. *Designing for Quality*. Milwaukee: ASQ Quality Press, 1990.
3. Hybert, Peter. "Five Ways to Improve the Contracting Process." *Quality Progress*, Feb. 1996, pp. 65–70.
4. Turbide, David A. "Japan's New Advantage: Total Productive Maintenance." *Quality Progress*, March 1995, pp. 121–123.
5. Ketola, Jeanne, and Kathy Roberts. "Product Realization." *Quality Digest* May 2000, pp. 39–43.
6. Arnold, Kenneth L. *The Manager's Guide to ISO 9000*. New York: Free Press, 1994.
7. Blanding, Warren. *Customer Service Operations*. New York: AMACOM, 1991.
8. Goldratt, Eliyahu M., and Jeff Cox. *The Goal: A Process of Continual Improvement*. New York: North River Press, 1986.

Measurement, Analysis, and Improvement

There are three ways for a company to establish the quality of its goods and services. The first is through folklore—you tell yourself how good you are. The second is through advertising—you tell others how good you are. The third is through measurement. Only the last method verifies that a product or service conforms to customer requirements, and it's the only method to interest auditors.

"I often say that when you can measure what you are speaking about and express it in numbers, you know something about it, but when you cannot measure it, when you cannot express it in numbers, your knowledge is of a meager and unsatisfactory kind," said William Thomson, Lord Kelvin, in 1891.[1]

Lord Kelvin makes short work of advertising and folklore, saying that without measurement, you simply don't know what you're talking about. An organization needs to measure performance for two very important reasons: to evaluate performance relative to goals, and to control its processes. You can't improve a process if you don't know how good it is or if you can't control it.

Therefore, measuring performance is a core criterion of ISO 9001, and its aspects are considered in several steps: making the measurement, understanding what you have measured, and using the results for improvement. Figure 14.1 shows how ISO 9001:2000 delineates these steps in five major requirements: 8.1 Planning, 8.2 Monitoring and measurement, 8.3 Control of nonconforming product, 8.4 Analysis of data, and 8.5 Improvement. The last requirement is a not-so-subtle reinforcement of the idea that improvement is the ultimate objective of a quality system.

PLANNING

The purpose of a measurement is to verify or validate some hypothesis. First, you must know what the hypothesis is, and then you must understand what parameters to measure that will verify or validate it, what metrics to choose, what measuring technique to apply, what device to use in making the measurement, and what data to record. Finally, you make the measurement. Then you must make sense of the data, particularly if it represents a random process. After you have decided exactly what it is the data reveals, you then must decide how best to use the results to effect an improvement in the measured process.

It should be clear by now that effective measurements require planning. In previous chapters we emphasized the notion that effective processes were *prima facie* evidence of good planning, indeed were better evidence than the plans themselves. Unfortunately, the same cannot be said for measurement because you cannot tell, by observation, whether a given measurement is effective. You must make inquiries and pursue the methodology.

Sometimes the wrong technique is used, sometimes the wrong equipment, and sometimes a measurement is made of a parameter simply because it's easy to mea-

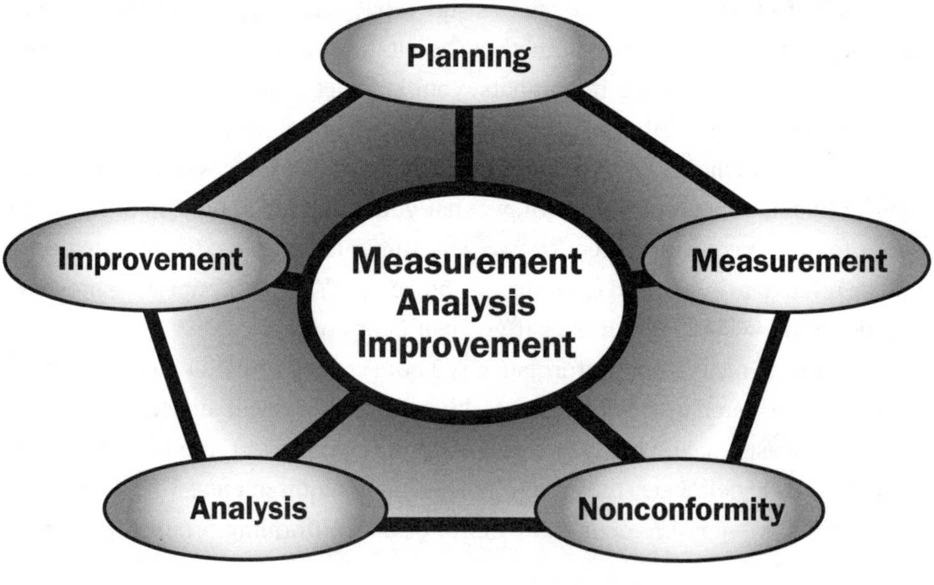

Figure 14.1 Performance measurement in the quality system

sure. There is a host of wrong ways to make a measurement. Perhaps, as an auditor, you can't validate a measurement, but you can verify that acceptable processes are used in determining the measurement criteria. These processes vary depending on the nature of the measurement, so we defer discussion of how to audit measurement planning to the next section on monitoring and measuring.

MONITORING AND MEASUREMENT

A company must define and implement measurement, analysis, and improvement processes to verify that a product or service conforms to specified requirements. Performance is measured at all levels of the company: system, process, and product or service. As a general rule, ISO 9001 does not dictate what is to be measured or what technique to use, with two exceptions. The first is that customer satisfaction must be measured, as a means to indicate the quality of system performance. The second is that an internal quality audit program is required as a means to measure system and process performance.

Customer Satisfaction

ISO 9000 defines quality as "the ability of a set of inherent characteristics of a product, system, or process to fulfill requirements of customers and other interested parties." This definition implies that it is the customer who decides what quality is; therefore, customer satisfaction is the metric of quality. It's not sufficient to declare quality. Advertising and folklore will not do. ISO 9001 requires that customer satisfaction be measured.

Each company will decide for itself how best to measure customer satisfaction appropriate to the business it is in. The standard goes farther, requiring the company to measure customer dissatisfaction as well. This additional twist heads off any sophistry or self-deception a company may employ in the absence of expressions of happiness from their customers. If you get complaints, they count as a measure of the customer's view.

Warren Blanding lists three basic ways to assess customer satisfaction, and your company should be doing at least one of them: personal interviews, telephone surveys, and mail questionnaires.[2] The advantage to the first is that it can be done at point-of-sale, but it can also be done anytime, either at your facility or at the customer's. Telephone surveys offer a follow-up procedure, and mail polls or questionnaires permit large-volume inquiry.

Your auditing job is to inquire after the methods used to obtain information on this subject and how often the measurement is made. You will also ask how this information is used in system improvement, looking for policies and procedures to ensure that these data are used effectively.

Internal Quality Audit

The purpose of an internal quality audit process is to determine whether the quality system established by the company conforms to the standard requirements and whether it is effectively implemented and maintained. As a participating member of the company internal quality audit (IQA) program, you are most knowledgeable of the planning and conduct of internal quality audits—who better than you?

It might seem, at first glance, a dichotomy for an internal quality auditor to audit the IQA function, a violation of the principle that "thou shalt not audit thyself." However, there are two conditions that save the integrity of the IQA self-audit. First, the owner of the IQA function is the quality assurance function. Therefore, those IQA members whose primary assignment is elsewhere in the company audit the IQA function. Second, the IQA process is formal, highly documented, and standardized. In a straightforward compliance audit, you perform the audit according to the book. Then you follow up with a brainstorming session for improvement initiatives.

Process of Measurement

An auditor must verify that measurements are being made and that they are effective. This task is more easily done if the auditor understands the process of measurement. The 10 steps in this process are: (1) determining the objective, (2) selecting the parameters, (3) determining the method, (4) selecting the metrics, (5) establishing validity, (6) choosing the measuring devices and references, (7) making the measurement, (8) performing the analysis, (9) drawing conclusions, and (10) improving the process. It's interesting to note that measurement is the "check" step in Shewhart's plan-do-check-act cycle, and the process of measurement itself follows that cycle.

Understanding the measurement process helps the auditor to formulate checklists and conduct inquiries. Most of the steps shown above need little explanation, but a few should be clarified. A valid measurement is one that allows prediction and extrapolation. For example, the number of school days in a year is a valid measurement of the quality of a school if there is a positive correlation between the number of days and the university acceptance rate of the school's graduates. The number of mechanics who work on your car is probably not a valid measurement of the quality of the repair.

Extrapolation is an important component of validity because it allows you to measure something that is observable, and from that, make judgments about something that is not. For example, we now measure engine temperature but no longer measure oil pressure, assuming that if the former is OK, then so is the latter. Similarly, in a valid measurement, we can make judgments about a large population while measuring only a small sample of it.

Selection of parameters refers to the characteristics that will actually be measured. For example, the color and fastness of a dye are two characteristics that might be measured in a dye shop. Smoothness and roundness may be measured parameters of a ball bearing. A metric is the unit to be used in measuring the parameter. An inch or a pound is a metric, as are the first-run ratio of a manufacturing line and the number of stitches per inch in a fabric. We shall examine many more metrics in the next section.

ISO 9001, in its wisdom, refers to "monitoring. and measuring." However, although it defines measuring, it does not define monitoring. The dictionary defines a monitor as something that warns or advises. Thus, we begin to understand what the standard is driving at. A company may prefer to observe a process in some sense without actually making a measurement. Measuring is a very formal process, although a great deal may be taken for granted in repeat measurements after the initial rationale is completed. Nevertheless, there is a cost to measuring that is over and above monitoring. On the other hand, measuring might suggest to someone that it is a one-time event, whereas monitoring goes on all the time.

In this book, we are interested in stable, capable, and improvable processes. This means that measurements of performance are made continually, and therefore "monitoring and measuring" is a redundancy. We use it when referring to the standard; otherwise we simply say "measurement."

Measurement of Process: Metrics

For a process to consistently meet customer requirements, it must be stable and capable. A company should want to know whether its processes are stable and capable because the cost of finding out is much less than the cost of not knowing. You find out by measuring key parameters of the process. To simplify things, let's arbitrarily adopt the following terms. Processes whose output is a product destined for sale in the marketplace are "productive" processes. Those whose output is a service—destined for sale in the marketplace are "service" processes. Those whose output contributes to productive or service processes are "support" processes. Very often support and service processes are the same because production requires services to achieve its ends. For example, accounting is a support process if it supports a factory and is a service process if it provides accounting to the marketplace. After all, a customer is a customer, internal or external.

Measuring Support Processes. Figure 14.2 provides a brief summary of support functions and related metrics. The list is hardly comprehensive and is offered solely to indicate to the auditor some of the processes that might be measured, and for which there must be policies and procedures.

Figure 14.2 Some metrics for service and support applications

Service/Support Function	Metrics
Accounting	Accounts receivable and payable; agreement to general ledger
Comptroller	Productivity measures; cost reductions
Computer programming	Defect density; percent of single-function modules
Contracts	Change orders
Data processing	Service volume; turnaround time
Finance	Return on investment; net present worth
Handling and storage	Damage incidence; retrieval rates
Information systems	Annual post hoc cost-benefit ratio
Inventory	Turnover rate; holding and shortage costs
Marketing	Market share, average time to market, return on investment
Planning	Forecasting variation
Publications	Defect density, timeliness of distribution, cost of rework
Purchasing	Price reductions, source selections, inventory control
Receiving and shipping	On-time schedules, condition, count, correct product
Safety	Accident rate, training rates
Sales	Contacts/bookings ratio, quotes/bookings ratio, new dealerships
Service	Percent orders entered once received, percent delivery on time
Traffic	Transportation costs per product
Training	Average and variance of annual training hours among personnel

Figure 14.3 Some metrics for productive applications	
Process Characteristic	**Metrics**
Stability	Constant mean and variance
Capability	Specification-variation ratio
Improvability	Cost function index
Productivity	Product price-cost ratio
Availability	Machine up time/production time ratio; reliability
Efficiency	Scrap and rework ratios; first-pass yields; setup times; percent of incoming product inspected; on-time delivery
Cycle times	Inventory turns; work-in-process inventory turns; order-to-shipment lead times
Customer factor	Customer reject rate; warranty costs
Innovations	Employee ideas adopted; new products

Measuring productive processes. Manufacturers usually track their productive processes quite well because a direct line can be traced from these systems to profitability. Some of the processes and metrics that are often used are listed in Figure 14.3.

Most of these indices are well known, though some of the terms may not be familiar. The improvability cost function is, for example, simply another name for the well-known Taguchi loss function. Other names might be "penalty function" or "opportunity loss." These names represent an increasing or decreasing range of values and hence an improving or deteriorating factor.

Measurement of Product or Service

ISO 9001 requires that an organization measure its products and services for conformance to customer requirements. The greatest enemy of quality is variation from target value of the quality characteristics of products and services, so statistical methods are often required. We'll discuss statistical methods in the next section on analysis; for the present, you should understand that evidence must be retained of measurement activities and acceptance criteria. Also, there must be procedures to ensure that nonconformities are prevented from being delivered to the customer.

ISO 9001 requires that products and services be measured to verify that they conform to customer requirements. Usually, this measurement is done by some scheme of inspection or testing. Such schemes not only help ensure conformance to requirements, they also provide a means to validate and verify the process. Indeed, the purpose of using sampling methods in the inspection and testing program is to evaluate the process. Of course, appropriate records must be maintained of the results of these activities because they are quality records. ISO 9001 doesn't specify how an inspection and test program is to be structured, but usually it is integrated with upstream and downstream activities from receiving through delivery.

Receipt inspection and testing. At the receiving station, incoming material may not be used in production processes until its conformance to specifications has been verified. This is usually achieved through inspection, either by verifying quality control data from the subcontractor, or by a receipt inspection in-house, such as acceptance testing. The receipt inspection process must be described in an associated procedure.

If the supplier is providing quality control of the incoming product, then there must be recorded evidence in the form of inspection results or statistical data from the final inspection conducted at the supplier facility. These data need to accompany the parts, and if they are separated—for instance, the parts go to storage and the confirming data to the quality assurance office—then there must be a procedure that describes this policy.

Incoming parts must arrive somewhere; usually there is a particular area within the plant that is designated for holding incoming inventory. This location should be clearly marked as a quarantine area to ensure that the materiel isn't integrated into production prior to its being inspected and approved for use. Some means of tagging or marking will serve to indicate whether the materiel has been inspected and accepted or not. Quarantine is needed for materiel not yet inspected, and rejection areas identified for unacceptable materiel. Auditors may find quarantined materiel in stock areas adjacent to materiel ready for use. The delineation of quarantine areas eliminates this ambiguity.

In urgent cases, incoming parts may be needed immediately and the receipt inspection therefore waived. This practice is acceptable, provided that the part is identified and recorded as having been so waived, and there exists a procedure describing the conditions of waiver and the policy behind it. The reason for identifying and recording this event is to be able to recall the final product and replace the culpable part in the event that a nonconformity is discovered.

In-process inspection and testing. People who perform value-added activity should also perform in-process inspection because each person is responsible for his or her own quality control. Testing is more complicated, and dedicated test personnel might be required, particularly at the final stage where the product is likely to have system characteristics. As with receipt inspections, you must maintain procedures and records for in-process inspections and testing. Product must be held until these verification activities have been completed, except under waiver rules previously discussed.

Final inspection and testing. In modern quality theory, each person is responsible for the quality of his or her own work. As a product or service proceeds from workstation to workstation, the quality control is continuous, assuming a process with integrity. Nevertheless, there is often a requirement for final verification and validation. The final product often takes on characteristics of its own that are arrived at synergistically. The sum total of quality is simply greater than its parts—for example, complex structures such as electronic systems.

Inspection and test records. A measurement program with integrity ensures that all specifications have been included; that inspections and tests overlap the specifications so that no characteristic, static or dynamic, is omitted; and that all of the scheduled inspections and tests, including the data, evaluations, and reports, are complete. Records verify that only a product that has passed the required inspections and tests is used in installation or delivered to the customer.

Auditing the Measurement Process

The auditable processes of measurement and monitoring include customer satisfaction, an internal quality audit program, measurement programs, measuring supplier performance, and the planning that goes into each of them. ISO 9004 also requires self-assessment, but we have not stressed this evaluation explicitly. Because it comes about quite naturally as a result of a program of continuous performance measurement and improvement, it is redundant. If your company conducts a continuous and comprehensive program of process measurement, then it is achieving self-assessment.

Customer satisfaction. You verify the process of determining customer satisfaction all along the line. First, find out who is responsible for planning programs of research into customer satisfaction. Then ask this group to describe how it plans its research. Determine which company function is the primary agent for contact with the external customer, and verify the use of personal interviews, telephone surveys, and polls and mail questionnaires. Verify that there is a follow-up procedure for every customer contact.

Ask how customer expectations are established, for without at least meeting expectations there will be no satisfaction. This is an important distinction. Don't be satisfied with learning how the company determines customer requirements; ask how it determines expectations. If the company doesn't pursue this inquiry, then you should raise the issue as an improvement initiative. Ask how the information is used that is solicited from the customer satisfaction process. You should expect it to be analyzed, sorted, and distributed to the various functions for later action.

Although many of the company functions won't have direct access to the customer, you still want to inquire, everywhere you go in your audit, how that process or activity determines customer satisfaction. A frequent answer from an operator might be that he or she simply follows the job order, under the assumption that this is what the customer wants. At the operator level this is a good answer. At the management level it's a terrible answer. The job order should never rise to the level of *nihil obstat* (no error). It should be the result of much research into customer requirements and expectations, and management everywhere should know its role in the determination.

Evidence of an active solicitation of customer satisfaction includes:

- Feedback on aspects of the product and service
- Customer requirements and contract information
- Market research
- Service delivery data
- Information on competitors
- Complaints and other direct communication with the customer
- Reports from consumer organizations
- Focus and brainstorming groups
- Surveys and questionnaires

Internal quality audit program. Figure 1.3 in chapter 1 portrays the structure of an IQA program and lists its elements. You begin by examining the program planning, directing your inquiry to the responsible person, probably the quality assurance officer. We have discussed the components of planning several times in this book—a plan specifies why, what, how, where, when, and who of a process, so the quality assurance officer's response should assign answers to each of these components. The major parts of the implemented IQA process are:

■ Adequate documentation
■ Performance measurement of processes that affect quality of product or service
■ Identification and active pursuit of process improvement

These issues should be interpreted broadly. For example, identification of nonconformities and corrective and preventive actions fall under the category of improvement. Evidence of an effective IQA process supports these activities, so look for a comprehensive quality manual including all supporting procedures and instructions, statistical results and analyses of tests verifying the stability and capability of each process, and reports and minutes of executive meetings in which improvement areas are identified and for which action items have been assigned.

Measuring processes. A great deal of verbiage can be expended on the subject of measuring the company's processes, but it isn't necessary. You want to verify three things:
■ Are the processes identified that affect the quality of product and service?
■ Are these processes being measured for stability, capability, and improvement?
■ Are the processes effective and efficient?

We have discussed at length the complicated process of measurement, most of which you can't verify because you aren't a process expert in what you are auditing. You will accept the word of the auditee that the methodology and metric of the measurement is correct.

Figures 14.2 and 14.3 provide numerous examples of metrics that apply to various functions in the company, and which measure various levels of aggregation (i.e., process hierarchy). They all come down to stability, capability, and improvement. So you ask every process owner the same simple questions: "How do you verify the stability of your process? How do you measure its capability? What is the procedure that you use to identify and implement improvement initiatives? How do you establish the effectiveness and efficiency of your process?"

The questions result in answers that are easy to understand. For example, capability is always measured the same way in every process; all you need to know is the metric.

In chapter 5 we learned that effectiveness is a measure of the extent to which planned activities are realized and planned results achieved, while efficiency is a measure of the relation between results achieved and resources used. Therefore, when you interview process owners, you expect to be answered in these terms.

Having established that the process is planned, you might ask for graphical evidence that the results compare accordingly. Similarly, you will inquire how the process efficiency is determined and verify the results.

Supplier performance. We have discussed supplier selection and evaluation in terms of policies and procedures in chapters 12 and 13. At this point we are concerned with suitable metrics of performance measurement. These can be simple measurements of timeliness, count, condition, and correct delivery, which offer easy-to-compute statistics. Although it might seem that timeliness is just a question of delivery no later than a specified date, some companies measure a supplier delivery time on a bilateral scale—too early and too late. The reason for this option is to avoid too much inventory. Thus, the supplier is given a window in which to make the delivery, and an early delivery can result in a poor evaluation just as much as a late one.

The policies and procedures for supplier performance may be handled by your company's purchasing function or by its quality assurance function. In many companies, Purchasing keeps these records and also performs the supplier audits. Having determined the responsible function, it's a straightforward matter to verify the company's supplier evaluation process.

CONTROL OF NONCONFORMITY

In medieval times, we understand, food not suitable for human consumption was simply thrown on the floor for the dogs. There isn't much you can say about this process, but it certainly established a clear and distinctive control of nonconformity. We face a similar dilemma with our quality system. After all our effort to design and construct quality products and services, and to measure our performance, we yet realize, as quality pioneer Walter Shewhart tells us, that variation is inevitable and at least some of that variation yields unacceptable product.

ISO 9001 requires a process to control product that fails to meet specifications, preclude its unintended use, and define how such product will be disposed. A company can do various things with its nonconforming product: scrap, rework, or regrade it, or provide it to the customer on a concession basis—i.e., the customer agrees to accept the product as is.

Nonconformity Review

Three processes are necessary for effective handling of nonconformity. The first is detecting the nonconformity. The second is deciding what to do with it. The third is investigating what caused it and taking some counteraction. Deciding what to do about the defective product is called "disposition." Deciding what action to take to counter nonconformity falls under the category of preventive and corrective actions, and will be discussed in the section on improvement.

Nonconformity review allows a board of experts to examine a defect within the context of similar events, perhaps discovering systematic problems. It should begin with an ad hoc meeting of those in operations most closely associated with the defective product. This approach provides the technical expertise that is needed to make a first-cut determination of whether the cause is common or special, systematic or random. The occurrence and identity of a defect and its cause should be filed as a defective material report, which will be the first documentation of the review process.

Disposition

The quality manual will describe the company's policy on the disposition of the nonconformity. Such products can be disposed of in several ways. "Scrap" is used as a general term to apply to nonconforming product that is rejected. It's not going to the customer. It may be thrown away as trash, returned to the vendor, or sold as scrap, but it isn't going to be used to make product.

The very first thing that must be done is to isolate the nonconforming product from good product. This must take place immediately, at the location of defect discovery, because it's in the vicinity of production that bad product is most likely to be inadvertently reinserted into the mainstream. The designation of nonconformity can be a colored label or sticker attached to the defective product by the discoverer, usually an inspector or tester. Once the nonconforming product is identified and labeled, it should be removed from the operations area and put into quarantine.

Rework refers to nonconforming product that must be refurbished, usually through repair. Bad product that needs reworking can be taken from the point of detection to the rework area, or it can remain temporarily in a rejection area if this is more efficient. Units to be reworked can be distinguished from other defective parts in the rejection area by a label on each. Then by some convenient mechanism—via a periodic daily schedule, for example—those parts destined for rework can be gathered from the rejection area and carted to the rework station.

Rework is a viable option if a cost-effective repair process can be developed. Usually, this depends on the nature of the product. Complex products often are repairable; fabrics usually are not. In any case, ISO 9001 is noncommittal on the subject, leaving the matter a decision of management. If there are rules of thumb to be used in the decision to rework or not, then they should be included in the policy described in the quality manual. This forces the company to think hard about what it wants to do relative to the business it is in.

Regrade refers to nonconforming product that will be reclassified as an alternate product. For example, a manufacturer of fabric makes a top-of-the-line product. Nonconforming product is not re-workable. Therefore, secondary product is sold as remnants at less than one dollar per yard; tertiary product is sold as rags at a few cents per pound.

Concession refers to nonconforming product that will be delivered to the customer despite its condition. A nonconforming product is one that fails to meet customer requirements, so why should a customer accept it? In fact, this sort of transaction happens all of the time and is one of the very good reasons why the term "nonconforming" is better than the term "bad." We often do this ourselves: You order, for example, a new car with options. All the options are written into the contract. After you wait five weeks for it, the car arrives but one of the options is missing. You decide to take the car anyway rather than wait another five weeks.

Everything in the preceding discussion is applicable to service as well. Usually, nonconformity in service is an incorrect entry on a form or document, or a lost or delayed document. For example, you may get your credit card bill too late to make the deadline for its payment. This nonconformity calls for rework of the bill in the form of a new payment deadline. If a billing form error is caught before the billing is sent out, and if the form is short, then it is scrapped and a new one made out. If it is a long form involving many pages and contains only a minor error, an ink correction may be written over and initialed. These options should be spelled out in procedures.

Auditing the Nonconformity Control Process

Nonconformity control is one of the universal processes of the company. Common policies and procedures are required, and they are applicable everywhere within the quality system. Because these policies and procedures are universal, they should be written in a tier one document such as the quality manual itself. At each audited function, you pose these questions: "How do you ensure that product or service which fails to meet specifications or objectives is precluded from unintended use? How do you dispose of it? Describe how 'scrap,' 'rework,' 'regrade,' and 'concession' are defined and implemented in your activity. Are there regulatory or industrial protocols governing your nonconformance policies and procedures?"

DATA ANALYSIS

Measurements yield data, but the data may have no meaning without analysis. Analysis is the examination of data to determine trends, stability, and capability, or to compare for indications of improvement. Analyzing data is how we achieve the objectives for making the measurements in the first place.

The standard requires data to be collected on the effectiveness of the quality system, trends, trends in operations, customer satisfaction, cost of quality, supplier performance, and conformance to customer requirements. The data can be gathered from a variety of measurements of process, product, or service, or from observations made during internal audits, corrective and preventive actions, customer complaints, and other processes. Much of the data will indicate variation and will require statistical analysis, so statistical techniques are an important part of quality measurement.

Statistical Techniques

In planning measurement processes, ISO 9001 requires a company to identify those statistical techniques needed to make valid measurements and to verify adherence to product specifications and system capability. In chapter 9, we agreed with Shewhart on several points, and sum them up here in the following, from Eugene L. Grant and Richard S. Leavenworth:

Measured quality of a manufactured product is always subject to a certain amount of variation as a result of chance. Some stable system of chance causes is inherent in any particular scheme of production and inspection. Variation within this stable pattern is inevitable. The reasons for variation outside this stable pattern may be discovered and corrected.[3]

Walter Shewhart tells us that variation is the enemy of quality. Therefore, variation must be measured everywhere it exists and affects product quality. This is potentially a large task because variation exists in all processes throughout a company, not just in operations, and it's difficult to imagine some process that doesn't affect quality directly or indirectly. Recognizing this reality, an effective audit program includes most of the processes within the company.

Once the processes to be measured are identified, then appropriate techniques are chosen for making the measurement. The auditor is concerned that there are policies and procedures in place to govern the measurements. There are a wide variety of statistical techniques: time series, run charts, Pareto diagrams, and cause-and-effect (Ishikawa or "fishbone") diagrams, to name a few. Whichever methods are adopted, a procedure should be drawn up that describes the events for which they will be used. ISO 9001 does not require a description of how they are done.

The auditor should be familiar with the most commonly used statistical methods, including those listed above and some of the techniques of designed experiments such as analysis of variance, factorial arrays, and response surface methods. The reason is obvious: If you are going to ask someone how he or she analyzes data, you need to understand the answer. Detailed knowledge isn't necessary. An auditor doesn't have to be a statistician. Nevertheless, knowledge of the strategic purposes of statistical methods and of the vocabulary will maintain the auditor's credibility.

Auditing the Analysis Process

You audit an activity's analysis process at the same time you audit the measurement of its functional process. When you ask for the results of the performance measurement of the stability, capability, improvement, effectiveness, and efficiency of a process, the results, if these measurements have been done at all, will be in graphic form: control chart readouts, histograms, pie charts, and so on. You verify the results, then ask the process owner how they were validated.

IMPROVEMENT

Improvement of product or process is achieved by correction or prevention of nonconformity, or by finding a better way to do something. We shall begin the discussion with correction and prevention because these strategies are relatively straightforward. Basically, they amount to this: You can wait until things go wrong or you can take steps to prevent a defect before it happens. Both strategies have their adherents. The first is described by the old saw, "if it ain't broke, don't fix it," more elegantly termed a run-to-fail philosophy. However, quality is not best served with an either/or approach. Correction and prevention are complementary. An effective quality system provides both corrective and preventive programs.

Corrective and preventive actions represent two different philosophies. Corrective actions are those taken to address a problem of variability that exists in the process. This problem may be due to a special cause (e.g., external disturbance) or to a common cause (e.g., a variation inherent in the system). Preventive actions are those taken to address a potential problem of variability that might occur in the process. The problems might be regarded as either potentially special or potentially inherent. In sum, corrective actions are remedial, whereas preventive actions are anticipative.

There is general agreement on the problem-solving process. The iteration is to (1) identify a problem, (2) analyze the problem, (3) evaluate alternate solutions,

(4) select and implement a solution, and (5) evaluate results. Corrective and preventive measures both use this process but employ different strategies in doing so, as indicated in Figure 14.4. As a general statement, correction tends to focus on product; prevention tends to focus on process.

Corrective Action

Figure 14.5 depicts a corrective action program and may help the auditor visualize the process. We begin by formalizing a problem with an identification (ID) number, date of occurrence, its description, and symptoms. An owner is assigned who will size the job of solving the problem: estimate the nature of the problem; determine functional contacts, if any; set up a status reporting process; determine appropriate analytical techniques to resolve the problem; and move to solution. The problem report will record these issues by evaluating the solution.

Once a problem is detected, corrective action is taken to determine the cause. The force behind both of these methods is often collective discussion, using some sort of committee analysis or brainstorming technique. After the cause is identi-

Figure 14.4 Problem-solving strategies for prevention and correction

Step	Prevention	Correction
Identify problem	Research, surveys, audits Maintenance, training Forecasts	Test, inspect Customer complaint Operator reports
Analyze problem	Environmental impact Process analysis Modes and interactions	Product analysis Root-cause analysis
Evaluate alternate solutions	Incremental changes Changes in kind	Redesign, repair, replace
Implement solution	Effect in the large Effect in test case	Effect in the large Effect in test case
Evaluate results	Evaluate in the large	Evaluate locally

fied, the investigation must include a confirmation period to verify that the corrective action has resolved the issue. In sum, a correction process will identify four phases: detection, identification, resolution, and verification.

A formal process may seem too cumbersome to be effective, but it is necessary to ensure a systematic solution. Furthermore, as the figure indicates, a formal process does not preclude a quick fix, which is an ad hoc, on-the-spot solution to a problem. It can be reasonable, economically necessary, and very often sufficient. Sometimes a problem is simple and its solution obvious—an assembler may notice that some of the cooling fins on an air conditioner may be bent. If they can be straightened out on the spot, why not do so? It should still be reported, if only to detect a systematic problem. The incident may be a recurring one. A good corrective action process will be formal yet accommodate quick fixes, and the auditor should look for both.

Preventive Action

Preventive action implies the ability to see into the future, to conceive the possible. It is quite similar to strategic thinking. Prevention focuses on potential failure and thus lies in analyzing and recognizing pervasive and persistent effects,

Figure 14.5 The structure of a corrective action process

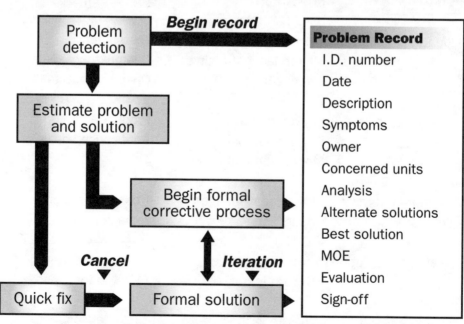

(William A. Stimson, 1998. With permission from AMACOM)

trends, and patterns of failure. Shewhart tells us that random failure will always be with us, but we can remove the causes of repetitive failure by a program of studying and analyzing processes.[4] Prevention is the main reason we take data and keep records—to look for systematic causes.

Preventive actions, too, require a formal framework. The purpose of a prevention program is to anticipate and identify systematic problems in product or process. An effective program includes regular scrutiny of operations, quality records, audit reports, customer complaints, and results of inspection and testing in order to detect, analyze, and remove potential problem areas. Additionally, a well-defined program improves employees' cognitive skills, which broadens their view, and includes employee empowerment, which increases their motivation.

Cognitive skills should be improved because the very nature of forecasting potential trouble implies human intellect. The better people understand the product, process, and environment, the better their abilities to see nuance and anticipate a problem. Systems-level training is the best vehicle for broadening an employee's view.

To understand the importance of systems-level training, we must start with a definition: "A system is a process in which, within a given period of time, a set of inputs will yield a set of outputs according to the state of the system"[5] Therefore, systems-level training provides the employee a top-down view of the process in terms of inputs, outputs, integration requirements, and contribution to the total effort. Everyone is an expert in his or her task, but understanding its strategic function increases the ability to see areas of improvement or opportunities for prevention.

Employee empowerment contributes to a continuous improvement program by making employees participants and stakeholders in the process. Thus, they are encouraged to use their expertise to identify potential problems. Some companies are cautious about empowering their employees, and Robert M. Tomasko reports resistance to the concept by employees themselves, either because they don't want what they perceive as added responsibility, or because sharing problems that have only management solutions proves frustrating.[6]

Many companies find that a workable employee empowerment program includes giving employees the authority to make a defined range of improvements in their own processes, and to serve on boards or in meetings where a bottom-up view enriches considerations.

Auditing the Improvement Process

By now it should be clear that customer satisfaction and improvement issues are, or should be, woven into the quality system's fabric. There may be no explicit "customer satisfaction" process or "improvement" process in the company. Rather, these factors are integrated as activities within each process of the system. Thus, when you have audited all the processes defined in the audit's scope, you have at the same time audited their improvement scheme. In this section, we will review what you look for in terms of evidence.

Corrective action. Corrections are initiated by customer complaints, nonconformance reports, outputs from management review, internal audit reports, process measurements, and quality system reports. Each source should result in some corrective action, so it's appropriate to examine some of these sources, and then ask what is being done about them. The corrective process described to you should include a definition of the causes of the nonconformities and defects, appropriate actions to avoid recurrence of the problems, and a record of this corrective activity and results.

ISO 9001 places great importance on finding root cause. Mending a nonconformity is a necessary but not sufficient first step in corrective action. Moreover, the follow-up period includes an assessment of the correction's effectiveness, which is measured in two ways: by restoring effectiveness and efficiency of the process, and by achieving a confidence level that ensures the defect will not recur. The corrective action should enjoy high visibility. Nonconformance reports are matters for an executive review board, where the assignment of action items is recorded. Subsequent analyses and root causes, too, are management concerns because resources are usually required for definitive corrections. Thus, you should trace the corrective action from point-of-discovery through to its executive review and back to final disposition. To summarize, the evidence of an effective corrective action process includes:

■ A corrective action program structured as shown in Figure 14.5, in both organization and in procedures

■ Reliance on sources: customer, executive review, IQA reports, nonconformance reports, process measurements, and quality system evaluations and reports

■ Root-cause analysis and elimination

■ Executive overview of corrective action from problem identity through resolution

■ Permanent-fix installation and quick-fix removal, where appropriate

■ Measures of performance to establish process restoration

■ Record keeping for long-term verification of problem elimination

■ Updating procedures where needed to preclude problem recurrence

Preventive action. Smallpox vaccination is regarded as a measure of preventive medicine. In that case, what is the evidence that a smallpox vaccination has saved you from that disease? There is none. The occurrence of smallpox is a random event, and the evidence of the effectiveness of a vaccine is statistical. Most preventive actions share this ambiguity; on a case-by-case basis there is little evidence that they work. By their very nature they *prevent*, thus a successful preventive action is followed by a nonevent.

And so it is with quality systems. If a company has a dynamic preventive action program, the best evidence of its effectiveness will be that the company has better indices of performance than competitors in the same industry that have weaker prevention programs. This evidence may be, of course, confounded with other interacting factors.

Therefore, as an auditor, your approach to assessing the effectiveness of a preventive action program is to look for evidence that things are being done that are believed to be effective in prevention. Everything starts with knowledge, so you want evidence that the company is open to sources that tell us how things work: customer expectations, market analysis, management reviews, data analysis, process measurements, and early-warning indicators. These sources may vary from process to process, so the process owner must explain his or her sources to you. For example, an early-warning indicator for inventory may be a ramp-type trigger that occurs when a certain level is reached. An early-warning indicator for a production line might be a moving average control chart.

I believe that very good sources for prevention are the operators themselves, and their ability to contribute to prevention is in proportion to their experience and breadth of training. The evidence for taking advantage of this source is found in company training programs, suggestion programs, and by employees participating in forums where prevention is an agenda item.

Specific evidence of preventive action is found in minutes and records as:

■ Identified potential causes of nonconformity

■ Defined actions for prevention

■ Review of action results

Improvement action. By definition, correction and prevention are improvement actions, but a comprehensive improvement program goes beyond corrective and preventive activities to explore the system environment, which, in systems engineering, is all that is exterior to the system. Thus, an effective improvement program includes:

■ Sources of information such as process measurements, market analysis, financial data, customer questionnaires, supplier evaluations and responses, and validation and verification data

■ Forums for improvement participated in by employees and management, with improvement initiatives explicitly on the agenda and open discussion of incremental and breakthrough ideas for product, service, or process improvement

■ Formal procedures for validating, testing, verifying, installing, and evaluating over the long term improvement initiatives as determined by measures of performance

The process of improvement is shown in Figure 9.3, which you can compare to the process used by your company to judge your quality system's effectiveness. A bottom-line indication of your system depends on the answer to two questions: If an employee has a "better way" to do something, is there a formal process for giving this idea serious consideration? If this better way is found feasible, is there a formal and ensured process for its validation, verification, and adoption? You should realize that there are two issues here. The first is whether the system of improvement exists; the second is whether employees believe that it works.

SUMMARY

A company must define and implement measurement, analysis, and improvement processes as a means of demonstrating that a product or service conforms to specified requirements. Performance will be measured at all levels of the organization—system, process, and product.

The company must have a process to measure customer requirements and expectations, must maintain an effective internal audit program, and must measure process performance. The purpose of measurement is improvement; however, because nonconforming product or service will necessarily be discovered as well, a process to control nonconformance is also required.

Measurements provide data, which are the real source of information and improvement, so a company must have formal processes and procedures for analyzing data, including validating the measurement processes themselves. Possibilities for improvement are enhanced with the knowledge gained from market, customer, and process measurements. Accordingly, there must be a formal improvement process for corrective action, preventive action, and for finding better ways to do things.

REFERENCES

1. Thomson, William. *Popular Lectures and Addresses*. Vol. 1, second ed. London: Macmillen, 1891.

2. Blanding, Warren. *Customer Service Operations*. New York: AMACOM, 1991.

3. Grant, Eugene L., and Richard S. Leavenworth. *Statistical Quality Control*. New York: McGraw-Hill, 1988.

4. Shewhart, Walter A. *Economic Control of Quality of Manufactured Product*. Princeton, N.J.: Van Nostrand, 1931.

5. Stimson, William A. "Principles of System Testing." *Naval Engineers Journal*, Nov. 1988, pp. 8–58.

6. Tomasko, Robert M. *Rethinking the Corporation*. New York, 1993.

CHAPTER 15

Summary and Conclusions

It's important for auditors to maintain the big picture of what an audit is all about. Rather than concluding this book with a review of its chapters, we shall end by describing this big picture. According to D. L. Beeler, the purpose of an audit is to examine three aspects of a company's systems:

1. *Adequacy*—do they have the potential to succeed?
2. *Implementation*—are they implemented as designed?
3. *Effectiveness*—are the systems achieving their intended results?[1]

ISO 9001 is designed to answer these questions by providing the auditor some requirements that help ascertain the degree of adequacy, implementation, and effectiveness. Unfortunately, auditors sometimes lose sight of the big picture and assume that the requirements are the audit's objectives. They are not; determining adequacy, implementation, and effectiveness are.

The auditor must make judgments about these traits based on observations of "facts." But when making a judgment, don't ask, "Is this observation a violation of a requirement?" The answers inevitably result in a list of nonconformities that often are irrelevant or trivial from a systems viewpoint. A host of venial sins does not a mortal sin make. Rather, the question should be, "How does this observation affect the adequacy, implementation, and effectiveness of the system?" An audit report with this perspective provides management with an informative evaluation of the quality system.

Beeler points out that *facts are not useful or meaningful in themselves*. They have meaning only to the extent that they shed light on how the systems perform. You can make up a list of nonconformities, refer them to requirements, put a cover on it, and call it an audit report, but it will be little help to line managers responsible for the processes. They will regard such a list as nitpicking, and they will be right. Furthermore, correcting the deficiencies revealed in this type of report will not necessarily improve the quality system.

Auditors must use inferential reasoning. Working from discrete bits of information gathered from reviewing documents, interviewing personnel, or observing work processes, they must draw conclusions about adequacy, implementation, and effectiveness. To the extent that an observation can indicate a level of attainment of these system aspects, it is useful to system improvement.

So what does adequacy mean? An adequate quality system is one that has the potential to succeed. The word "potential" is the key to adequacy. No quality system is perfect, and according to Walter Shewhart, it never can be.[2] But if the quality system is comprehensive, complete, and built on a structure that conforms to quality principles, then it is eminently improvable. It will succeed because it can get better and better. ISO 9001 describes a comprehensive and complete quality system, and the auditor's job is to assemble observations that can assist in its effectiveness.

A quality system that is correctly implemented is adequate in both written and physical forms. It's important to distinguish between these schemes; one represents form, the other represents substance, and both are absolutely necessary. In the United States, whose history is one of discovery and development, we often overlook the importance of form. The emphasis is on substance, in accordance with the old saying, "it's all form and no substance," itself a scornful condemnation. Yet, form provides both the guiding light and the corporate history necessary to sustainability. Form keeps you from patricide and continually reinventing the wheel.

Auditors must understand this duality in the quality system and evaluate both. It's tedious to audit documents. We've said before that the devil is in the details, and when you audit the written quality system, you must critically read these details. Technical reading isn't easy. Your mind wanders or goes numb; I have seen a few auditors doze off.

It's easier and more exciting to audit the physical system, but what are you going to audit it against if you are not thoroughly familiar with the quality manual?

Too, it is the physical system that we sample, so the physical audit must be well planned and executed if it is to be effective.

A quality system is effective if it gets us where we want to go. This is effectiveness on a grand scale—big-picture effectiveness, not the control-by-control effectiveness that ruled in times past. The auditor contributes to a constructive, formative audit when he or she verifies both the documented system and the implemented system.

Getting us where we want to go means continually improving the quality of process, product, and service. This is not the same as adequacy. A system is improvable when it is structured so that it *can* lead to improvement. A system is effective when it *does* lead to improvement. Again, these subtle differences are the business of the auditor. An inadequate quality system cannot be effective; an ineffective quality system cannot be made effective unless it is adequate, so the auditor must verify both. These are big-picture notions that go well beyond looking for nonconformities.

The auditor's task then, is to focus on the system, posing all questions in the light of adequacy, implementation, and effectiveness, and work with the system owner toward a constructive conclusion about system performance and improvement. As a rule of thumb, the internal quality auditor should use a simple technique in conducting a formative audit:

- Build facts to a conclusion
- Use judgment
- Think systems
- Avoid nitpicking

REFERENCES

1. Beeler, D. L. "Internal Auditing: The Big Lies." *Quality Progress*, May 1999, pp. 73–78.
2. Shewhart, Walter A. *Economic Control of Quality of Manufactured Product.* Princeton, NJ.: Van Nostrand, 1931.

Sampling for Internal Quality Audits

Although you may not have thought about it, auditing is done by taking samples. All conformity audits use some form of sampling, explicit or implicit. However, if you are to make inferences from your observations, as all auditors must do, the integrity of your audit will depend on how you go about selecting your evidence. You can use sampling well or badly, and if you use it without consideration, you will probably use it badly. In recognition of this reality, it's best to use a formal sampling approach so that valid conclusions can be drawn from the audit findings.

There are two kinds of sampling plans—statistical and nonstatistical. Statistical sampling applies the laws of probability to the sampling scheme to measure the sufficiency of the evidence gained and to evaluate the results. However, sometimes it's impractical or difficult to meet the requirements of statistical inference in a quality audit. For example, randomness and sample size may be difficult to achieve in a partial audit; given a pre-selected audit basis and scope, a large number of the system controls will not be sampled at all. Therefore, quality auditors may prefer to conduct an audit using nonstatistical techniques.

A sampling plan is nonstatistical when it fails to meet the criteria required of a statistical sampling plan. Nonstatistical sampling plans rely primarily on subjective judgment derived from experience, prior knowledge, and current information to determine sample size and evaluate results. A properly designed nonstatistical sampling plan can provide results just as effective as those from a statistical sampling plan, except that it cannot measure sampling risk. Therefore, the choice of a statistical or nonstatistical sampling plan depends upon the tradeoff of costs and benefits relative to sampling risks. Bear in mind that just because you do not measure sampling risks in a nonstatistical audit does not mean they do not exist. They always exist. You must decide on the effectiveness of a control, and, either way, you could be wrong.

The purpose of an internal quality audit is to improve the quality system, and we want to stay focused on this objective. Either a statistical or a nonstatistical sampling plan will move you in the direction of improvement—the former gives you a more accurate measure of where you're at, the latter relies more on judgment—therefore we'll discuss both techniques. Although there are many variations of sampling plans, in keeping with the focus of the book, we will discuss just two, one statistical and one not, that are suitable to internal quality audits.

Even if you prefer to implement a nonstatistical sampling plan, you should use procedures similar to those of statistical plans to safeguard the integrity of your conclusions. This means you must understand the vocabulary and principles of statistical sampling. In the next few paragraphs, we'll discuss some basic statistical notions and then proceed to a discussion of two statistical sampling plans: fixed size and stop-or-go. Following this, we'll discuss how to set up a nonstatistical sampling plan that is valid for an internal quality audit.

POPULATIONS

Sampling is the process of taking samples from a parent population and, based upon the statistics of the samples, making an estimate of the population's properties. "Population" is a statistical term for a set of objects under study. It could be what we normally think of as a population—say, the population of cod off the coast of Iceland or the population of people in Muncie, Indiana. But population also can refer to any large set—the professional football games played between 1960 and 1990, the crop of vinifera grapes in Monterey County in 1968 through 1988, the customers that use a local bank on Saturdays, or the week's production of integrated circuit cards in a factory.

Auditors are interested in the population of control procedures and specifically in the mean value, variance, and distribution of the population. Its mean and variance are called its "parameters." The samples provide estimates of the mean and variance, which are called "statistics." The sampled data also can indicate the distribution of the parent population. Knowledge of a population's distribution enables an estimate of whether a sample is representative of that distribution or of some other. This is important to an auditor because it serves to measure the effectiveness of the controls.

Sample Populations

The purpose of a quality audit is to verify the existence and effectiveness of the controls of various processes. Usually, there are too many controls to verify within the limits of the allowable time, so it's necessary to sample them. The controls that are sampled become the sample population. In this sense, the controls are those policies, procedures, documents, and actions that the company employs to ensure the compliance of the quality system to the standard. A nonconformity in the sampled population is often called a "deviation" because the control deviates from the standard.

Barbara Apostolou and Francine Alleman describe it this way: An auditor tests controls to see if they are functioning properly. The auditor measures compliance with the control procedures in terms of deviation rates. Compliance in a given test means the control works (i.e., control is present). Noncompliance means that the control does not work (i.e., control is absent). A deviation exists. The judgment is made by comparing an estimate of the process deviation rate made from sampling to an acceptable deviation rate determined during the audit's planning.[1]

This sounds very similar to an acceptance sampling scheme used in manufacturing, as well it should. Acceptance sampling is similar in kind to a product audit. Many audit-sampling schemes were developed by the accounting profession. For example, certified public accountants (CPAs) conduct audits that are required by law but may use sampling because of the sheer scope of their audits. Noncompliance may be against the law and carry severe penalties, so a CPA must use sampling techniques correctly, and much of the literature on audit sampling derives from them. This is all to the benefit of quality auditors, who are free to use the same techniques.

The objective of sampling is to make inferences about a parent population based on the statistics of a sample population. The inherent variation of the parent population is called "system noise." The variation in the sample population will be an estimate of system noise. Because of the nature of randomness, each sample will yield a different value as an estimate and, as the number of samples increases, the average value of sample noise will more closely approximate the value of the system noise. In addition, it's possible to introduce added variation into the measurement, caused by the measuring technique, which is not itself part of system noise but will appear to be so. Great care must be taken in designing a sampling plan to avoid introducing noise.

Homogeneity

In planning an audit, you must define the population to be audited, and you should strive to define it on the basis of homogeneity. The members of a homogeneous population are pretty much alike, relative to the purpose of the audit, which allows you to make valid statistical inferences about it. Consider the effect of homogeneity of a poll taken to determine the proportion of the population that buys a particular product made by your company. Suppose the product is a stain used for decks and home exteriors. The results of the poll may vary greatly, depending upon whether the polled population was general or strictly homeowners. An effective and efficient marketing poll strategy might be aimed at homeowners only, and by geographical area, too, because the durability of a stain is a function of the variability and severity of the weather.

As another example, suppose your company makes a large variety of heaters, ventilators, and air conditioners, and decides to audit overall sales, in dollars, during the next five years. This can be done but the result is almost meaningless. In any given period, the markets for some products are increasing, some are decreasing, and some are dying out. If the audit's purpose is to set up marketing strategies, then the production should be audited by product type, defining products in similar blocks: the heat-pump block, the chiller block, the ventilator block, and so on. In this way, the average and variance in sales of each kind of product can be determined, and the results used to formulate strategies in terms of customer requirements and competition.

Blocking lets you divide a nonhomogeneous population into groups such that each group is homogeneous, then sample from the groups. Then, based upon the statistics of each of the grouped samples, you can estimate the groups and certain properties of the total population. The division of populations into homogeneous groups for purposes of sampling is called "blocking" or "stratified sampling"; it's required to maintain the study's integrity.

As an auditor, you can see where this discussion is heading. When you establish your audit's goals, you must also define the controls because the population of most quality audits is not homogeneous. We audit many departments against different requirements and consider a great many different operations. However, you can cleverly define the controls so they will be homogeneous, creating a total population sufficient for statistical analysis of the overall quality system, yet still allowing for assessment of the performance of each process. We'll see an example of how this is done in the next section in a discussion of controls and treating decisions as attributes.

ATTRIBUTE SAMPLING

In everyday language, an "attribute" is a synonym for a characteristic or a property of something or someone. We might say, for example, that George Washington had the attributes of courage and resoluteness or that mica has the attribute of translucence. In the quality profession, however, the definition of attribute is narrow: it refers to a binary property of good or bad. A thing either has a defect or it does not; it is either in conformance or it is not. In general terms, there are two measures of the quality of a product or service. If the quality can be measured dimensionally—it has thickness, length, or weight—it's called a "variable quality." It takes on values over a continuous range. If the quality is measured as simply either good or bad, then its quality is an attribute. It takes on only two values, zero or one.

We saw in the previous section that compliance at a given inquiry means the control works—control is present. Noncompliance means that the control did not work-control is absent. The presence or absence of a control is an attribute. Therefore, attribute sampling can be used by quality auditors to arrive at a numerical evaluation of the effectiveness of a quality system's controls. Let's say you are auditing the engineering department, and the quality manual requires that all drawings have a dated approval signature on them. You select a random sample of 50 drawings. One of the drawings lacks an approval signature; another is signed but isn't dated. Then the deviation rate of that sample is 4 percent. Whether this is good or bad depends upon the acceptable deviation rate for that process.

Acceptable Deviation Rate

We concede that variation exists in any production or service scheme. In any given phase of a continual improvement program, we must define an acceptable rate of bad product or service, similar to an acceptance number in acceptance sampling. We call this rate the "acceptable deviation rate" (ADR). The notion of an "acceptable" deviation rate is controversial. Charles A. Mills states that any nonconformity in the sample requires corrective action; therefore, the auditor is looking for error-free performance and a zero acceptance number. Any failure is intolerable, and the ADR is specified simply to determine a sample size.[2] This is true, but there will always be a system deviation rate and therefore a need to define and work with an ADR, with a goal of continuously decreasing both through system improvement.

If you conduct an audit and find zero nonconformities, it doesn't mean that there are none; it simply means that you didn't find them. Conversely, if you find one or some nonconformities, it doesn't mean that the quality system is ineffective. It means that the company must take a hard look at the amount of variation it is willing to accept in any epoch in the development of its quality system. A good strategy for internal quality audits is to define an acceptable level of performance, and then, using measured indices, track and improve the system continuously.

System Deviation Rate

In this book, the terms "system" and "process" are equivalent. Moreover, whether any given entity is a system, subsystem, or element in a system is a matter of perspective. The term "system deviation rate" as used here can refer to the quality system or to any subset of the quality system, including the block of "processes" that is being audited in a partial audit.

We usually don't know the system deviation rate but instead, we derive an estimated rate determined from control samples. However, we really need to make two estimates—a pre-test estimate and a post-test estimate. The pre-test estimate, or the expected system deviation rate, can be estimated from prior records, if the controls and personnel have not changed, or from a pilot sample, and is used to determine sample size. The post-test estimate is the measured estimate of the true system deviation rate.

The auditor compares the measured system deviation rate to the acceptable deviation rate. If the measured rate is lower than the acceptable rate, subject to appropriate confidence level and sampling risk, then the control procedures are deemed effective. Otherwise, they are ineffective.

Controls

We have established that the presence or absence of a control is an attribute. It either works or it doesn't, thereby verifying the compliance of the process. It's very important, therefore, that the auditor understand what is a control and what is not. A measurement, for example, is a control—the value measured is not. Suppose a process produces plastic film that must be clear of spots. Periodically the operator measures the spot count according to an acceptance criterion: One spot per square meter is acceptable, two or more means rejection. As an auditor, you are not particularly interested in this count—that's the operator's job. You are interested in the measurement process and whether it is being conducted according to the quality manual.

As another example, your company has implemented a receipt inspection process to prevent unverified parts from being used in production. The quality manual defines the process in six steps:

■ *Receiving*—The parts are received at a point designated as the receiving station.

■ *Holding*—An operator labels the parts "not inspected" and puts them in a quarantine area until they can be tested.

■ *Inspection*—An inspector inspects or tests the parts for conformance to the purchase order, according to a specified acceptance scheme.

■ *Labeling*—The inspector labels the good parts "Inspected OK," and labels the bad parts as "Inspected and Unacceptable: Return to Vendor."

■ *Recording*—The inspector records the measurement results as a quality record, sending a copy to purchasing.

■ *Traffic*—A forklift operator moves the good parts to inventory and moves the rejected parts to a specified shipping dock.

The company uses the receipt inspection process as the control to ensure that only good parts are used in products. If you've been tasked to audit this process, then you want to verify that the steps described in the quality manual are being followed. The actual rejection rate of the received parts is the concern of the inspector and not yours, unless you've been explicitly assigned to verify it, perhaps as one task of a product audit.

So how do you evaluate this control? Suppose that on the day you inspect, you find one of the steps isn't being followed, but the rest are. Whether you assess receipt inspection as a nonconforming process or as a process with a deviation rate of 16.7 percent (i.e., one defect in six steps) depends on your company's assessment policies. In any case, you must make a binary decision—either go or no-go—and this is true for every control that you verify.

Your assessment is a go/no-go decision no matter the nature of the control. According to Mills, defining all control assessments as yes or no decisions means the entire control population can be treated as homogeneous.[3] This provides a sufficiently large population, which as we shall see in the discussion on statistical sampling plans, is one of the considerations necessary to valid statistical inference.

SAMPLING RISKS

A risk is a probability of loss, often associated with a decision. Auditors who have studied manufacturing processes are familiar with two business risks: *producer risk* and *consumer risk*. In acceptance sampling it's possible to ship a lot of product containing defectives. The probability of doing this is called a "consumer risk" for obvious reasons: There are bad products in the lot, and some customers will purchase them. On the other hand, it's also possible to condemn for rework or further inspection a lot containing few defectives. This is called a "producer risk" because it adds unnecessarily to the production cost. These risks exist because no sampling plan is perfect, but there are statistical techniques that can assess any sampling plan's inherent producer and consumer risks. Consumer and producer risks are inversely related, and management must make a decision about the acceptable level of these risks.

Control Risk

A control risk is the risk that a control will be ineffective. CPAs spend much effort in deciding the control risk of a procedure or process, and if you peruse the literature on statistical sampling in audits, you will see the concept repeatedly. We won't use this risk explicitly in our evaluation of a quality system because it leads to unnecessary complication. However, it should be understood that in auditing, sampling risks always refer to the assessment of control, and not to the assessment of product or service per se.

Alpha and Beta Risks

The best sampling plan in the world can provide only an estimate of system performance. The statistical deviation rate is only an estimate of the system's true deviation rate, and the statistical variance is only an estimate of system variance. Yet, the auditor must make a decision about the system based on these estimates. There is a certain risk that he or she will be wrong, one way or the other. This is called "sampling risk" and will work out as either an *Alpha* or *Beta* risk. For an Alpha risk, the sample will indicate that an effective control is ineffective. For a Beta risk, the sample will indicate that an ineffective control is effective.

The auditor makes an *Alpha error* by deciding, on the basis of the sample, that the control is ineffective and there is a high risk that bad product is going out. In reality, the control is very effective, with little bad outgoing product. Thus, the auditor has contributed to producer risk, causing management to take steps to correct a problem that doesn't exist.

Figure A.1 Alpha and Beta errors related to audit decisions		
Decision Indicated by Sample	**Control Procedure Is:**	
	Effective	*Ineffective*
Accept	Correct decision	Beta error
Reject	Alpha error	Correct decision

The auditor makes a *Beta error* by deciding, on the basis of the sample, that the control is very effective, with low risk of bad product. In reality, the control is ineffective, with an unacceptable level of bad outgoing product. Thus, the auditor's decision contributes to consumer risk, allowing an unacceptable rate of bad product to be delivered to the customer. Figure A.1 relates these concepts to the sampled data and to the quality system.

According to Dan M. Guy, the audit profession doesn't regard Alpha and Beta errors as equally bad.[4] Suppose an auditor commits an Alpha error, deciding that a good control is not effective. If he or she stops there, then harm is done because a producer's risk is assigned. The producer must take corrective action where none is really needed. However, usually an auditor doesn't stop there because if a sample indicates the control should be rejected, the client will insist that the auditor look for more evidence and take more samples. Presumably, larger samples will be more informative. Hence, an Alpha error can lead to an inefficient but effective audit.

If the auditor commits a Beta error, deciding that a poor control is effective, then there is no motivation to continue, the audit stops (at least with respect to the verification of that process), and harm is done because a customer risk exists. Thus, a Beta error leads to an ineffective audit. For this reason, auditors use Beta risk as a measure of audit effectiveness.

Confidence Level

The objective of audit sampling is to measure the effectiveness of a set of controls by estimating the true system deviation rate with the sample deviation rate. For clarity, we will use the acronym SDR to represent the true system deviation rate, and use the symbol $\hat{p}$, as the sample deviation rate. If we take a sample of size n and find x deviations, $\hat{p} = x/n$.

Given a sample, $\hat{p}$, the question is, "How close an estimate of the SDR is it?" If it is less than a predetermined acceptable deviation rate, we will assess the control as effective, otherwise we will assess it as ineffective. So we must have some confidence that $\hat{p}$ is a good estimate of the true system deviation rate.

A visual interpretation of the problem is shown in Figure A.2, which depicts a possible probability distribution of the system deviation rate, with a mean value, SDR. A sample is located at some arbitrary value, but we can't know for certain whether the sample is really drawn from this distribution or from some other. The tails of the distribution represent values with very low probabilities of occurring in this distribution, so that if the sample lies in the "α area," we say that there is a very low probability that the sample is from this distribution. Conversely, if the sample value lies in the greater area to the left of the tail, then we say that there is a very high probability that it comes from this distribution.

We can specify the size of the α area to gain confidence about the estimation. This is done by simply assigning a value, p_c, as a critical value of the system deviation distribution, beyond which all values will be assumed as probably be-

Figure A.2 A possible distribution of a system deviation rate

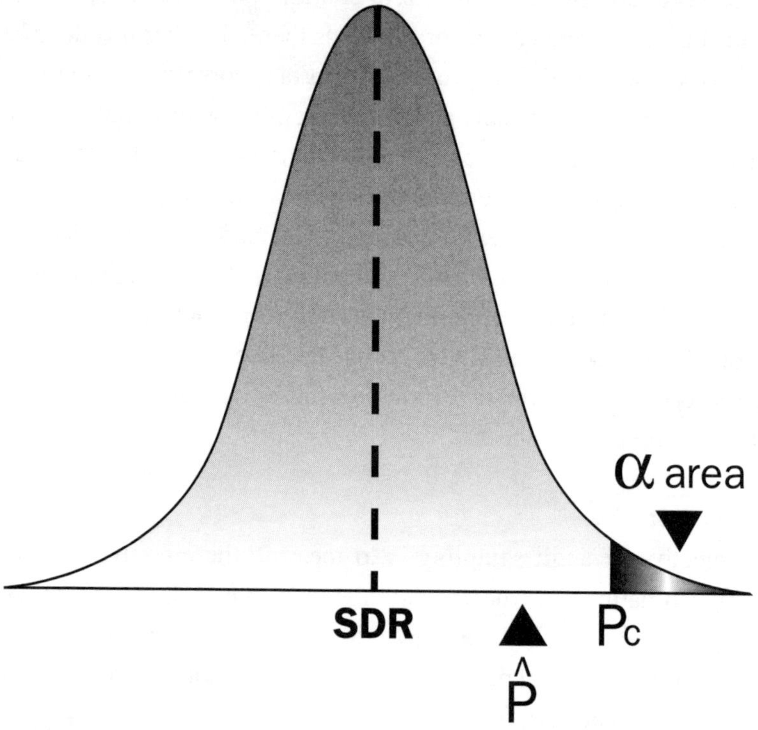

(The distribution has two tails, but we consider only one of them for purposes of this discussion because we are usually concerned that a system deviation rate be less than some value.)

longing to some other distribution. Let the α area comprise 5 percent of the distribution's total area. Then $\alpha = 0.05$, and a sample with a value found in α area range of values would have at most a 5-percent chance of being drawn from this distribution. On the other hand, if the sample lies in the larger area to the left of the α area, then there is a 0.95 probability that the sample was drawn from this distribution. Thus, the α area is defined as the "rejection area." If a sample has a value in this range, we reject the hypothesis that it's drawn from the distribution with a mean value of SDR. Conversely, all of the area of the distribution to the left of the α area in Figure A.2 is called the "acceptance region." If a sample has a value in this range, we accept the hypothesis that it is drawn from the SDR distribution.

Two important and related terms of statistics are involved here: "level of significance" and "confidence level." The first refers to the statistical significance of the test-i.e., the level at which the cause of a measured variation can be distinguished. Thus, a $= 0.05$ means we can distinguish designed effect from noise down to 5 percent. It follows that the confidence that we can have in the measurement is related and is defined by a "confidence coefficient," shown in Equation A.1 below:

$$Cc = 1 - \alpha$$

When the confidence coefficient is expressed as a percentage, it is called the confidence level. Thus, if $\alpha = 0.05$, then $Cc = 0.95$, and we have a confidence level of 95 percent that a given probability interval contains the true system deviation rate.

In auditing, confidence level refers to the probability of accepting an effective control and is expressed by Dan Guy as equal to $100(1 - \alpha)$. This agrees with the definition of confidence level used in statistics. A sample taken from the parent population will return a value, $\hat{p}$, which is an estimate of the SDR. We specify a confidence level to establish that the system distribution has a mean deviation rate such that there is a 0.95 probability of yielding the given sample.

REFERENCES

1. Apostolou, Barbara, and Francine Alleman. *Internal Audit Sampling*. Altamonte Springs, FL: The Institute of Internal Auditors, 1991.
2. Mills, Charles A. *The Quality Audit*. New York: McGraw-Hill, 1989.
3. Ibid.
4. Guy, Dan M. *An Introduction to Statistical Sampling in Auditing*. New York: John Wiley, 1981.

Statistical Sampling for Quality Audits

A statistical sampling plan follows the laws of probability, allowing you to make valid inferences about a population from the statistics of the samples taken from it. It also lets you determine in advance the magnitude of Alpha and Beta sampling errors. You commit an Alpha error when you assess control risk too high, saying the control is ineffective when, in reality it is very effective, with little bad outgoing product. You commit a Beta error when you assess control risk too low, saying the control is very effective when, in reality the control is ineffective, with an unacceptable level of bad outgoing product or service.

There are many different statistical sampling plans, but we shall discuss just two, whose characteristics lend themselves to the partial audits of internal quality auditing. The first, fixed-size attribute sampling, can accommodate developing quality systems where system deviation may be relatively high and easily measured. The other, stop-or-go sampling, can be used in very good quality systems with very low deviation rates and hard-to-find errors.

FIXED-SAMPLE-SIZE ATTRIBUTE SAMPLING PLAN

Sampling is efficient and practical where there is a trail of documentary evidence, or when the auditor can take the time to observe a process in action. David N. Ricchiute proposes a seven-step strategy for a fixed-size attribute sampling plan:[1]

1. Determine the objectives of the test.
2. Define the attribute and deviation conditions.
3. Define the population.
4. Determine the method of sample selection.
5. Determine the sample size.
6. Perform the sampling plan.
7. Evaluate the sample results.

Determine the Objectives

The objective of controls tests is to assess the effectiveness of control procedures. One control might be a required signoff signature. Others might be a receipt inspection, revision date on a document, or completeness of a purchase order. The auditor's basic job is to determine if the error rate of a controls system is below the acceptable level. We have asserted that no control is perfect, that there will always be variation in any quality system. The objective of an ongoing audit program is to work toward system improvement. Therefore, given that a system of controls isn't perfect, how good is it? Specifically, how does the measured system deviation rate compare to the acceptable deviation rate? If the measured deviation rate is lower than the acceptable rate, then the control procedures are deemed effective. Otherwise, they are ineffective.

Defining Attribute and Deviation Conditions

Acceptable Deviation Rate. By "attribute and deviation conditions," we mean the measurement statistics—acceptable and system deviation rates. When performing controls tests, you must specify the maximum number of deviations from the prescribed control procedures that can be accepted and still regard the procedures as effective. This measure is known by various names, such as tolerable deviation rate and acceptable error rate. To accommodate several disciplines, we'll use the term "acceptable deviation rate."

System Deviation Rate. We usually don't know the system deviation rate, but instead, we derive an estimated system deviation rate determined from the control samples. As noted in Appendix A, we really need to make two estimates—pre-test and post-test. The post-test estimate is, of course, the measured estimate of the true system deviation rate.

Why is it necessary to "estimate the estimate"? The sample size needed to measure the effectiveness of a control depends on the difference between the system and acceptable deviation rates. Thus, how well we can estimate the true system deviation rate depends on the sample size. This literally puts the auditor in a Catch 22 situation: You need to know the deviation rate before you can estimate it. You need some idea of how good the system is in order to determine a valid sample size; an invalid sample size can give you a wrong measure of the system deviation rate. You can base this pre-test estimate on observation, inquiry, or experience, but you must have some knowledge of system capability. All this should not dismay us; George Box et al. stress repeatedly that statistical techniques are most effective when they are combined with appropriate subject matter knowledge.[2]

In keeping with our convention on the equivalency of "system" and "process," the term "system deviation rate" here can refer to the quality system or to any subset of the system, including the block of processes that are being audited in a partial audit. Don't assume that system deviation rate refers just to the quality system. When we speak specifically of that larger system, we always use the full term—the quality system.

Defining the Population

As we discussed in an earlier section, the population of concern is all the items constituting a class of controls or events. They must all have, nominally, the desired attribute and time period. For example, if the attribute you are verifying is a properly authorized document change over the past three months, then any document changes beyond this 90-day period does not belong to the population. A calibration schedule change within the 90 days does not belong either because you aren't looking for changes per se, but rather authorizations. The internal quality audit (IQA) team must work together to arrive at a coherent sampling plan of nonredundant, homogeneous controls.

According to Charles A. Mills, defining all control assessments as yes-or-no decisions means the entire control population can be treated as homogeneous, though those decisions may relate to different technical points.[3] The homogeneity lies in the decision to accept or reject a control. Whether the control is a measurement, a document signature, observing a task, or recording a result, the verification must be posed so that you arrive at a decision of acceptable or not acceptable. This convenience carries with it a proviso on decision homogeneity: The block of controls should have similar acceptable deviation rates and sampling risks.

Determining the Method of Sample Selection

We have decided on a strategy and are well on our way to developing a sampling plan. Now we must consider how the sampling itself will be done—i.e., taking data. Some common methods of sampling include random sampling, systematic sampling, and haphazard sampling.

Valid statistical sampling requires randomization. Random sampling occurs when each member of the population has an equal chance of being selected. Suppose, for example, you want to assess job orders for a given week. You shouldn't randomly choose from a set offered to you by the production supervisor but must contrive to choose randomly from the entire set. They will probably be stacked in some kind of order, so you must factor this bias in with your selection. You might suppose that taking a few near the top, a few in the middle, and a few near the bottom are a random selection. They are not because the job orders that are not near the top, middle, or bottom of the stack have no chance of being selected. If you have defined the control population as all the job orders for the week, then each must be given an equal chance at being selected. You can, for example, assign numbers to the job orders, and then use a random number generator to help you in the selection. If this method causes you to end up with a random sample containing most of the job orders early in the week, so be it.

You might also choose systematic sampling, which is choosing every nth member of the population, with the first determined randomly. You need to know the population size and sample size. Suppose you are looking at job orders during the past year and there are 5,000 of them. You decide upon a sample size of 200. Then you begin at some random point and select every 25th member (5,000/200 = 25).

You must avoid using haphazard sampling, which seems to be random but is not. This method consists of selecting samples without special reason but without conscious bias. Many auditors practice this, believing it is fair, but haphazard sampling can lead to samples that are not representative of the population. Things are rarely arranged randomly; haphazard sampling will invariably include items that are not homogeneous. For example, suppose you are in the customer service office, and you ask to examine a batch of customer orders lying on one of the service agent's desk. Will this batch represent that office's quality of service? Not likely. If there were six agents in the office, it would be better to select randomly from each one's work. In this way, each record has an equal chance of being selected. Haphazard sampling should *not* be used in statistical sampling, but it can be effective in nonstatistical sampling.

Determining the Sample Size

The advantage to statistical sampling is that the audit's sampling risks and confidence levels can be determined from the sampled data. One of the factors governing the validity of statistical inference is sample size. In order to determine an appropriate sample size, five factors come into play:

1. Size of the total audit population
2. Acceptable deviation rate
3. Expected system deviation rate
4. Alpha risk
5. Beta risk

The first of these must be large. Population sizes in excess of 5,000 can be considered effectively infinite. According to Barbara Apostolou and Francine Alleman, even a parent population of only 500 will have small effect on sampling size.[4]

The expected system deviation rate can be estimated from prior records—if the controls and personnel have not changed—or from a pilot sample. Pilot samples often are integrated into an audit sample. Suppose your initial estimate of the system deviation rate suggests a sample size of 120. You can select a pilot sample of 50, then test for accuracy. If the measured rate appears to support the initial estimate, you continue with the remaining 70 tests.

Alternatively, suppose your initial estimate of the system deviation rate called for a sample size of 50, but the measured data indicate that a sample size of 120 should have been taken. Although your initial estimate was in error, the 50 tests are still valid, so that you need to take only 70 more samples to arrive at a valid estimate of the system deviation rate. In this case, the initial 50 served as a pilot sample.

Because sample size is a function of five factors, it's usually found from tables rather than computed directly. Figure B.1 shows the required sample sizes for a plan with an Alpha risk of 10 percent, a Beta risk of 5 percent, and various acceptable and expected system deviation rates. Sample sizes greater than 250 are omitted as impractical for quality audits.

Generating this figure is explained in Appendix D. A similar figure can be generated for any combination of Alpha and Beta risks by programming the equations in Appendix D into your spreadsheet software.

Figure B.1 reinforces the fact that as the interval between the system and tolerable deviation rates decreases, the required sample size increases in order to distinguish the rates and maintain the prescribed risks. This is because a smaller interval between deviation rates leaves less room for sampling error, so smaller sampling risks are needed. The relationship of these statistics can be summarized in Figure B.2.

Figure B.1 Sample sizes for control tests

Percent Sample Size	Percent Acceptable Deviation Rate								
	2	3	4	5	6	7	8	9	10
0.00	114	76	56	45	37	32	28	24	22
0.10	148	87	60	46	37	30	26	22	19
0.25	224	120	79	58	45	37	31	26	23
0.50	*	179	110	77	58	46	38	32	28
0.75	*	*	146	98	72	56	46	38	32
1.00	*	*	191	123	88	67	53	44	37
1.25	*	*	249	152	105	79	62	50	42
1.50	*	*	*	188	126	92	71	57	47
1.75	*	*	*	232	150	107	81	65	53
2.00	*	*	*	*	179	124	93	73	59
2.25	*	*	*	*	214	145	106	82	66
2.50	*	*	*	*	*	168	121	92	73
2.75	*	*	*	*	*	197	138	104	81
3.00	*	*	*	*	*	231	158	116	90

Beta risk = 5 percent; Alpha risk = 10 percent.

Performing the Sampling Plan

Let's look at a few examples. The auditor begins taking samples. In the worst case, if a large number of deviations are found up front, it may be well to cancel the sample plan as not cost-effective and conclude that the control procedure is ineffective. If you plan to take 88 samples and you find 11 nonconformities in the first 20 or 30 tests, why continue the plan?

Generally, things will go according to plan if your pre-test knowledge of the system is good. Assume that we expect a deviation rate of 1 percent, are willing to accept a deviation rate of 5 percent, and want to limit the Beta risk to 5 percent. In these conditions, Figure B.1 gives a sample size of 123. If the measured deviation rate is approximately equal to the initial estimate, then this sample size was appropriate. If the measured deviation rate was 0.5 percent, then you find that the sample size should have been 77. You took more tests than was necessary but still conducted an effective test program. A pilot sample strategy would have been useful here, which would have indicated that fewer tests were going to be needed than originally supposed.

On the other hand, if you measure a deviation rate of 1.5 percent, then the sample size should have been 188, and you have another 65 tests to make. This increased requirement occurs because the interval between deviation rates is sufficiently small that you need many more samples to ensure the desired sampling risks. However, we can anticipate a problem here because the total 188 tests approaches a size too large for many partial quality audits.

Figure B.2 The relationship of Beta risk and deviation rates		
Factor	**Change**	**Sample Size**
Beta	Increase	Decrease
Acceptable Deviation Rate	Increase	Decrease
System Deviation Rate	Increase	Increase

Evaluating Sample Results

Initially, our estimate, $\hat{p}$, of the system deviation rate came from historical data, pilot data, or knowledge of the process under test. After sampling, we update the estimate with the measured rate determined from Equation B.1, where x is the number of deviations found in the sample, n:

$$\hat{p} = x/n$$

When the sampling is completed, you have taken a sample size of n and have found x deviations. You determine that $\hat{p} = x/n$, but how accurate an estimate is this one sample of the true system deviation rate (SDR)? Another sample might yield a different value altogether. A better question is: "What is the highest system deviation rate that is likely to yield that sample at a given level of significance?" You can get this information from tables in a book on audit sampling, but you can do just as well with a binomial distribution function using spreadsheet software such as Microsoft Excel.

Proportions have binomial distributions as shown in Figure B.3. The abscissa displays the range of the number of events, x, which for audits represents the number of deviations that are discovered in a sample of n controls. However, implied at each value of x is a deviation rate, x/n, so that the abscissa also can be scaled for a deviation rate, $\hat{p} = x/n$. Indeed, this is how a p-type control chart is made. In Figure B.3, an envelope has been drawn around the discrete plots of x to accent its form. Notice that the tails of the envelope are not even. This is because the peak is near the lower tail, which stops at zero, whereas the upper tail continues to the value n.

Good quality systems have low deviation rates, and it will not be unusual to draw zero or few deviations in a sample. Thus, the binomial distributions of audit deviations will tend to have lower tails of small area. As explained in Appendix D, this means that a normal approximation to the binomial distribution often cannot be used to determine confidence intervals.

To answer the question of the highest value of the SDR likely to yield the given sample, you must define "likely." Let's assume Figure B.3 represents a binomial distribution of a system with a mean deviation rate, SDR. Let this distribution slip along the scale to the right, in the direction of increasing deviation rates. At some point, the sample, $\hat{p}$, will appear in the lower tail defined as the α area. In the discrete distribution of Figure B.3, we will define the tail as the set of all values of p to the left of p_c, which delineates the rejection and acceptance values of $\hat{p}$. Values of $\hat{p} = p_c$ correspond to the test's level of significance. Usually, values of 0.01 to 0.1 are chosen for the a area because it represents the probability of an Alpha error.

We arbitrarily reject values of $\hat{p}$ in the α area as members of the system distribution on the grounds that they have a very low probability of occurring in that distribution. Given a value, $\hat{p}$, if we slip the distribution to a point where $\hat{p} = p_c$ and define the level of significance as 0.05, then we can be 95 percent sure that the sample does not derive from the distribution with a mean of the SDR. It follows that we are therefore 95 percent sure that the SDR is the upper limit of a system deviation rate likely to yield the given sample. As described by George Box et al., this procedure effectively establishes one limit of the confidence interval on the SDR.[5]

Figure B.3 Locating the estimate *x/n* with respect to a distribution centered at SDR

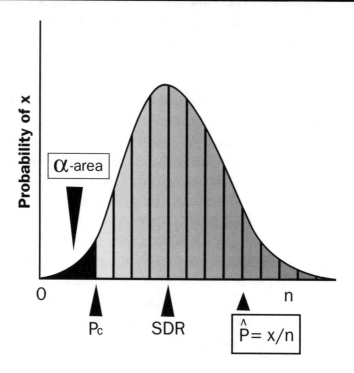

To locate a maximum SDR for a level of significance of 0.05 and for a given sample, go to the spreadsheet and select the binomial function, then set the cumulative logic to "true," and enter the number of deviations and trials into the appropriate windows. Then vary the value in the probability window until the result reads 0.05, or as close as you can get to it.

To clarify what we are doing here, and how to use a spreadsheet to do it, suppose you audit 100 controls and find two deviations. Your initial estimate of the system deviation rate is then 2/100, or 2 percent. When you adjust the constant probability in the spreadsheet until the cumulative probability value is 0.05, you establish a binomial distribution with a mean value, SDR, such that $\hat{p} = p_c$ located just in the a area of Figure B.3. You can then be 95 percent certain that the SDR is no greater than that in the spreadsheet probability window, for if it is greater, the probability of obtaining a statistic of 2/100 is less than 0.05.

In our example, at the spreadsheet you enter $n = 100$ and $x = 2$. You select "true" for cumulative distribution, then vary values of the SDR probability until the cumulative probability is 0.05. Where do you start? Because 2/100 = 0.02, you can start there. For this case, 0.02 is a bit low, and the cumulative value won't reach 0.05 until the SDR = 0.0616, or 6.16 percent. Thus, as an auditor you can conclude, with 95 percent certainty, that the system deviation rate is less than 6.2 percent, and hence if the acceptable deviation rate is 8 percent, the control is effective.

The reason we look for the highest deviation rate likely to provide the obtained sample is that it's not possible to determine exactly the system deviation rate on the basis of one sample or even several samples. In principle, even a system of very high deviation rate has a probability of providing a sample of only 2 percent deviations. However, the probability is quite small—a rare event. For example, a system with a deviation rate of 9 percent may yield a sample of 2/100, but the probability of doing so is 0.005, a rare event indeed and, therefore, "unlikely" to occur.

The reader might ask why we choose a confidence level of 95 percent. Why not 99 percent? In fact, you *can* choose 99 percent—confidence levels usually range from 90 percent to 99 percent, but you pay a price for greater confidence. As with most things, there is a tradeoff to be made. When you choose a confidence level of 99 percent, you decrease the α area of the process distribution, and hence reduce the Alpha risk. However, as is demonstrated in Appendix D, decreasing the Alpha risk increases the Beta risk, as they are inversely related. We noted in Appendix A that a Beta risk is regarded as a measure of audit effectiveness and can lead to an ineffective audit.

Conversely, when you decrease the confidence level to 90 percent, you increase the α area, which increases the Alpha risk. Although this will decrease the Beta risk, it is by definition increasing the risk of designating an effective control procedure as ineffective.

STOP-OR-GO SAMPLING

The fixed-size attribute sampling plan is appropriate for audits of developing quality systems because it can measure systems having relatively large deviation rates, or modest expectations. Quality systems that are performing at a high level will have a lower percentage of deviations, and in such cases there are sampling strategies that are designed to detect the relatively hard-to-find events. One of them is stop-or-go sampling.

Stop-or-go sampling is an attribute sampling strategy used for quality systems whose expected deviation rate is nearly zero. It is more efficient than a fixed-size attribute sampling plan because it uses small sampling populations as long as the measured deviation rate is very low. If the measured rate is higher than expected, the auditor has the option of increasing the sample size and continuing or stopping that control system's audit. Only two factors are specified to conduct stop-or-go sampling: confidence level and acceptable deviation rate. We discussed confidence level in Appendix A, so we need only address the latter issue here.

Acceptable Deviation Rate

The acceptable deviation rate (ADR) and its corollary, the acceptable performance level (APL), are system-level measures that will be used frequently hereafter, so acronyms are convenient. Strictly speaking, the acceptable deviation rate is not a statistic; it's simply a declared value. Yet, it's derived from our knowledge of past system performance, itself based on statistics, so it's not completely deterministic either. Stop-and-go sampling uses an acceptable deviation rate to create a sample size and to provide a standard of comparison for the measured system deviation rate. In a binomial distribution, the probability that x events will occur in n trials is shown in Equation B.2:

$$P(x) = \binom{n}{x} p^x q^{n-x}$$

where p is the probability of a single event occurring, and $q = 1 - p$. From Equation B.2, the probability of no events is shown in Equation B.3:

$$P(0) = q^n$$

Because the events we are concerned with are deviations, then P is the probability of a deviation and q is the converse. Therefore, the probability, q, is a measure of an acceptable performance. For example, if $q = 0.99$, this implies that the system deviation rate is 0.01. In order to determine the sample size needed for an audit, we specify an ADR as the maximum system deviation rate that we will accept. Thus, we have an acceptable performance level (APL) defined in Equation B.4 as:

$$APL = 1 - ADR$$

(Careful readers will note that $APL = q$, and therefore $ADR = p$, but I prefer to use the acronyms because they are terms of system performance, rather than p and q of mathematical notation.)

Initial Sample Size

Quality systems that perform very well have, by definition, very low deviation rates. Samples with zero deviations can be expected. However, zero deviations should not be considered a norm. No system is perfect, but if there are just a few deviations, we want a sampling plan that will find at least one of them. Charles Mills meets this challenge with an interesting approach, using a new definition of confidence—i.e., the confidence that the sample size will detect at least one deviation.[6] This can be expressed in Equation B.5 as:

$$C = 1 - P(0)$$

Where $P(0)$ is the probability of finding zero deviations in a sample of size n and a quality level of q. Although not readily apparent, Equation B.5 is entirely in keeping with the definition of confidence coefficient presented in Appendix A. To see this, refer to Equation B.3. For a given quality level, q, we can choose a sample size, n, such that $P(0)$ will have some arbitrarily low value. Values at $P(0)$ or lower effectively become a rejection range.

However, it is critical to understand exactly what this confidence index, C, is—the confidence that the sampling plan can find a deviation, if it exists. It is *not* the confidence in the estimate of the system deviation rate. At this point we are only setting up the sampling plan. No samples have yet been taken.

Using the notations C = confidence index, and ADR = acceptable deviation rate, we can solve Equations B.3 and B.5 for n, which is shown in Equation B.6:

$$n = \frac{ln(1-C)}{ln(1-ADR)}$$

The terms C and ADR are deliberately substituted in Equation B.6 in order to focus on the big picture and not bog down in p's and q's. Confidence indices and acceptable deviation rates are system-level metrics. Knowing something of the system, we can specify C and ADR for any given audit, then easily determine the necessary sample size. Moreover, although you can solve Equation B.6 with a spreadsheet, you can also solve it easily on a hand-held calculator, and it is a one-time-per-audit calculation.

As an example, suppose that for a system audit you choose a confidence level of 95 percent as your baseline, and from recent records you determine the acceptable deviation rate is 0.04. Then, using Equation B.6, you will need a sample size of $n = 73$. If no deviations are discovered, the evaluation is thus: "There is a 0.95 probability that the system deviation rate is less than or equal to 0.04." Figure B.4 provides sample sizes for a range of confidence levels and acceptable deviation rates.

Comparing figures B.1 and B.4 shows that good systems require smaller sample sizes and, hence, less auditing than developing systems. This satisfies our moral sense; there are rewards for maintaining good systems, and this is one of them. However, even good systems sometimes stray, and the proof is in the evaluation. Stop-and-go sampling plans respond appropriately if a system is beginning to drift in effectiveness, as demonstrated in the next section.

Evaluation

In a previous example, you chose a confidence level of 95 percent and a tolerable deviation rate of 4 percent, resulting in a required sample size of 73. Now suppose the sample contains one deviation. What does this imply about the system deviation rate? As in fixed-rate sampling, you aren't so much concerned with estimating the true system deviation rate from a single sample as you are in determining its probable upper limit—the worst-case scenario, so to speak.

Again, you repeat the spreadsheet process, using a binomial function to enter the sample size, n, the number of deviations, x, in the sample, and the expected system deviation rate, the SDR. You select the cumulative distribution, "true," and vary the SDR until the cumulative probability in the value window reads 0.05, or as close as you can get to it. Where do you start? As in the previous example, you have a sample mean deviation rate of 1/73, so you can start there. The final result is SDR = 0.063. As with fixed-size sampling, this means that there is only a probability of 0.05 that the sample comes from a distribution with a mean of the SDR; it is an upper limit on acceptable system deviation rates. The conclusion is: You are 95-percent certain that the system deviation rate is no greater than 6.3 percent.

Figure B.4 Stop-or-go sampling sizes for an expected deviation rate of zero			
Percent Acceptable Deviation Rate	**Confidence Levels**		
	90 Percent	95 Percent	99 Percent
	Sample Sizes		
10	22	28	44
9	25	32	49
8	28	36	55
7	32	41	64
6	37	48	74
5	45	58	90
4	56	73	113
3	76	98	151
2	114	148	228
1	230	298	458

To summarize, you want to assess the effectiveness of a control system of procedures, where the acceptable deviation rate is 4 percent, the desired confidence level is 95 percent, and the sample size is 73. If zero deviations are discovered, you are 95 percent sure that the true system deviation rate is 4 percent or less, and if one deviation is found, then you are 95 percent sure that the deviation rate is 6.3 percent or less. However, in the latter case, the acceptable deviation rate is only 4 percent, so you must decide whether to stop or go. Your options are:

■ If the sample contains zero deviation, stop. The system meets performance criteria.

■ If the sample contains one or more deviations, the audit fails to demonstrate acceptable performance. You must them decide to:

    a.   Stop the audit. The control system fails performance criteria

    b.   Continue the audit, extending the sample size.

Sample Size Extension

Stop-or-go sampling means that you can continue the sampling after studying the first results, or you can stop sampling and pursue a subjective evaluation. If you choose to continue, then you want to build on what you have learned—i.e., that if you draw one deviation from a sample size of 73, the highest likely system deviation rate is SDR = 0.063, and the mean number of deviations is $\overline{X} = (73)\,(0.063) = 4.6$. We use this information to find the size of an augmented sample. Let $\tilde{n}$ be the new, required sample size. This updated sample size must take into consideration that the highest likely system deviation rate is closer to the acceptable deviation rate than we had initially expected. Figure B.2 shows that if the system deviation rate increases, the new sample size must increase, too, in order to distinguish between the closer rates and maintain the prescribed Alpha and Beta risks. We can determine a new sample size by developing a desired relationship as shown in Equation B.7:

$$SDR \leq ADR,$$
$$(n)\,(SDR) = (n)\,(ADR),$$
$$\overline{X} \leq (n)\,(ADR)$$

Therefore, according to Equation B.7: $n \geq \overline{X} / ADR = \tilde{n}$

Equation B.7 results in an updated sample size requirement of *(4.6/0.04) =115*. Because you have already sampled 73, you must sample an additional 42 to verify the effectiveness of this system.

There are two lessons here. First, stop-or-go sampling is efficient for good performers. Second, if the system has degraded slightly, it may be necessary to extend the sample size, but if it has degraded greatly, then the audit should probably stop. The size of the extension, with its associated increased cost in time and effort, may be the deciding factor on whether to stop or go.

APPLICATION: AN ATTRIBUTE SAMPLING PLAN

It's fairly easy to determine sample size in attribute sampling. You can use tables or make a few simple calculations. However, internal audits are usually horizontal or vertical. Assuming a horizontal audit for the sake of demonstration, it becomes clear that the sample size must be judiciously partitioned among the various functions to be audited, as in the following example.

Wild Rover Inc. is an ISO 9001-registered company. Its internal quality audit team is due to conduct a horizontal audit of the company's documentation control procedures and has selected a stratified attribute sampling scheme. The IQA team's strategy is depicted in Figure B.5, showing the documents, owner functions, and estimated document populations to be examined. In adjacent columns, the relative percentage of the subgroup population is also shown, with the associated number of documents to be drawn at random from that subgroup population. The following considerations were included in the audit plan:

Figure B.5 Wild Rover IQA Team Sampling Strategy				
Function	**Document Type**	**Document Population**	**Percent of Population**	**Sample Size**
General Manager	Management Reviews	15	0.416	1
All Departments	Quality Manual	80	2.22	3
Acquisitions	Purchase Orders	250	6.94	9
Production	Job Orders	1,500	41.6	51
	Calibration Records	60	1.67	2
Customer Service	Delivery Orders	1,500	41.6	51
Personnel	Training Records	200	5.55	7
Totals		3,605	100	124

- A control test confidence level of 95 percent was required
- A deviation rate maximum of 5 percent would be the tolerable rate
- The expected deviation rate would be low, about 1 percent

Column one displays the company functions to be audited. At Wild Rover, all functions are performed in a departmental structure. Column two displays the document type that will be audited and to which appropriate questions are addressed in the checklist. Column three lists the population of documents that will be audited. This population is defined not only by type of document, but also by time period. The documents will be examined for the previous 12-month period, the time since the last audit. For example, it's known that there were 15 management reviews in this period, all of them recorded per requirements. This column shows the document population for each function. The total number of documents is 3,605, which is considered a "large" population for statistical purposes. Indeed, the control population may be much greater than this if each document has several controls to it such as authorization, revision date, and clarity.

Column four shows the percentage of each function population to the overall document population. Because the acceptable maximum and expected deviation rates have been declared, 5 percent and 1 percent respectively, the required sample size can be found from Figure B.1. The required sample size for this audit is 123.

Accordingly, the percentage of 123 to be sampled for each subgroup is determined and rounded off to the next highest integer. This number, shown in column five, is the required sample size for each subgroup. Notice that the sample size actually taken is 124. This is due to rounding up at each subgroup to ensure that the individual function meets its own sample size criteria.

After finishing the inquiry phase, the audit team sums up the number of deviations found in each department—let's say two deviations total—then takes the proportion 2/124 as the estimate of the deviation rate of documentation control. Performing an evaluation from a spreadsheet using a binomial distribution function described earlier, Wild Rover finds that it can be 95 percent certain that its documentation control deviation rate is not greater than 5 percent and therefore meets its performance requirement.

Note that the test is of the total documentation control system's effectiveness, not of any one function. Some functions will have better rates, some worse. The reason for proportioning the sample size over the functions was to give proper weight to each function in arriving at a valid estimate of the total system.

REFERENCES

1. Ricchiute, David N. *Auditing*. Cincinnati: South-Western Publishing, 1992.
2. Box, George; William G. Hunter; and J. Stuart Hunter. *Statistics for Experimenters*. New York: Wiley and Sons, 1978.
3. Mills, Charles A. *The Quality Audit*. New York: McGraw-Hill, 1989.
4. Apostolou, Barbara, and Francine Alleman. *Internal Audit Sampling*. Altamonte Springs, Florida: The Institute of Internal Auditors, 1991.

Nonstatistical Sampling
for Quality Audits

Internal quality audits are usually partial audits of the quality system with predetermined goals that often preclude the criteria required for a valid statistical sampling plan, which are:

■ Each member of the audited population is representative of the population

■ The process is stable

■ The drawing of samples is random (i.e., each member has an equal chance of being selected)

■ Each sample is independent of the other samples

You must meet these criteria to conduct a statistical sampling plan. If they cannot be met, then you can conduct a nonstatistical plan. We have asserted that a properly designed nonstatistical sampling plan can provide results just as effective as those of a statistical sampling plan, except that it cannot measure sampling risk. Yet, even here we can make rough estimates of sampling risk if we select as randomly as possible from a stable process.

AUDIT PROCEDURES

Audit procedures are the same for both statistical and nonstatistical plans. Even though you don't use probability laws in a nonstatistical sampling plan, using statistical procedures enhances objectivity. For example, during the audit, you may meet people who strike you as particularly bright or unusually dull. Perhaps you are scheduled to examine training records and are tempted to inquire after the records of these persons. If you do, your audit has just lost its objectivity. The selection of people to be interviewed and records for inquiry should be done randomly even if the sample size is too small to make assumptions about the distribution of the population. Dan M. Guy proposes the following criteria for any sampling plan:

- Selection of a representative sample
- Determination of sample size based upon materiality, risk, and population
- Projection of sample error based on acceptability of sampling risk[1]

"Materiality" refers to a judgment of the sample relative to the whole in terms of potential error and the importance of that error. Obviously, this is subjective, but it satisfies the need to focus on critical parts of an audit, where true randomness cannot differentiate. Shipyards provide a good example. A typical repair contract will contain more than 5,000 work items, but only about one-tenth of those will be on the critical path. These are called "controlled work items," and are usually the focus of an audit. Just as with the example of the training records, once you have decided upon a set of controlling work items, or any type of record for examination, then you should randomly select from that pool.

The selection of samples is made either by haphazard, blocking, or judgment techniques. You should recognize the difference in these selection techniques and choose one deliberately. Haphazard selection is one made without bias, and this is best done through randomness if possible. You must be satisfied that the sample is representative of the population.

Block selection means you select a homogeneous subpopulation (e.g., all the job orders for a given day or week). To ensure fair representation, many blocks should be selected. Randomness can be introduced by randomly selecting the days or weeks for which you will examine the job orders. Suppose, for example, you want to examine job orders during the last 30 days. Using block selection, you choose all the job orders for, say, a randomly selected set of five or 10 days, depending upon the time available.

Judgment means that samples are taken from areas you believe have high control risk, either due to the nature of the process or past audit results. This is where materiality comes into play; it's a departure from randomness, but may be needed for a cost-effective audit.

Figure C.1 Estimating control risk as a function of the acceptable deviation rate		
Assessment	**Acceptable Deviation Rate**	
	Kelly	*Guy*
Substantial Reliance	2 percent–7 percent	≤ 5 percent
Moderate Reliance	6 percent–12 percent	≤ 10 percent
Little Reliance	11 percent–20 percent	≤ 20 percent
No Reliance	Omit Test	Omit Test

Risk Estimation and Error Rates

The nonstatistical sampling plan also uses risk assessment, but it's estimated qualitatively. You make an Alpha error by assessing the control as ineffective, when in reality the control is very effective, with little bad outgoing product. You make a Beta error by assessing the control as effective, when in reality the control is ineffective.

Although nonstatistical sampling plans can't measure Alpha and Beta risks, you need to know, to a "reasonable" degree, whether a quality system is effective. A properly conducted nonstatistical plan will yield a valid proportion of deviations to sample size, and you are free to preselect an acceptable deviation rate (ADR). It's the interval between these two rates that can't be accurately measured, but you can still make a good estimate of control effectiveness. There is consensus among audit experts on assigning numbers to a qualitative assessment of a control. Figure C.1 compares the value system of James W. Kelly[2] and Dan M. Guy. The term "reliance" isn't related to the engineering notion of reliability but is popular among auditors. In the context of this figure, reliance is the complement of risk and represents confidence in the estimate.

The ADRs shown in Figure C.1 may seem unacceptably large to production people, but they must be understood in context. They apply to the deviation rate of controls, and not to the deviation rate of quality characteristics of a product or service.

As with statistical sampling, when deriving a nonstatistical sampling plan you use knowledge of past performance to pre-assess the quality system in order to arrive at a sample size. If you have no previous quantitative assessments, you de-

Figure C.2 How changes in deviation rates and Beta risk interact

Factor	Change	Sample Size
Beta Risk	Increase	Decrease
Acceptable Deviation Rate	Increase	Decrease
Expected System Deviation Rate	Increase	Increase

cide on the basis of qualitative assessments whether the controls to be audited are "substantially," "moderately," or "slightly" reliable, and then select an ADR that is associated with this estimate. With this ADR, and with expected system deviation rates based on past experience, you determine an appropriate sample size for the audit from Figure B.1 in appendix B. Then you evaluate the control, based on the difference between the sample and acceptable deviation rates.

Effect of Sample Size

Nonstatistical sampling plans don't measure Beta error, but you know that it exists. You must make some effort to reduce it, and sample size has much to do with that. We repeat that sample size is affected by the risk and error rate factors as shown in Figure C.2. For example, suppose you want to choose a smaller sample size. Then you must be willing to increase the chance of Beta error (i.e., the risk of assessing a control as good when, in fact, it is a weak control).

If you want to increase the ADR, then you can decrease the sample size. The reason should be clear: A lower sample size will result in less accuracy, and you want less accuracy to be on the fail-safe side. A larger ADR offers a less effective control, or a less accurate sample of a good control. But if you want to tighten the system assessment by decreasing the ADR, then a larger sample population is needed, again to err on the fail-safe side.

Finally, if you expect a low system deviation rate, then you can use a lower sample size, knowing that the decreased accuracy is unimportant for a very good system. If you expect a high system error rate, possibly above the acceptance rate, then you need a large sample size to be sure of the margins. These considerations require judgment, experience, and profound knowledge of the system, but they enhance the validity of a nonstatistical sampling plan.

Evaluating Sample Results

Because nonstatistical sampling does not provide a reliable estimate of sampling risk, the auditor must judge whether the difference between the ADR and the measured deviation rate is an adequate allowance for sampling error. For example, suppose the auditor will accept a deviation rate of 8 percent, and suppose further that in a sample of 53 the auditor finds one error. Then the sample deviation rate is 1/53, or about 2 percent, but how good is this as an estimate of the system deviation rate?

Now is the time for judgment. The auditor doesn't know on the basis of a single sample what the system deviation rate is. Indeed, the sample, 1/53, is just as likely to derive from a distribution centered at 0.005 as at 0.05. The auditor doesn't know where the upper tail α area of its distribution is found, so he or she can't measure the sampling risks.

Yet, the auditor does have a past history of system performance and a level of confidence in his or her knowledge that was used as a basis to determine sample size. The auditor determined an acceptable deviation rate from Figure C.1, and then, using this ADR, selected a sample size according to Figure B.1. Because the sample deviation rate is greater than that estimated for the sample size, there is a greater Beta risk in the measurement.

The auditor accepts the statistic 1/53 as a reasonable estimate of the SDR if it is in accord with his or her knowledge of past system performance and level of confidence. As for the increased Beta risk, the auditor has two choices. First, take more samples, if feasible. Figure B.1 shows that an expected SDR of 2 percent requires a sample size of 93, so the auditor needs to take 40 more samples to ensure a Beta risk of 5 percent.

If it isn't feasible to take more samples in this measurement, the auditor can still estimate the increase in the Beta risk because it is nonlinearly related to the interval between the estimated SDR and the ADR. In the case under discussion, the expected SDR is changed very little. This is why a high ADR value provides a good cushion against increases in Beta risk. Nevertheless, in the next audit of this process, the auditor would be wise to use 2 percent as his or her expected SDR when calculating sample size.

THE VALIDITY OF AUDIT SAMPLING

Almost all audits use some form of sampling and it's both reasonable and appropriate to conduct the sampling in a systematic way so as to draw valid conclusions from observations. The Achilles heel of audit sampling plans is their infrequency. A random sample will yield one value, another random sample from the same population will yield another value, and so on. The variance can be significant. Therefore, it usually takes a large number of samples before you can attain a high level of confidence in an estimate of some parameter of the audited population.

We have shown in appendix B that valid conclusions can be made on the basis of a single sample if you ask the right questions. The wrong question is, "What is the deviation rate of the control process?" You cannot determine the control procedure deviation rate from the evidence of one sample. However, one sample *can* answer the question, "What is the highest system deviation rate that is likely to yield that sample at a given level of significance?" Moreover, a good statistical sampling plan, such as those shown in this book, will provide a sample size that offers a desired discrimination of Alpha and Beta risks, and a strategy that will protect the selected risk levels.

Nonstatistical sampling provides even less accuracy in evaluating control effectiveness. You use subjective judgment primarily to verify system conformance. Yet, a well-designed nonstatistical sampling plan can provide results as effective as those from a statistical sampling plan if it's based on profound knowledge of the system, adherence as closely as possible to the audit procedures used in statistical plans, and on objective evidence.

REFERENCES

1. Guy, Dan M. *An Introduction to Statistical Sampling in Auditing*. New York: John Wiley, 1981.
2. Kelly, James W. *How to Use Statistical Sampling in Your Audit Practice*. New York: Matthew Bender, 1986.

Sampling Analysis

By its very nature, a sample from a population can provide only an estimate of a parameter of that population. Nevertheless, it is possible to determine the "goodness" of the estimate by statistical inference. In particular, statistical inference allows us to measure the errors in our sample. Inference is appropriate to a process that follows certain laws of probability with regard to randomness and independence.

STATISTICAL INFERENCE

In appendix C, we reviewed the criteria required for a valid statistical sampling plan. The first criterion is that each member of the audited population be representative of the population. This is a requirement on homogeneity, to prevent comparing apples to oranges. For example, if a projected audit population contains both variable and attribute controls, you would be obliged to define two different populations. If the population contained subgroups of the same kind but with significantly different parameters, it would be nonhomogeneous. Homogeneity of a population can at times be achieved by how the population is defined. Charles A. Mills convincingly shows that even diverse controls can be made homogeneous if they are defined as simple yes or no decisions.[1]

The second criterion concerns process stability. You can't estimate the mean value or variance of a population if none exists, nor can you estimate the sampling risks. A stable process has a defined, if unknown, distribution, and the whole purpose of sampling analysis is to assess the control effectiveness by estimating certain properties of the system distribution.

The third criterion is randomness. As described by George Box et al., randomness is at the heart of much statistical analysis.[2] A random sample is one in which each member is a random drawing from the audited population. A random drawing is one in which each member of the audited population has an equal chance of being drawn. A member of a sample is a random variable if it was drawn from a known distribution. Introducing randomness into the sample improves our ability to locate the sample in the parent population.

The fourth criterion is that each member of the sample must be independent of other members. This ensures that each member, a random variable, has the same distribution, so that the sample distribution, too, is stable. Randomness and independence let you make inferences about the parent population with a relatively small sample. You can use statistical inference without these properties but you'd need a very large sample in order to make valid estimates of the parent population.

Sample Distributions

The probabilities associated with drawing samples from a finite population are described by a hypergeometric probability model. Acceptance sampling, for example, is the process of drawing samples from lots of manufactured product. Because the lots tend to be relatively small—fewer than 500—the hypergeometric model is required to relate the sample's probabilities to the lot's. Unfortunately, the hypergeometric distribution is difficult to work with because it involves four variables: the population and defect rate of the lot, and the population and defect rate of the sample. If, however, the sampling is a Bernoulli process done from a very large population, then a binomial probability model can be used in lieu of the hypergeometric model. Since the former involves only two variables, simplifying calculations ensue.

A sequence of n trials is a Bernoulli process if the trials are independent, with each trial having only one of two possible outcomes, and if the probability of success remains constant from trial to trial. The term "success" simply refers to a designated result; it could be the set of ones or it could be the set of zeros, whichever we're keeping track of. The random variable, x, that denotes the number of successes in n trials, has a binomial distribution. Assume that a very large population of controls, n, are audited as either in conformance or not, and that each control is selected randomly. Then the audit sequence is a Bernoulli process. More-over, if x deviations are found, then the ratio, x/n, is a random variable with a binomial distribution.

Population Size

How large must the audited population be for it to be considered "very large"? Experts offer a variety of views on the matter. Barbara Apostolou and Francine Alleman state that a population greater than 500 would be sufficient; other sources say that several thousand would be necessary.[3] Grant and Leavenworth state that as long as the parent population is at least 10 times the sample population ($n/N < 0.1$), the binomial distribution can be used.[4] Charles A. Mills, too, suggests that in auditing generally, the parent will be much larger than the sample popula-tion and simplifying statistics can be used.[5] Dan M. Guy uses the case where $N = 1000$; $n > 20$, and $n/N < 0.1$.[6] These numbers are similar to those expected of an internal quality audit. Therefore, it is reasonable to use the binomial distribution in audit sampling in lieu of the hypergeometric distribution.

Figure D.1 Distributions of acceptable and unacceptable product or service

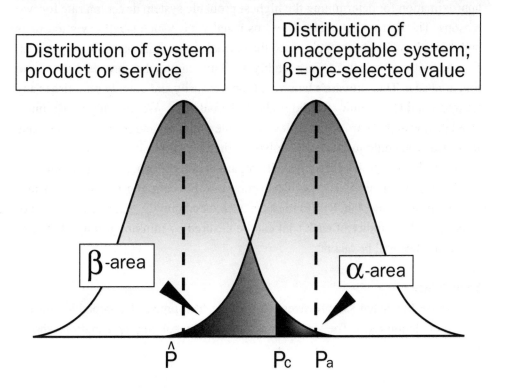

Central Limit Theorem

Using a binomial distribution in lieu of a hypergeometric distribution is an important simplification because it reduces the number of variables needed to determine probabilities. Sample probabilities can be simplified even further by approximating a binomial distribution with a normal one. The central limit theorem provides the justification for doing so, stating that for sufficiently large n, the distribution of a sample mean, X, is approximately normal, where X is defined in Equation D.1 as:

$$X = \frac{(x/n) - p_0}{\sqrt{(p_0 * q_0)/n}}$$

That is, X is normally distributed with a mean value of 0 and a variance of 1. Thus, we can find values of X from a table of $N(0,1)$ distribution. In particular, we can exactly measure the tails of the distribution, which are areas of very low probability, and hence quantify a rare event in the audit. P_0 is the system deviation rate, and $q_0 = 1 - p_0$. (The * means multiply.)

In appendix B, we took advantage of normal distribution in computing the data of Figure B.1, as will be discussed momentarily. However, we don't use this approximation for determining the highest probable system deviation rate for two reasons. The first is that quality systems usually have such small deviation rates and thus, given feasible sample sizes, the normal approximation is not very robust. Second, with statistical software readily available in popular spreadsheets, we no longer need it. The software's binomial function easily and quickly establishes any desired confidence limits for the highest estimated p_0. We are only really interested in how high the true system deviation rate might be, and so solve for only one limit. But you could just as easily solve for the other limit, if desired.

By following probability rules with regard to independence and randomness in conducting the audit, it is possible to measure the sampling risk involved in a statistical sampling plan. Randomness is introduced into the test by the method of selection. The stability of each trial can be ensured by thinking through how and when samples will be taken.

Sample Size

Figure B.1 listed sample sizes appropriate to a range of acceptable and expected deviation rates. The sizes were calculated by solving the equations shown in D.2:

$$\frac{p_c - p_a}{\sqrt{(p_a * q_a)/n}} = Z_\alpha \quad \text{and} \quad \frac{p_c - \hat{p}}{\sqrt{(\hat{p} * \hat{q})/n}} = -Z_\beta$$

Figure D.1 explains the statistics used in equations D.2. P_a is the acceptable deviation rate, while $\hat{p} = x/n$ is the measured system deviation rate and is unacceptably high if it is greater than a value such that β exceeds a pre-selected value. In the case used to generate Figure B.1, the factor, $Z_\alpha = 1.282$, establishes $\alpha = 10$ percent, and $Z_\beta = 1.645$, establishes $\beta = 5$ percent. The value p_c defines the rejection region of the $\hat{p}$ distribution and sets the confidence level needed to solve for n. (The $*$ in equations D.1 and D.2 means multiply.)

REFERENCES

1. Mills, Charles. A. *The Quality Audit*. New York: McGraw-Hill, 1989.
2. Box, George; William G. Hunter; and J. Stuart Hunter. *Statistics for Experimenters*. New York: Wiley and Sons, 1978.
3. Apostolou, Barbara, and Francine Alleman. *Internal Audit Sampling*. Altamonte Springs, FL: The Institute of Internal Auditors, 1991.
4. Grant, Eugene, and Richard Leavenworth. *Statistical Quality Control*. New York: McGraw-Hill, 1988.
5. Mills, Charles. A. *The Quality Audit*. New York: McGraw-Hill, 1989.
6. Guy, Dan M. *An Introduction to Statistical Sampling in Auditing*. New York: John Wiley, 1981.

Index

Figures in *italics* represent charts and graphics.